ADVANCE

Revolutionary STEM Education

"At this particular historical moment, when the national security state has forced humanity to claw its way out of the structurally generated vaults of inhumanity, Jeremiah J. Sims has penned a book that addresses one of the key features of this inhumanity, the vicious attacks on black males in a country that has fallen prey to new species of racism against people of color. Calling for a dramatic shift in STEM pedagogy for black males that combines critical-reality pedagogy, critical race theory, and innovations that cut across the field of urban education, Sims cultivates a pathfinding approach to social justice. Join his paradigm-shifting revolution by reading this book."

—Peter McLaren, Distinguished Professor in Critical Studies,
Donna Ford Attallah College of Education, Chapman University;
Author of *Pedagogy of Insurrection*

"*Revolutionary STEM Education: Critical-Reality Pedagogy and Social Justice in STEM for Black Males* explores the complex relationships between learning processes, student identity development, and deep equity-focused work in an out-of-school STEM learning environment focused on Black boys. Jeremiah J. Sims provides a comprehensive view of how the MAN UP program supports Black male youth's learning of STEM concepts, STEM identity development, and understandings of how to use STEM to affect social change in their communities, filling a sore gap in the equity-focused STEM education literature. Teacher educators and teachers (both preservice and inservice) will find the book useful for use in methods courses, professional development sessions, or professional learning communities (PLCs) to engage in teacher learning about equity-focused STEM teaching and learning; the examples of teacher-student and student-student interactions, along with guiding questions at the end of each chapter, will undoubtedly spur conversations and lesson ideas."

—Tia Madkins, Assistant Professor, Department of Curriculum
and Instruction, University of Texas, Austin

"In *Revolutionary STEM Education: Critical-Reality Pedagogy and Social Justice in STEM for Black Males*, Jeremiah J. Sims argues that positioning students as STEM-savvy, social justice-oriented change agents increases both their STEM identity and their STEM competency. In so doing, Sims provides what STEM education truly needs. This book offers readers both description and explanation. Many contemporary research projects and text simply describe the problem with access to STEM; Sims' text offers us a revelation. It describes the problem, explains the source of the problem, and tells us what to do about getting students critically involved in STEM."

—Bryan A. Brown, Associate Professor, Education;
Associate Dean for Student Affairs, Stanford University

Revolutionary
STEM Education

Educational
PSYCHOLOGY

Critical Pedagogical Perspectives

M. Cathrene Connery and
Greg S. Goodman, *General Editors*

Vol. 36

The Educational Psychology series is part of the Peter Lang Education list.
Every volume is peer reviewed and meets
the highest quality standards for content and production.

PETER LANG
New York • Bern • Berlin
Brussels • Vienna • Oxford • Warsaw

Jeremiah J. Sims

Revolutionary
STEM Education

Critical-Reality Pedagogy
and Social Justice in STEM
for Black Males

PETER LANG
New York • Bern • Berlin
Brussels • Vienna • Oxford • Warsaw

Library of Congress Cataloging-in-Publication Data

Names: Sims, Jeremiah J., author.
Title: Revolutionary STEM education: critical-reality pedagogy and social justice in STEM for black males / Jeremiah J. Sims.
Description: New York: Peter Lang, 2018.
Series: Educational psychology: critical pedagogical perspectives; v. 36 | ISSN 1943-8109
Includes bibliographical references and index.
Identifiers: LCCN 2017051872 | ISBN 978-1-4331-4950-4 (hardback: alk. paper)
ISBN 978-1-4331-5760-8 (paperback: alk. paper) | ISBN 978-1-4331-5254-2 (ebook pdf)
ISBN 978-1-4331-5255-9 (epub) | ISBN 978-1-4331-5256-6 (mobi)
Subjects: LCSH: African American boys—Education. | African American young men—Education. | Science—Study and teaching—Social aspects—United States. | Social justice—United States. | Racism in education—United States.
Classification: LCC LC2731 .S54 2018 | DDC 507.1/073—dc23
LC record available at https://lccn.loc.gov/2017051872
DOI 10.3726/b13074

Bibliographic information published by **Die Deutsche Nationalbibliothek**.
Die Deutsche Nationalbibliothek lists this publication in the "Deutsche Nationalbibliografie"; detailed bibliographic data are available on the Internet at http://dnb.d-nb.de/.

© 2018 Peter Lang Publishing, Inc., New York
29 Broadway, 18th floor, New York, NY 10006
www.peterlang.com

"There's not just one way to be an African-American male, to be Black. Sure, we can try to do sports or music or whatever. We can do anything we set our minds to. And, we can also do STEM. I think it's important that we know that all of us know that."

—Michael, 6th grade MAN UP scholar

Table of contents

Preface   xiii
Overview of this book   xvii

Acknowledgements   xxiii
Do it for the culture   xxvii

Chapter 1 Male aptitudes nurtured for unlimited potential   1

Why am I fighting to live if I'm just living to fight?
Internalization on imminent Black death   2

Canaries in the coalmine: Black males and STEM education   4

Reimagining what it means to MAN UP   7

Real recognize real: Operationalizing critical-reality pedagogy   8

Identifying the real issue: It's not just about achievement   10

Chapter 1 review: Considerations and questions   13

References   14

Chapter 2 Cutting straight the truth: Interrogating White supremacist-based racism's role in perceptions of Black maleness 17

Behind the mask: Uncovering whiteness 18

Playing with house money: Whiteness commoditized 21

The construction of "Whiteness" vis-à-vis "Blackness" 23

Psychological consequences of othering, ideological inculcation and cultural misidentification 24

It's not just about White privilege: Whiteness must be abolished 26

The transmogrification of Black Males: Thugs and threats 28

The 21st century urban colonized 30

The archenemy of hope: The nihilistic threat 31

The other and "otherness" 33

Black ghettoes: Our "Other" America 35

Going viral in the 19th century: The minstrel show 37

Nihilistic threat illustrated in Black literature 39

I am my brother's keeper: Fratricidal violence in the Black community 42

Innocence lost: The adultification of Black males 43

Chapter 2 review: Considerations and questions 45

References 47

Chapter 3 Standing in the gap: Black boys and STEM 51

Where we at, though? Black males' conspicuous absence in STEM spaces 52

Criminal minds? The criminalization of Black males 53

Where I come from, this approach is called keeping it 100 56

Identifying the educational gap in STEM 57

Pedagogy that oppresses: Exclusionary nature of traditional STEM education 58

Minding the opportunity gap 59

Real talk: Demystifying stereotype threat 60

Getting it right: STEM education can and should center criticality 63

Shifting the paradigm: Critical-reality pedagogy in STEM education 67

Ring the alarm: Social justice and STEM education 69

We are what we speak: Dissin' Black English and the correlation between language skills and scholastic expectations 73

Flipping the script: Connecting cultural-linguistic
identities and STEM competencies   75
Bridge building over troubled waters: Connecting
STEM learning and social justice   78
Greater than hope: Insisting on high expectations for Black boys   80
The consequence of low expectations   82
Out with the old: (Re)Conceptualizing rigor   82
Does this approach work: Data analysis procedures   86
Shakers, makers, and takers   89
Reevaluating competency: Identification and socially just
applications of STEM   90
Chapter 3 review: Considerations and questions   90
References   92

**Chapter 4 Changing the game: The role of critical contextualization and
socio-academic synergy in developing STEM identities**   97
Critical contextualization explicated   99
Emerging critical contextualization   101
Evidence of emergent critical contextualization of STEM   101
Manning UP: Shifts in students' STEM identities   102
Remixing identity: Developing identification with STEM   103
We have lift-off: Shakers, makers, and takers   105
Cases studies: From a taker to shaker and from makers to shakers 111
Context matters: Further connecting STEM
identities in the courses   115
Chapter 4 review: Considerations and questions   120
References   122

Chapter 5 Showing out: Developing competencies in STEM and beyond 123
"It was easier for me to learn here because I felt like what
I said mattered"   124
Achieving socio-academic synergy: Yearend Post-Satisfaction
Survey (YPSS)   126
We can do math, too: Yearend focus group interviews   127
Decoding success: Computer science course concept inventory   128
Our voices matter: The rhetorical analysis of manhood   129
Chapter 5 review: Considerations and questions   131
References   133

Chapter 6 STEM for good: Creating socio-academic synergy for the
development of socially just applications of STEM   135
Equity by design   137
Socio-academic synergy: Cultivating and curating an
educationally nutritive atmosphere   138
Doing for self: Positive shifts in self-efficacy   140
Putting the tools to work: Examples of socially just
applications of STEM   145
Chapter 6 review: Considerations and questions   149
References   152

Chapter 7 Love conquers fear: The efficacy of critical-reality
pedagogy at MAN UP   153
Paradigm shifting approach to STEM education   154
Why the critical contextualization of STEM mattered   156
Time to switch it up: Focus on relationship building   156
Real talk: Focusing on students' real lives
in and out of school   157
Chapter 7 review: Considerations and questions   159
References   161

Chapter 8 It takes a village: Highlighting the indispensability
and strength of the three-fold cord   163
What's love got to do with it: Two contrasting tales of
parental advocacy Justin and Judah   164
U-N-I-T-Y: Working against racial isolation for our scholars   169
Chapter 8 review: Considerations and questions   171
References   173

Chapter 9 The revolution will be digitized   175
All power to the people: Cultivating student voice
through critical-reality pedagogy   177
Expect the unexpected: The importance of high
standards for Black boys   178
In conclusion: Please, allow me to keep it 100 with you   180
References   183

Final consideration (Epilogue) 185
Running the race: A level playing field is not enough 186
This is not just meaningful work, it's life and death 188
References 190

Appendix A: Pre/post identification survey 191
Appendix B: Manhood survey and rhetorical analysis concept inventory 193
Appendix C: MAN UP yearend program satisfaction survey (YPSS) 195
Appendix D: Teacher interview questions 199
Appendix E: Yearend focus group and individual interview prompts 201
Index 205

Preface

I remember my response to my high school English teacher like it was yesterday, though this conversation is more than two decades old. Ms. Horrigan asked me if I planned to go to college—which was an entirely reasonable question as she taught my 12th grade English class. I responded, only semi-jokingly, that I hadn't planned on attending college because, well, the life-expectancy for Black males in my city was only twenty-one years of age. So, I told her that, following my high school graduation, I planned to just take life one day at a time because, clearly, growing up in Richmond, California did not hold the promise of another day for me or any other young man that grew up like me. Admittedly, I was the class clown, so I fully expected Ms. Horrigan to simply laugh this statement off—but, instead, I remember the sheer anguish—instantiated by her suddenly crestfallen countenance. I tried to reassure her that I was only joking. But, she saw something that I could not apprehend at the time: she saw that I was resigned to my fate. Because, like the majority of the students that animate this book, I grew up in urban-poverty, with a single-mother who had to function as both my mother and my father. I grew up in a city that during my high school years, in the early 1990's, boasted the highest murder rate per capita in the United States. I grew up in Section 8 Housing. The ever-present threat of intentional and or unintentional (cases of mistaken identity) fratricidal violence informed my every step from the age of twelve until my early twenties. It formed in me something that, from time to time even today rears its ugly head: Persistent Traumatic Stress Disorder.

I was only 17 when this conversation took place, but I was already carrying around a lifetime of trauma, disappointment, abandonment, and pain. I was normally jovial in Ms. Horrigan's class; and, even though I was sometimes borderline disruptive, I knew that I was one of her favorite students. She was someone whose care for her students caused her to be innovative. She was what I aspire to be: a caring, nutritive, critical pedagogue—long before I had any idea that that those modifiers could be strung together to form an identity. Here she was a middle-aged (possibly older) European American women, teaching in the hood (albeit at a top high school) simply out of love. She'd made a small fortune—enough to own, outright, two houses in the Bay Area—selling 501 jeans to tourists all over Northern California. She did not need to teach; however, she loved to teach. And, she did it in a way that was and still is paradigm-shifting for me.

Throughout my K12 experience, I repeatedly got in trouble for being a "class clown". What I know now, that I couldn't have known then, was that my flippant attitude was a defense mechanism that allowed me to laugh despite pain, and to chuckle in the face of a constant, deeply-internalized fear of failure. When I got to Ms. Horrigan's class, I was still class clown. But in her class, I never got in trouble for it. Instead, she carved out the last 5 to 7 minutes of class, at least once per week, to invite me to do stand-up comedy during school hours. This was diametrically opposed to anything I'd ever experienced before. In every other instance my wit carried sanctions. But, instead of castigating me, Ms. Horrigan invited what was at the time the leading aspect of my identity kit into the meaning making process that was her 12th grade English class. As a result, I excelled in her class; as a result, I wanted to become an English teacher. She changed my life academically; and, it is not an overstatement to say that she quite possible contributed to saving my life. She gave me hope. That is what critical educators do. Sadly, I was never able to share this with her.

This, of course, is beginning to read in a way that is commensurate with the staid narrative. This meta-narrative, instantiated by movies like Dangerous Minds and or the Blindside—celebrates a benevolent white educator's (or caretaker in the latter example) willingness to go native and function as a messianic figure that helps poor students of color find their voices and realize their erstwhile unknown or misrecognized potential. And, while the characters in my personal play are consistent with this narrative, something altogether different was taking place. Ms. Horrigan did not help me find my voice; clearly, I already had one that I used with self-appointed impunity. I know this because prior to her class my voice got me in trouble quite often. Instead of viewing me as deficient or in need of a savior, however, Ms. Horrigan allowed me to be exactly who I was, while still holding me to high expectations. More than that, she encouraged me to do well as myself, not as some false persona that required me to repudiate and or abdicate the socio-cultural identity that I was painstakingly developing. The pedagogical dexterity that she displayed provided me with an entry point, for the first time in long time, into my own academic trajectory and ultimately my own academic success. More simply put: she worked alongside me, not for me; and, certainly not against me. *Ms. Horrigan was keeping it one-hundred (percent); that is to say, she was her authentic self, which encouraged and empowered her students to be, at least in some small measure, authentic in return.* This is a theme that I will return to throughout this book, the idea of keeping it 100. If we, as educators, ever want to create spaces for our students to learn as their authentic selves, we have to be authentic as well. In fact, like Ms. Horrigan, we have to take the lead. Ms. Horrigan was an exemplar because she had a genuine care and concern, perhaps even love, for us.

The argument can be made that Ms. Horrigan, well before the term had been coined, was engaging in a form of critical-reality pedagogy precisely because she allowed and, frankly, even invited me to bring elements of my lived experiences into her 12 grade English class. And while my experiences at that point were localized and somewhat narrow, those experience represented who I was as a person. She made me feel that my personhood was so integral in the constitution and meaning making of her course. I began to engage in here class as started by preparing for my 5 to 7 minute routines; soon, I was fully engaged in her class and my engagement was no longer limited to my "comedy" skits. Holistically, I began to feel as though I had a place in that course. This is what reality critical-reality pedagogy does—it invites students to be who they are without asking them to repudiate their cultural affinities or cultural identity's. To be clear, this is only one component of a critical-reality pedagogical approach. But, it is a requisite component. There also needs to be a laser-focus on creating opportunities for students to disambiguate, deconstruct, and ultimately redress societal injustice using whatever material is covered in a given course of study.

Nevertheless, inviting traditionally-marginalized students to work through course material that is predicated on their interests, concerns, and ways of being is indispensable to this approach; and, in this book I argue, it is indispensable to student empowerment as well. There is an analog to be made between *keeping it 100* and enacting critical-reality pedagogy because both concepts require educators to eschew the trappings of the banking model of education by presenting their authentic selves in their educational spaces so that students will know that there is space for them to be reciprocally authentic. We know a lot about Ms. Horrigan's life. We knew that she wanted kids but, unfortunately, had none of her own. We heard her stories of vulnerability and stories of triumph. Like Ms. Horrigan, we, educators, have to be willing to be authentic and come with our whole selves so that they can create an environment where students can be exactly who they are and still be view as young people full of promise and potential. This pedagogical orientation is diametrically opposed to the stultifying banking model of education wherein educators insist on maintaining their authority while either misrecognizing or failing to recognize the expertise that students also bring to the fore. Student expertise is not limited to just knowledge of self, which is undoubtedly important, nor is it limited to knowledge of their immediate localized environment, though this, too, is certainly included. In order to understand what it is that students know, and how it is that they want to engage, we have to give them every opportunity to demonstrate what they know to us and to themselves. This is what Ms. Horrigan did; and, this is what I strive to do as well. For me, this is being authentic, this is *keeping it 100*; and, when this approach is conjoined with a focus on redressing social injustice and social inequity, it is an application of critical-reality pedagogy. Ms. Horrigan, though she could not possibly have been aware of this terminology, was a caring, committed educator. My guidance counselor in junior high, however, was not. Ms. Horrigan was the exception; this man, sadly, was the rule.

"No one cares what you do in junior high, Jeremiah; you'll eventually be socially passed." My middle school guidance counselor (who would later become principal) spoke these words to me. I know that some of the young men that I have been blessed to work with have had similarly dismissive conversations with adults entrusted to guide them on their educational journeys. I wonder how many more experienced this but were reticent to speak up. If my memory serves, I was once again in trouble for talking out of turn in class. This was a common theme during my first year in middle school as I worked diligently to carve out a "cool" identity for myself. I will not soon forget this moment, however, because it is when I began to see both school and myself differently. This counselor had given me license to free myself from academic struggle, which I did not know at the time, was analogous to freeing myself from academic growth. This was especially true where math was concerned. After excelling in elementary school, middle school brought struggles that I was ill prepared for, none more so than in math. I was stuck and never got unstuck because according to my counselor, I didn't have to.

Sadly, this story is all too familiar for many young, low-income, urban Black males, and especially so in STEM. Moreover, often we, or our parents, or our culture are blamed for our struggles in STEM. In truth, structural and institutionalized racism in educational policy and practice is to blame. Structural and institutionalized racism in educational policy and practice result in stultifying low expectations for perhaps the most educationally marginalized group in this country, Black males. Rhetoric around persistent educational struggles of Black males foists the locus of failure on us; and in so doing, this very same rhetoric exculpates the racist structures and institutions that function to ensure inequitable educational opportunities for Black males (and other traditionally marginalized students). Fortunately, as an adult I had people in my life who encouraged and assisted me in pushing forward with my education. However, this is not always the case for young men that grew up like me: poor, Black, and enmeshed within a violent, unrelenting environment.

I was saved by love, by the love of my Savior, by the love of my hard-working single mother, by the love of teachers like Mrs. Searles and Ms. Horrigan, by the love of my church, and when I needed it most, by the love of the women who would become my partner in love and in life. Though my environment was in many ways loveless, somehow, I still felt love and that love saved me. Far too many young men that grow up like me do not get to experience the holistic love that I was blessed to receive. I am not okay with this "reality"; I never will be. No one should be. In time, I was presented with the opportunity to create a program that would begin to address and hopefully, in some small measure, ameliorate this saddening reality by creating a STEM focused academic program for Black boys that was predicated on love. Despite the reticence that my own math-phobia induced in me, I felt I had no choice but to move forward in developing a STEM focused program for predominately low-income, urban Black males: Male Aptitudes Nurtured for Unlimited Potential (MAN UP).

Overview of this book

This book is separated into nine chapters—an overview of each chapter is provided below. It is important to note that at the end of each chapter, as with the preceding chapter (with the exception of the final chapter) there is a page with considerations and questions for both educators and students. These considerations are not meant to be the final word nor raise the only important questions around equitable educational practices in STEM for Black males. Rather, they are included to catalyze intra-group conversations between educators, writ large, and students so that these two groups can, hopefully, come together in a meaningful way to begin both intra and intergroup conversations that hold the potential to transform the pedagogical practices that characterize STEM education for Black males (as well as other marginalized groups). These questions should also help both students and teachers think, reflectively, about the roles that they occupy within the teaching and learning continuum.

"Cutting straight the truth: Interrogating White supremacist-based racism's role in perceptions of Black maleness?" is split into two parts. Part one reviews literature on the inclusion of critical and reality based pedagogical practices in STEM education. I discuss literature that speaks to the root causes of underperformance in STEM for Black males: white supremacist-centered notions of Black inferiority and the pedagogical practices that are predicated on the erroneous, stereotypical depictions of Black males that have been normalized by the apparatuses wielded by this very same white supremacist agenda. In order to paint this picture, I discuss literature that perniciously positions Black males as threats and thugs who, irrespective of their age, are not afforded the notions of child-like innocence that buttresses the lived-experiences of the European American (i.e., White) counterparts. Next, I review literature that works to deconstruct white supremacy and the undeniable role it plays in catalyzing and promulgating negative stereotypes of Black males in education generally and in STEM specifically. After this, I review the work of scholars who have discussed the negative effects of stereotyping on Black males' learning and identity. Then, wanting to move the conversation forward, I transition into an analysis of the literature that speaks to the potential benefits of a critical-reality pedagogical approach to STEM education of urban, middle school Black males by using Freire's conception of problem-posing education as the frame for the critical MAN UP pedagogical approach.

This chapter also introduces two terms that are central to this study: the critical contextualization of STEM, and socio-academic synergy. Part two of this chapter, "My Approach", delineates the design of this study including the central guiding question of this work as well as a description of the site where the intervention took place. Additionally, part two of this chapter provides detailed demographic information regarding the focal cohort. I also discuss the data collection procedures and data analysis procedures, and I discuss both the limitations of the research as well as my varied role as the researcher.

The title of Chapter Three is, "Standing in the gap: Black boys and STEM". In this chapter, I discussed literature that speaks to the root causes of underperformance in STEM for Black males: white supremacist-centered notions of Black inferiority and the, related, pedagogical practices that are predicated on the erroneous, stereotypical depictions of Black males. These negative stereotypes have been normalized through mass media such that they are accepted as fact in far too many educational circles. This chapter also spoke in greater detail about the many of the negative stereotypes are associated with us, Black males, and how these stereotypes are part and parcel of a larger systematic push to Black boys (and men) for our academic struggles instead of identifying the real culprit: race-based, structural inequity. However, let me keep it 100 right now. These stereotypes are false. There is nothing innately inferior or deficient about any Black male or any other student from a non-dominant group. We all have the same capacity to realize our fullest potential, because intelligence grows over time; it does not remain static. Additionally, I present the analysis of and findings from my data by analyzing the focal cohort's math pre-and post-test scores, their shifts in their Manhood Development Concept Inventory, shifts in their Rhetorical Analysis Concept Inventory, as well as shifts in their CS/Mobile Apps course: Technology for Social Justice Concept Inventory (CS), respectively. As a result, my analysis of the pre-survey data, three categories of participation came to the fore. In this chapter, I highlight five students as case studies for the larger focal cohort to demonstrate the shifts in STEM identity experienced by these students as microcosms of the overall shifts experienced by the entire focal cohort. Following a discussion of these case studies, I return to a discussion of the entire focal cohort. Additionally, I investigate how students began to identify as applied STEM practitioners; drawing on data, I seek to uncover what contributes to and or the limits positive development of STEM identities for the focal students.

In Chapter Four: "Changing the game: The role of critical contextualization and socio-academic synergy in developing STEM identities," I explicate the three terms that I introduced in the previous chapter, socio-academic synergy and critical contextualization as well as the critical contextualization of STEM. Additionally, I analyze the focal cohorts' shifts in STEM competency as captured by both their pre-post CS and Math concept inventories. In addition to working to facilitate MAN UP student's development of a positive STEM identity, this program also focused on developing specific STEM competencies required for college and careers. In addition, I chronicle the focal cohorts' shifts in STEM competency as well as their shifts in competency in their non-STEM RAM course to speak to the ways in which their increases in STEM identity contributed to their demonstrated increases in competency vis-à-vis the courses offered at MAN UP. I work to illuminate the potentially powerful connection between the intentional development of a positive STEM identity—as an applied STEM practitioner—to their confidence and demonstrated ability to excel in the STEM course content covered in MAN UP.

Chapter Five is entitled: "Showing out: Developing competencies in STEM and beyond." In this chapter, I discuss how the intentional atmosphere developed and curated at MAN UP facilitated and/or contributed to the focal cohorts' desire, willingness, and ability to apply their increased STEM knowledge for social justice as well as their self-directed applications of STEM for social justice, which, when present, provides evidence that students had begun to critically contextualize STEM. This chapter also looks at the effects of synergizing atmosphere that worked diligently to include students' voices and their lived-realities into the curriculum as well as the overall ethos of this program. This chapter also speaks to the importance of centering critical-reality pedagogy in STEM and understanding the power of student agency via application, and why it is that a critical-reality based STEM pedagogical approach is a matter of social justice. And, I discuss surveys that students completed that speak to their relationship with MAN UP vis-à-vis their own home schools and draw implications regarding what, if any, elements of MAN UP's atmosphere contributed to student increases in the considerations described in this studies' guiding question. I conclude this chapter by making the argument that the critical contextualization of STEM was in fact taking place and was evidenced by the focal cohorts' positive shifts in STEM identity, competency and in their socially just applications of STEM. I also underscore the innovative nature of the MAN UP program. And, I speak to the importance of MAN UP's philosophical-pedagogical and material setting insofar as the role of this program's positioning played in catalyzing a nutritive educational atmosphere that worked to ensure socio-academic synergy between students' real lives and the course content.

In Chapter Six: STEM for good: "Creating Socio-academic Synergy for the Development of Socially Just Applications of STEM", I assess the pedagogical atmosphere that characterized this program and how it created and curated a nutritive educational space that afforded the focal participants the opportunity to become applied STEM practitioners by realizing the critical contextualization of STEM. And in doing so, I reiterate the primary position of this study: that a critical-reality pedagogical approach to STEM education was integral to the creation of just such a positive, transformative atmosphere because it carved out a space for the realization of a socio-academic synergy, which, then, encouraged students to envision themselves as applied STEM practitioners as evidence by their demonstrated critical contextualization of STEM.

In Chapter Seven: Perfect love casts out all fear: The Efficacy of Critical-reality pedagogy at MAN UP, I underscores the importance of a reimagined STEM pedagogy that encourages, empowers, and equips hyper-marginalized students to become increasingly adroit at critically contextualizing STEM so that they experience increases in their STEM identity, competency, and demonstrated ability to apply STEM for social justice. In this chapter, I lay out the foundational argument of this book, i.e., that socio-academic synergy should be a goal of any program seeking to work effectively with and for Black boys because it holds the potential to catalyze both critical contextualization proper and the critical contextualization of STEM, more specifically by taking into account, both pedagogically and curricularly, the specific needs, interests, obstacles, life-experiences and joys of Black boys.

In Chapter Eight, "It takes a village: Highlighting the indispensability and strength of the three-fold cord", I discuss the necessity and benefit of integrating parents/guardians into both the construction and maintenance of the intentional atmosphere developed and curated at MAN UP. Again, a commitment to becoming a more critical, emancipatory, social justice centered educator is wholly necessary in this work. It is also wholly necessary to work alongside and in solidarity with students and parents. We cannot continue the trend of presupposing that we know exactly what our students need to feel safe and encouraged to being realizing their fullest possible potential. Instead, we have to create opportunities for students and parents/guardians, respectively, to help shape the educational atmosphere by listening to and addressing the issues, concerns, and needs of both the students and their primary advocates.

Acknowledgements

With much gratitude and respect, I acknowledge the MAN UP educational team: Professor Jabari Mahiri, who graciously volunteered his time to work with the MAN UP instructional team with pedagogical considerations as well as overall, programmatic components. We were a group of graduate students with varying levels of experience in program development; however, this particular task was larger than anything we had endeavored to develop on our own. Professor Mahiri, your guidance, experience, expertise—your presence in our planning meetings or on site gave us the confidence to move forward into what was uncharted territory. I also acknowledge the MAN UP instructional team. Kenyatta Weathersby, my brother, you were our rock. Your experience as a professional teacher and your loving-concern for the young men that this program served were invaluable. Now you're at the helm, bro, and I have every confidence that you will continue to push toward the vision we all created. To my brother, soon to be Dr. Sepehr Vakil, an engineer by training and an activist at heart, you are the instantiation of the work that we were endeavoring to do: to raise up socially-conscious, committed, applied STEM practitioners. You constantly challenged me in the best way possible to reflect on and iterate my pedagogy. I'm eternally grateful. This is just the beginning. My brother, Pierre, your contribution and your spirit, not to mention your educational and technical expertise were invaluable. To Jarvis,

I cannot thank you enough for the mentorship you provided professionally and personally. I appreciate you, brother. Like Sepehr and Kenyatta, you represent the goal for all the young men that this program touched. Geronimo, even though we had courses together because we are in the same cohort, I always looked to you as a mentor. Our conversations while co-teaching, or in class, or just eating lunch together continue to push me to do better by the young people I'm blessed to work with. Dr.'s Dawn Williams, Aaminah Norris, Nora Kenny, Genevieve Negron-Gonzales, Rick Ayers, and Allison Scott, you incredibly powerful scholars/intellectuals have all touched me and informed my work. I thank you all from the bottom of my heart.

As for my dissertation committee, I already spoke to the matter-of-fact, yet altogether empowering mentorship that Professor Mahiri has provided over the last 6 years and change. Professor Glynda Hull, you made me want to be a critical pedagogue. Your infectious joy in teaching education 140 gave me hope again. Sometimes I struggled, largely due to my background, with my place in a doctoral program at the nation's preeminent public university, but you always made me feel I had something of value to add. Thank you.

Professor Rodolfo Mendoza-Denton, thank you for agreeing to help guide my dissertation work. Your input has been invaluable. I am inspired by your work and personal commitment to equity that has been acknowledged this year with the Chancellor's Award for Advancing Institutional Excellence. I very much look forward to continued work with you in the future.

And to Professor Zeus Leonardo, I fully expected to wow GSE folks with my handle on critical theory based on my undergraduate degree in Rhetoric; then I took your class. You challenged me in ways that'd I'd never been challenged before—ways that strengthened as opposed to enervating me. I appreciate your stance, and I appreciate the way you received me. I knew you could tell I was still rough around the edges, but you always made me feel that I could take part in the conversations in your classes.

And, to the beautiful, brilliant, youth who are forced to traverse a rugged, inhospitable educational terrain: I feel you, I hear you; and, please know that in whatever way that I can—I'm here for you. And, specifically, to the young men that made up and continue to make up the MAN UP program and to the young men that I worked with through AAMA: I love you all. Each one of you has inspired me in your own way. Collectively, you all helped me find my direction in life; I'm eternally grateful.

To my family: Rachel, my dearest sweetest Rachel: You took a chance on me because even though you'd already graduated from Cal, and was busy making lots of money, you dared to fall in love with a guy with a desultory past and only a high school diploma. Well, all these years later, here we are still in love. I have been in school our entire marriage. In that time, you found your professional passion and excelled in serving the underserved, in remembering the forgotten, and in empowering the disempowered, and you did all this while bearing and beautifully mothering three perfect, albeit rambunctious little boys. You are my heart. Nothing I do in life would matter to me if you weren't there to share it with me. This is our work, baby; and, I could not have a better partner. You are the light of my life.

Judah, what can I say about Mr. Judah Zaire Sims? You are an old soul, young man; it's like you've been here before. Your perspective is far beyond your nearly eight years of existence. Little bro, I'm so elated that I get to be your daddy. Every time I hear you call me, my heart fills with joy, and I am made full. I love you, Judah. You appeared on the scene and immediately made me want to be a better person, for you. Not sure if that's happening or not, but outside of marrying mommy, your birth is the greatest thing that has ever happened to me. That you are my son, for me, is proof of God's love.

Malachi Jeremiah Sims, my mini-me. I love you Kai Kai. I thought that I could never love another child the way that I loved Judah. I was wrong. Kai Kai, you proved me wrong. I love you so much. I love your sense of humor, your disposition and your overall Kai Kai-ness. Even though you've only been here for five years, I now know that my life will forever be better because you're in it. Kai Kai, air hug; air kiss!

Zion Alexander Sims, my little "Poots." Zion, the three years that you've been on this planet, have, undoubtedly been the best three years of my life. Don't get me wrong, life was already great—but somehow it got even better over the last three years or so—because of you. Your smile animates me, Zion; your laugh makes me joyous; your face fills me with pure delight. I love you, Poots! You are brilliant, a little mischievous, and altogether wonderful.

Freedom Joseph Sims, I love you little boy. It'll be a little while before you can read this—but no worries—your big bros will read it to you. Baby boy number four, you are amazing. You're a beautiful boy like your brothers; and, even though you're just over 90 days old, you make my heart full.

To my brothers, Joseph & Tosh, quite frankly I wouldn't be here without the two of you always having my back. We didn't have it easy, but still we continued to push because we have each other to fall back on. That will always be the case.

To the family I married into: Henry & Sylvia, Tim & Shyra, Phil & Liza, and Sarah, Sho, and beautiful Yaelle, all of you have played a role in getting me to this point. And, more importantly, in your own ways, each of you has cared for me and my crew both spiritually and practically.

And, last but certainly not least, mom, thank you for raising me all by yourself. Thank you for waking up early to go to work at low-paying jobs so that we could be cared for. I don't say thank you enough. There are no words that truly express the way I feel: I love you, mom.

I also need to thank a host of people who made my education journey empowering, edifying, and encouraging (in no particular order): Joey Lample, G. Reyes, Sarah Fong, Dr. Dale Allender, Dr. Melanie Sperling, Dr. Laura Sterponi, Dave Starks, Justin Martin, Dr. Alexis Martin, kihana ross, Patrick Johnson, Dr. Daniel Coffeen, Dr. Rakesh Bandari, Professor Abdul Jan Mohamed, Dr. Felipe Gutierrez, Dr. Bryan Brown, Dr. Chris Emdin, Dr. J.B. Rodgers, Dr. Paul Dobenmeyer, Gerald Lau, Larry Chen, Donald Mangold, Gopal Shetty, Paul Hon, Chaz Shoenig, Christyna Serrano, Sumaiya Taldukar, James Sarria, Ramon Chairez, Rafa Velasquez, Ilka Williams, Karen Sullivan, Dr. Ron Fortune, Dr. Freada Kapor Klein, Mitch Kapor, Cedric Brown, Dave Starks, Dr. Cheala Delgado, Chris Chatmon, Jerome Gourdine, Lasana O. Hotep, the IDEAL Scholars crew…the list goes on and on. I know full well that I didn't simply pull myself up by my bootstraps—I was helped, cared for, and encouraged all along the way. I thank you all.

Do it for the culture

I am writing this book for my neighborhood, for my community, even for my entire demographic. I grew up in Richmond, California. I grew up amidst career drug dealers, hookers, gang-bangers and pimps. I was able to extricate myself from those negative influences because I held fast to my belief in the value of education, and because in spite of the overall toxicity of my environment, there were people who cared for me and guided me. To this day, sadly, I am one of few males from my neighborhood that has gone on to graduate from college. My mom raised my younger brother and me all by herself. My brother and I have different fathers; my mom and my father were never married. He was not in the picture.

"Fast Eddie", which is what I knew him by, was a career criminal. Still, we got along okay—when he came around. When I spent time with him, because my mom was working, I saw all types of things that someone my age should not have been exposed to: I saw my father shoot Heroin into his veins; I also got a glimpse of the 80's drug trade first hand watching him sell pounds of weed to assorted buyers. Fast Eddie disappeared from my life altogether when I was 12, up until that point I would see him every two months or so. It turns out he started robbing banks, 15 banks in fact. I did not find this out until 10 years later. I went to look for him when I was 13 and he was nowhere to be found; one of his longtime neighbors told me that he had died. So, that is where I left it. To my surprise, when I was 23, I received a letter from Fast Eddie; he was not dead, not physically anyway. He had been in prison for the past 10 years experiencing the recurrence of psychosocial and socioemotional death that the prison industrial complex all but ensures. After three months of freedom, Fast Eddie died of full-blown AIDS due to years of intravenous drug use. Seventeen years later, I still have not cried. That was the story of my biological father, the story of my stepfather is also worth telling. My mom got married when I was 4 years old. My stepfather turned out to be an abusive alcoholic. I witnessed him beat my mom repeatedly. I saw him kick a hole in her throat; she almost died. He pushed her out of a car they were in while it was moving, leaving me in the car alone to crash into a pole. I was 4 years old at the time. I was only bruised, physically—but the emotional toll was much more injurious.

All these experiences have made me appreciate the opportunity that I have now: I get to share elements of my story and stories of the young men I was fortunate to serve, while highlighting a potentially paradigm-shifting pedagogical approach to STEM education for young men (and women) that grew up like me. This book is not really about me; my story is but a footnote. Nevertheless, I am eternally grateful for the opportunity to share it with you all. We did it for the culture! As evidenced by the comments of the young men included in this book, our youth are powerful. This quote captures collective ferocity of the MAN UP scholar crew:

> There's not just one way to be an African-American male, to be Black. Sure, we can try to do sports or music or whatever. We can do anything we set our minds to. And, we can also do STEM. I think it's important that we know that all of us know that. (Michael, 6th grade MAN UP scholar)

Thank you for reading this work! To be in a position to work alongside and in service of a group people whose needs are often times misunderstood, elided, and or intentionally ignored means everything to me.

1

Male aptitudes nurtured for unlimited potential

I grew up in the inner city. The fierce poetry of the late great 2Pac (Tupac Amaru Shakur), melodically juxtaposed with rhythmic beat after beat, was the score from my personal educational screenplay from high school into my early twenties. Even after his premature death, his music lived on constantly inflecting and infracting the mise-en-scene of my personal motion picture. One song resonated with me for much of my young adult life because it served as a homage to the sometimes-perilous realities of my life growing up in the inner city: I See Death around the Corner. In retrospect, I know why this song resonates with me: it painfully captures my psychosocial reality growing up as a Black male ensconced within a violent, unforgiving environment that was absent easily accessible levers for upward mobility and positive role models to emulate. I had no aspirations precisely because I had come to believe the purported reality that, as a Black male in the inner city, I was on borrowed time. What I know now is that I was suffering through Persistent Traumatic Stress. I am not yet willing to say that I was or am suffering through a disorder; maybe it is my pride. And, in reality, I truly believe in the power of holistic spiritual healing. However, what I can say, looking back, is that I had internalized the statistics that were rampant during the last years my high school experience. Black males that grew up in my city were only expected to live to be 21. So, for me and many of the Black and Brown males that I grew up with, there was no point in living for tomorrow—because I, we, saw death ominously looming right around the corner.

Why am I fighting to live if I'm just living to fight? Internalization on imminent Black death

I had continuous nightmares during this stretch of my life. In my nightmares, an indistinguishable figure would pull a shotgun from his waistband, aim it at me, then pull the trigger. Boom. Then, I would awaken, all at once—out of breath. These dreams were steeped in reality. I had never been shot at before, but, by this point in my life I had several interactions with police and would be assailants where a gun was drawn on me or someone that I was with. In the dream, the buckshot always approached in slow motion. All I needed to do to survive was make it to the end of the building were this pseudo-attempted murder was taking place. Every time I made it around the corner, until one time I did not. Well, that is not entirely true; if my memory serves, I did in fact make it around the corner. However, instead of the bullets continuing in a straight line commensurate with the rules of physics, like me, the buckshot also turned the corner. This time I was hit. I woke up gasping for air. I prayed to calm myself. The prayer worked. I went a few years before this erstwhile recurring dream recurred.

Some years later, coming back from a raucous summer concert with a group of friends, we pulled into the closest gas station, which was filled with other concertgoers. Music blaring, the gas station, much to the owner's chagrin, had been transformed to a continuation of the concert that had ended only minutes earlier. As a few of my friends were coming back from buying wares at the gas station's mini-mart, one of them, Zeke, got into a staring contest (mean-muggin') with another Black male. Soon, this young man had his hands raised to the sky; he was twisting and contorting his fingers. I would come to find out later that in gang culture, this is called "stacking", i.e., to send rapid fire messages, usually warnings, to a potential or known adversary. In my part of the East Bay Area (this was the South Bay), Black males were not gang affiliated in the same way. Only Latinos in my community claimed colors.

My friend, Zeke, yelled out, threateningly: "what's that supposed to mean?" The other young man continued stacking. Soon, two more cars full of potential problems joined him on this night. One young man emerged from one of the cars that had just joined the fray. Almost in one motion, he got out of the car while pulling a revolver from his waistband. At this point, the driver, Eric, sped off.

They gave chase, firing into the darkness. We made it to the freeway unscathed, at least physically. On this night, once the adrenaline wore off and I fell asleep, the nightmare returned. For the next year, I got shot nightly. Sometimes, I could see my funeral in a kind of out of body experience. People would lament that I was gone too soon; however, they would also speak to continuing on—continuing to live. They had no choice. Black people in this country, according to Sharpe (2016) have been relegated to living in the wake of the peculiar institution of American Chattel Slavery. This peculiar institution, which produced America's first million-aires, left violence, death, and despair in it its wake, in the pluperfect tense. The wake comports us Black peoples as non-beings (Fanon, 1968). Because, if we are beings, then, our lives cannot be expendable, right? If we are beings, our lives must matter, too, right? So, even amid senseless death (here, I am speaking to the real deaths of countless Black males throughout this country), we must admonish each other to cling to hope and continue to live. According to Sharpe (2016), we must come to terms with the reality of the wake:

> What happens when instead of becoming enraged and shocked every time a Black person is killed in the United States, we recognize Black death as a predictable and constitutive aspect of this democracy? What will happen then if instead of demanding justice we recognize (or at least consider) that the very notion of justice … produces and requires Black exclusion and death as normative. (Sharpe, 2016, Kindle locations 284–287)

While Sharpe's quote seems pessimistic—but it is real; and, it does beg consideration. I think that the response in my dream, responses that I have seen firsthand in real life at the end of another young person's real life, are a way to navigate the wake by rejecting what we have been told is the inevitability of Black death. And, to be fair, in laying out her argument, Sharpe is desirous to catalyze scholarship that goes deeper while simultaneously accounting for the myriad considerations that the wake insists upon:

> In the midst of so much death and the fact of Black life as proximate to death, how do we attend to physical, social, and figurative death and also to the largeness that is Black life, Black life insisted from death? I want to suggest that that might look something like wake work. (Sharpe, 2016, Kindle locations 469–472)

Whether this book qualifies as wake work is not for me to judge, though that is my goal. Nevertheless, I do remember a particular awakening related to the recurring nightmare that I mentioned above. One night, upon falling asleep, I was in the same predicament yet again. There I was at the corner; the gunman again had me in his sights. I started to run, but this time my gait was not impelled by terror—instead, it was perfunctory and seemingly obligatory. For some reason, I was not scared. He shot; I turned the corner. However, this time was different. As the bullets turned the corner in hot pursuit, I raised my hand to stop this act mid scene. I was tired of dying. I yelled to the gunman: "bullets cannot turn corners! I know that this is a dream; I am tired of running; and, I am done dying!" Then, I awoke. No more terror. I was free. From that point forward, though at the time a struggling community college student, I committed myself to working alongside other equity-minded sisters and brothers to work towards the emancipation of young people who grew up just like me. I want them to be free, too.

Throughout this book, I will interweave aspects of my personal narrative into the text because this work *is* personal for me, for several reasons. However, in reality, this is not so much my story as is my story a microcosm of the macro-level injustices that Black males (as well as other traditionally and hyper-marginalized) must face in order to survive and thrive in a society that was built upon and designed to serve the interests of White supremacy. Like Sharpe, I accept the imminent threat of Black death; and like Sharpe, I want to disrupt this seeming inevitability by focusing intentional work that "attend[s] to physical, social, and figurative death and also to the largeness that is Black life" (Sharpe, 2016, Kindle locations 469–472). The MAN UP program was an attempt to do wake work. The curriculum spoke to calling out the pernicious vicissitudes of Black life while, in this case, empowering, encouraging, and equipping the young Black boys that we served to use STEM to deconstruct and, potentially, restructure the inimical environments that they were compelled to participate in.

Canaries in the coalmine: Black males and STEM education

Black males represent the proverbial canary in the mineshaft in this country. In many ways, the plight of Black males in this country is analogous to the canaries that were used as unwitting proxies for coal miners. It is no secret that coal mining is an incredibly difficult and dangerous profession, replete with potentially fatal, yet accepted, occupational risks. There is the possibility of methane poisoning, cave-ins, explosions, and if these immediate threats are avoided—a more gradual death by black lung disease is disproportionately high in this profession. For centuries, to determine whether a potential mine was safe to enter, a simple (and inhumane) early warning system was concocted: canaries were released into mines, and if the canaries returned, the cave was considered safe to enter. However, if the canaries failed to return—because the undetectable methane gas poisoned them—the determination was made that the concentration of methane gas was too high for miners to enter. The canaries functioned as expendable, living gauges of toxicity. Sadly, this is not unlike the realities that many poor, urban Black males face. Black males are overwhelming impoverished and, consequently, are forced both socio-economically and juridically, to live in under-resourced, violent urban enclaves where high levels of environmental and social toxicity are present (Alexander, 2010). Unfortunately, as with coal mining, being a Black male in this country, seemingly, comes with an acceptable amount of risk. What is more, according to Skinner (2008) a community's health can be gauged by how well Black men and boys are doing within it. If Skinner's claim is accurate—we are all in trouble. To this point, Noguera (2008) writes:

> Black males in America are in trouble. With respect to health, education, employment, income, and overall well-being, all of the most reliable data consistently indicate that Black males constitute a segment of the population that is distinguished by hardships, disadvantages, and vulnerability. (2008, p. 11)

Noguera's troubling observation is, sadly, yet unsurprisingly, supported by report after report, year after year. For example, the 2012 Level Playing Field Institute (LPFI) report on STEM Educational Inequality (Scott and Martin, 2012) found that there are still glaring inequalities in our state's educational outcomes. This is especially true for Black males, especially when the level of specificity for the data collected is disaggregated for STEM-related educational preparedness and attainment. The schooling of Black boys does not foment the nutritive educational space that all children need (Marsh, Mendoza-Denton, & Adam Smith, 2010); instead, traditional schooling normalizes and reifies the pressures, pejorative stereotypes (Duncan-Andrade & Morrell, 2008; Leonardo, 2010; Steele, 2010), and academic failings of Black boys. Far too often (purportedly oppositional) the culture, ethnicity, community, pigment, parenting and or the attitude or comportment of Black boys is used to obfuscate or elide, altogether, authentic and potentially transformative conversations about the systemic, institutionalized racist apparatuses at the root of the educational underperformance of Black boys.

According to reports from the Level Playing Field Institute (Scott, 2010; Scott & Martin, 2012), the STEM opportunity gap for Black students is profound. For example, just 43 percent of Black students reach proficiency in 5th grade science compared to 80 percent for Asians and Whites. By 6th grade with respect to math proficiency, 46 percentage points separate Black (35 percent) from Asian students (81 percent). Throughout middle and high school, proficiency rates in math and science continue to decline insuring that Black students are less likely to access and be successful in rigorous college preparatory coursework in these subjects. Predictably, very few graduate from college with degrees and career opportunities in STEM, the fields with seven of the top ten fastest-growing occupations between 2010 and 2020 (Scott & Martin, 2012).

These statistics are troubling for Black students generally, and though not disaggregated by gender, they are even more problematic for Black males who have the highest school dropout rates of any demographic category. For example, data on Black males and public education in all 50 states in the U.S. indicate that they remain at the bottom of high school graduation rates in all but 13 states, and in those 13 states, Latino males are on the bottom (Scott & Martin, 2012). Clearly, there is a need to dramatically change the language, curriculum, and pedagogy utilized for learning STEM as well as other academic subjects as a human right in education for Black students and, ultimately, for all students.

So, in 2011, I took charge of developing a revolutionary, out-of-school education program aimed at transforming the language and pedagogy of curricular approaches to learning STEM in order to counter some of the problematic constraints on Black male academic achievement in these subject areas, and, potentially, in related careers. In addition to these academic considerations, I also wanted to contribute to an educational space that encouraged middle school Black males to explore their epistemological curiosities regarding the way that the world works and their role/s within it. The MAN UP program featured three core classes—math, Computer Science and Mobile Apps (CS), and the Rhetorical Analysis of manhood (RAM). These three classes were taught on two Saturdays each month throughout the school year to Black males in each of the three grades of middle school (i.e., 6th, 7th, and 8th grade). And, while we did not have to adhere, lockstep, with the strictures of standardization that characterize urban, public schools, we did have to adhere to the standardized metrics, derived from the Common Core, that MAN UP's sole funder insisted on.

This program was hosted and funded by a neighborhood-based non-profit organization, located in the San Francisco Bay Area. After an application process that required transcripts, letters of recommendation and standardized test scores as well as phone and in-person interviews, I selected the participants, which were mainly drawn from under-resourced, under-performing public schools in several Northern California, urban municipalities. The acronym of the program, "MAN UP," stands for Male Aptitudes Nurtured for Unlimited Potential.

Reimagining what it means to MAN UP

With origins in Black vernacular, (to) MAN UP has several meanings. One is to rise to the occasion to complete a task. Another is to take care of one's responsibilities while eschewing any kind of emotionality. A third is to prepare oneself for a fight. Implicit within all three of the definitions of MAN(ing) UP provided above, lies a tacit invoking of rigidified gender roles and the potential for manifestations of toxic masculinity precisely because manhood is defined vis-à-vis womanhood or any other gendered or orientational positionality. Much like whiteness vis-à-vis Blackness, this dialectical relationship positions manhood as the thesis and non-manhood in its panoply of manifestations as the antithesis. Thus, manhood is not only anti-womanhood, it is also homophobic and transantogonisitic as well. According to Butler (1990, 1997) gender performativity is socially constructed. However, it has had and continues to have pernicious material effects for Black men and boys because their perceived hyper-masculinity is a threat that must be controlled. (Starting with criminalization in school, then, the prison industrial complex, and in an alarming number of incidences, sanctioned murder by people entrusted to uphold the laws of the land, Black men have been positioned as public enemy number one.)

Notions of manhood, though they do vary, have seemingly been forever placed in contradistinction to womanhood in this country. This false binary is rife with problematic, seemingly irreconcilable contradictions. Not least of these is a myopic and stubborn insistence on a false dialectical relationship between manhood as the thesis, and womanhood, as the antithesis. Contiguously, notions of manhood are also rife with tensions that are not predicated on the problematic manhood/ womanhood distinction precisely because gender normativity is measured, valued, and ultimately inscribed vis-à-vis one's perceived proximity to heteronormativity. Therefore, "performances" of gender (Butler, 1990) that are incommensurate with prevailing notions of heteronormative manhood are considered to be incrementally and in some case exponentially less manly than more static, socially-constructed definitions of manhood. Furthermore, perceived/purported non-identification with the gender performance most closely associated with one's biological sex is considered strange or queer. This is the result of a patriarchal, heteronormative idealization of manhood that, simultaneously, constrains and contorts notions of what a "man" can look like, dress like, talk like, act like, and who he can or cannot love (and marry).

So, then, this begs the question: why was this acronym selected, if according to Butler, "Those who fail to do their gender right are regularly punished?" (1997, p. 405). Here is why: In selecting the acronym, MAN UP, we were purposeful in including the notion of nurture to this appellation, with the expressed aim of eschewing contrived, toxic hyper-masculinized notions of Black manhood. More simply put: we wanted to first deconstruct and, subsequently, rehabilitate (i.e., to rid it of its toxicity) notions of manhood alongside the students we served. I readily admit that this concept may be beyond saving for the reasons listed above as well as many others. That said, because Black manhood has always been subaltern and subordinated in contradistinction to manhood proper (i.e., white manhood), I wanted to afford our scholars a chance to wrestle with prevailing and historical conceptions of both manhood and Black manhood so that they could determine for themselves whether there was anything redeemable about this concept. My hope was that in so doing, we would provide spaces for MAN UP students to interrogate their conceptualizations of manhood, generally, and Black manhood, specifically, to develop more inclusive, more expansive understandings of their role in society as framed by a personal and collective commitment to equity and justice for all.

The team of instructors led by myself (Mr. J) for the RAM class, Mr. K for the Math class, and Mr. S for the CS/Mobile Apps class implemented the program to leverage all three meanings, in part, by seamlessly incorporating Black language, culture, and daily life experiences into STEM learning. Within this framework, we designed learning experiences that uniquely nurtured the participants' aptitudes—their innate or acquired capacities and talents—for STEM and, then, in turn worked diligently to encourage, empower, and equip them to use, or apply, their STEM knowledge and talents for social justice at the local, national, and even global level. We experience success, which I will speak to detail later in this book. To achieve this goal, or at the very least set the stage so that this goal is in reach, I am proposing a revolution in STEM pedagogy.

Real recognize real: Operationalizing critical-reality pedagogy

The MAN UP educational team consciously and collaboratively instituted a critical-reality pedagogical approach as a deliberate way to develop the students' identities with and competencies in STEM as well as their capacities to conceptualize, develop, create, and test socially just applications of STEM. A critical-reality pedagogical approach, which alloys the critical pedagogical work of Freire (1997),

Giroux (2011), Duncan-Andrade, and Morrell (2008) and others with Emdin's (2010, 2016) work on reality pedagogy, is in many ways akin to the metaphor used to explain critical thinking. To be considered a critical thinker—according to this metaphor—one must be willing to think outside of the confines/paradigm of the seemingly concretized box. However, a critical-reality metaphor goes further in that simply thinking outside of the "box" is not sufficient. Rather, a critical-reality pedagogical approach holds that students should not only be encouraged to think outside of the box, but, rather, that they should also be empowered, encouraged, and equipped to critically analyze the box (i.e., paradigm) to determine if its positionality is victimizing particular groups of people while, simultaneously, illuminating the beneficiaries of the box's positionality. The goal of this pedagogical approach is to (re)position students to use their knowledge and skills to deconstruct the box (i.e., white supremacist based structuralized inequity) in a way that is commensurate with social justice.

Critical-reality pedagogically not only looks at macro level injustices, ala critical pedagogical, but it also positions students to understand, identify, and began to deconstruct and subsequently redress individualized issues while also helping students realize that the individualized, localized injustices that inform their lived experiences are part and parcel of a larger, macro-level system of oppression that is disproportionately injurious to ~~people~~ poor people of color.

And while both critical and reality pedagogy emphasize student voice and student empowerment, the primary goal of critical-reality pedagogy extends beyond creating comfortable safe-spaces and equipping students with critical analytical tools. A critical-reality pedagogical approach is chiefly concerned with action. Reality pedagogy, which I must point out is intrinsically critical, is concerned with action; however, the action consists of creating opportunities for students to thrive in their classroom spaces by co-creating knowledge, by positioning them as co-teachers and by inviting aspects of their variegated cultures into their learning spaces. These are all vital considerations and necessary components of equitable educative spaces. Critical-reality pedagogy is predicated on these components as well. That said, there is an important tenet that critical-reality pedagogy espouses: while creating opportunities for students to co-create knowledge in a classroom/educative space is indispensable to efficacious, equitable pedagogy, students must also be empowered, encouraged, and equipped to take their classroom learning out of the classroom and apply it to issues that are important to them. Students, then, are encouraged and empowered to develop critical analytical thinking so that they can use their knowledge to shift the socio-political constraints that oppresses them. In the words of North Oakland legend, Oakland Raiders' running back,

Marshawn Lynch, critical-reality pedagogy is: "'bout that action, boss." Critical-reality pedagogy is not in opposition to nor critical pedagogy or reality pedagogy, respectively; instead, it represents an extension by amalgamation of these two indispensable pedagogical positionalitites.

At MAN UP, we were not interested in teaching our students how to fight for the crumbs that fall off the master's table, so to speak. Rather, the goal of the MAN UP critical-reality pedagogical approach was to provide our students with the necessary analytical tools to create access to power for traditionally marginalized students, like themselves, by deconstructing the current power structure and reimagining, and ultimately, re-forming it so that it is commensurate with social justice. This is a shift away from anachronistic views of Black male success, which hold that creating opportunities for Black males to access some scintilla of power from the existing power structure is the final goal. So, to be clear, I am not calling for a reforming of critical pedagogy or reality pedagogy, per se. What I am calling for, however, is a reconceptualization of criticality. In this book as derived from the work that catalyzed this book, criticality is not achieved until transformative, socially just action takes place. In line with this approach, we saw the linguistic, theoretical, and discursive components of Rhetorical Analysis of Manhood (RAM) as a tool kit that was central to the students' development. The RAM course afforded them with critical perspectives to not only absorb STEM, but, concomitantly, to intellectually wrestle with the applications and ethics of STEM knowledge and skills. Although RAM classes were key to this approach, critical-reality pedagogical practices were woven throughout the teaching and learning of all three courses.

Identifying the real issue: It's not just about achievement

"A message for the newborns waiting to breathe: If you believe then you can achieve—just look at me." This was one of my favorite lines from a 2pac record, released in 1997, entitled: Smile for Me Now (featuring Scarface). I, like many of the students that I would eventually come to serve, traversed a terrain like the one 2pac was forced to overcome. I grew up in Section 8 housing in Richmond, California's notorious Iron Triangle. Because of the things that I both endured and witnessed, my work has inhered around creating opportunities for students to hone their agentive voices by committing to real, transformative community change using education as a lever for upward mobility and community uplift. Creating spaces for hyper-marginalized students to be exposed to and enmeshed within critical, rigorous, and transformative education is a matter of social justice and should result in both college-readiness and a strong commitment to their communities. Returning to 2pac, if we are to believe the myth of meritocracy, to lift himself out of the deleterious realities that he was faced with, 2pac simply had to work incredibly hard; he had to demonstrate indefatigable grit, and dogged perseverance, while maintaining his undying belief in his abilities and talent. This, according the notion of rugged individualism that undergirds our national ethos, is what is necessary in order to achieve, which is why when talking about the differential educational outcomes between hyper-marginalized students vis-à-vis mainstream students, conversations that over-determine the achievement gap are incredibly problematic. There is ample data that highlights the disproportional, negative educational outcomes for hyper-marginalized students of color. This is true from kindergarten through college. Hyper-marginalization occurs when a group that faces marginalization due to on identity contingency, for example, socio-economic status also faces a different kind of marginalization based on yet another identity contingency, for example, ethnicity. For example, a poor, non-educated, single Latina mother for whom English is her second language can be marginalized for any one of those identity contingencies; however, when those three contingencies function in concert along with and predictive of living in an economically underserved community—this is hyper-marginalization. According to Wacquant (2010), hyper-marginalization is not happenstantial; instead, hyper-marginalization, which produces hyper-ghettoes, is a necessary component of perverse capitalistic greed.

There is ample data that highlights the disproportionate, negative educational outcomes for Black males, from kindergarten through college. Much of the data is positioned to explicate and in some cases, explain what has been termed the achievement gap. However, the so-called "achievement gap" is a red herring that obfuscates the real problem: there is a real, protracted opportunity gap (or gulf, to be more accurate) between low-income, first in family, underrepresented students of color (i.e., hyper-marginalized students) and their more well-resourced Asian American and European American counterparts. More simply put: hyper-marginalized students are not afforded the same opportunities that that their more affluent European and Asian American counterparts are. So, the issue is not truly predicated on achievement, which connotes intrinsic drive and perseverance; rather, the real issue is that equitable educational opportunities are rare for poor Black and Brown students (Freire and Macedo, 1997). This understanding is an important and necessary piece to the larger puzzle, i.e., how to best empower, encourage, and equip hyper-marginalized students to identify as and, subsequently, succeed as college ready students. Many hyper-marginalized students are pushed out or drop out of school before they can experience scholastic success. The conjoined

MAN UP curricular-pedagogical approach was designed to disrupt this alarming trend by centering the lived-experiences of the students that we served. We listened to our students so that we could work collaboratively, in solidarity, to ameliorate their individual suffering as well as the suffering experienced within their communities. We were careful not to pathologize our students by over-determining suffering. That said, coming from where I came from, I do know that impoverished, violent communities can produce a kind of nihilism that is pervasive and stubbornly difficult to shake free of. Therefore, the mission, goals, and structure of the MAN UP program were designed to provide an opportunity for our students to challenge their understanding of their potential to learn, excel, and change their material realities by using STEM as a lever for social justice.

In developing MAN UP, the instructional team was fully aware of the reality that the young men we were endeavoring to work with faced a slew of circumstances that are specific to them, but due to no fault of their own. Simply because they were low-income (as determined be eligibility for Free and Reduced Lunch), urban, middle school Black males, there were educational and social-civic obstacles that they need to be prepared to overcome. Contrary to the negative stereotypical depictions promulgated in mass media and in K-12 education, nationally, we were convinced that there were no innate deficits in the young men we planned to serve. We were also convinced that much of the low educational achievement of this group, the so-called achievement gap, is in fact based on structural and institutionalized, long-standing racist apparatuses (Delpit, 2012; Leonardo, 2010), which inform all aspects of their lived experiences. This is something that we spoke openly about to the powerful young men that we served. Deeply-entrenched structural and institutionalized racism carry the negative potential to adversely affect, seemingly, every facet of Black males' personhood, from identity formation and development to material advancement opportunities and actual, legal freedom (Alexander, 2010). The realities of limited access to equitable, STEM education for Black males, functions as a microcosm for this macro-level reality (Mahiri and Sims, 2016). Therefore, the goal of the MAN UP program was to arrive at a measure of educational equity, which, for me, is intentional work towards the creation of positive, nutritive educational spaces that actively combat structural and institutionalized inequity so that all students are empowered, encouraged, and equipped to succeed academically precisely because they have been afforded rigorous and rich educational opportunities that allow them work towards the realization of their full academic and human potential. Again, this book is interspersed with recollections of the vicissitudes of my own navigation of the world as a Black male. However, the inquiry into the efficacy of a STEM focused program, predicated on critical-reality pedagogy, on the identification, competency, and socially just applications of STEM for a group of urban, predominately low-income middle school Black males is the focus, heart of this book.

Chapter 1 review: Considerations and questions

Considerations: In this chapter, I discussed the impetus of the curricular design and pedagogical approach to the MAN UP program. This program was create to foster an educational environment wherein Black boys could be exactly who they were and still be viewed as students full of promise and potential, not students who are in any way cognitively, culturally, or linguistically deficient.

Questions for students:

1. This chapter spoke in detail about many of the negative statistics that characterize the academic struggles that we have had in STEM education, specifically, and in education overall, generally. How does it make you feel to know that while we are personally responsible for our own academic success, the struggles that we face are not due to any in-born lack but, instead, are the direct result of a system that was created to limit our success?

2. This chapter also spoke in detail about many of the negative stereotypes that have been associated with us—how does it make you feel to know that these, false, stereotypes were created to make you think less of yourselves and your abilities?

3. How are you going to use your understanding about structuralized inequity and negative stereotyping to make sure that other Black males as well as other marginalized students are no longer negatively impacted by these lies about their ability?

4. What does it "keeping it 100" mean to you; and, what does it look like in a STEM class?

Consideration:

Black males in this country face myriad obstacles precisely because they are compelled to participate in a compulsory educational system that has not and arguably, largely, does not have their best interest at heart (Duncan-Andrade & Morrell, 2008). Knowing this, we all have to devise ways to engage these young men, meaningfully, while ignoring any impulse to coddle them in any way. Because, high expectations are integral to Black males' academic success (Darling-Hammond,

2010); however, high expectations without proper supports are not only unrealistic, they are also burdensome. One of the tenets of this book is that authenticity is key. This is what I am referring to as keeping it 100, i.e., carving out opportunities for reciprocal authenticity between teachers and students and students and teachers.

Questions for educators:

1. This chapter outlined some of the pressing issues and obstacles that Black males face simply by virtue of the families that they are born into due to structural and institutionalized racism and inequity—how will you account for the obstacles that they have to face and support them, academically, without lowering your expectations for them?
2. How will you disabuse the pernicious effects of structural and institutionalized racism in developing your classroom culture, pedagogy, and curriculum?
3. How will you create spaces for students, especially Black males, to interrogate and deconstruct the stereotypes that have been sutured to them because of their race, ethnicity, socio-economic status, etc.?
4. If there is indeed value in thinking through ways to revolutionize, even at the micro-level, your pedagogy—what can you/will you do differently in order to carve out sustainable spaces for Black males to participate in the meaning-making and knowledge-creating processes that take place in your class?
5. How do you or will your work towards educational equity for the hyper-marginalized students that you serve while, simultaneously, empowering them to work towards the development of their own agency.

Keywords:

Opportunity gap, critical-reality pedagogy, toxic masculinity, Black death, achievement

References

Alexander, M. (2010). *The new Jim Crow: Mass incarceration in the age of colorblindness.* New York, NY: The New Press.

Butler, Judith (1997). *The psychic life of power: theories in subjection.* Stanford, California: Stanford University Press.

Butler, J. (1990). *Gender trouble: Feminism and the subversion of identity.* New York, NY: Routledge.

Darling-Hammond, L. (2010). *The flat world and education: How America's commitment to equity will determine our future.* New York: Teachers College Press.

Delpit, L. (2012). *Multiplication is for White people: Raising expectations for other people's children.* New York, NY: The New Press.

Duncan-Andrade, J., & Morrell, E. (2008). *The art of critical pedagogy: Possibilities for moving from theory to practice in urban schools.* New York, NY: Peter Lang.

Emdin, C. (2010). *Urban science education for the hip-hop generation: Essential tools for the urban science educator and researcher.* Ithaca, NY: Columbia University Press.

Emdin, C. (2016). *For white folks who teach in the hood … And the rest of y'all too: Reality pedagogy and urban education.* Boston, MA: Beacon Press.

Fanon, F. (1968). *Black skin, white masks.* New York, NY: Grove Press.

Fanon, F., & Sartre, J. (1965). *The wretched of the earth.* New York, NY: Grove Press.

Freire, P. (1997). *Pedagogy of the oppressed* (20th Century Anniversary ed.). (Myra Bergman Ramos, Trans.). New York, NY: Continuum Publishing.

Freire, P., & Macedo, D. (1987). *Literacy: Reading the word & the world.* New York, NY: Continuum Publishing.

Giroux, H. (2011). *On Critical Pedagogy.* New York, NY: Bloomsbury Academic

Leonardo, Z. (2010). *Race, whiteness, and education* (Kindle edition).

Mahiri, J. (2017). *Deconstructing race: Multicultural education beyond the color-bind.* New York, NY: Teachers College Press.

Mahiri, J., & Sims, J. J. (2016). Engineering equity: A critical pedagogical approach to language and curriculum change for African American males in STEM (55–70). In Z. Babaci-Wilhite (Ed.), In *Curriculum change in language and STEM subjects as a right in education.* Rotterdam: Sense Publishing.

Marsh, J. H., Mendoza-Denton, R., & Adam Smith, J. (2010). *Are we born racist? New insights from neuroscience and positive psychology.* Boston, MA: Beacon Press.http://1.usa.gov/nwHbku

Noguera, P. (2008). *The trouble with Black boys: And other reflections on race, equity, and the future of public education.* San Francisco, CA: Jossey-Bass.

Scott, A. L. (2010). *Dissecting the data: The STEM education opportunity gap in California.* Retrieved from http://www.lpfi.org/sites/default/files/dissecting_the_data_-_STEM_ed_opportunity_gap_lpfi_report.pdf

Scott, A. L., & Martin, A. (2012). *Dissecting the data 2012: Examining STEM opportunities and outcomes for underrepresented students in California.* Retrieved from http://www.lpfi.org/sites/default/files/dissecting_the_data_2012_final.pdf

Sharpe, C. (2016). *In the wake: On Blackness and being* (Kindle edition). Durham, NC: Duke University Press.

Sims, J.J., Hotep, L.O., James, K. (Forthcoming). The whole 10 yards: Increasing educational opportunities for African American males in Community College. In *Engaging African American men in Community College.* Charlotte, N.C: Information Age, Inc.

Skinner, R. (2008). *Black Caucus highlights disparages and suggests philanthropic solutions.* Retrieved from http://www.atlanticphilanthropies.org/news/black-caucus-highlights-disparages-and-suggests-philanthropic-solutions…

Steele, C. (2010). *Whistling Vivaldi: And other clues to how stereotypes affect us*. New York, NY: W. W. Norton.

Wacquant, L. (2008). *Urban Outcasts: A Comparative Sociology of Advanced Marginality*. Cambridge: Polity Press.

2

Cutting straight the truth

Interrogating White supremacist-based racism's role in perceptions of Black maleness

Racism, which is predicated on a delusional and perverse notion of white supremacy (Roberts, 2011; Roediger, 1994; Mahiri, 2017), rests upon a pernicious, manufactured and patently false dialectical relationship with whiteness positioned as the *thesis*, and, Blackness, seemingly forever positioned as its *antithesis*. This dialectical relationship was overt, violent, and ubiquitous and—both socially and juridically accepted—for much of American history. However, more recently whiteness has transmogrified. The overt hatred characterized by the peculiar institution of American Chattel Slavery, the three-fifths compromise, lynching, Jim Crow Laws, Separate but Equal Laws, segregation, and personified by the KKK, are no longer palatable for the general populace. So, racism has become less overt, in many respects (Leonardo, 2009). Groups of whites can no longer lynch young Black men with impunity; unless, of course, in place of a noose, there is a gun, and in the place of angry white mobs, there are uniformed law enforcement officers or overzealous pseudo-peace officers like the man that murdered Trayvon Martin. As is always the case, white supremacy is going through yet another pernicious iteration due to the white fragility that resulted in the election of President Number 45 and his band of white Nationalists. What has not changed, however, is that Black youth culture has been forcibly and dangerously conflated with macro-level societal ills like violence and crime (Mahiri & Conner, 2003). This recriminatory strategy, which blames those victimized by white supremacy for their injurious relationship to it, employs ideological state apparatuses (e.g., schools, media, etc.) in the place of the more expensive and resource-intensive repressive state apparatuses (e.g., KKK, militia groups, police, military, etc.) it once relied heavily upon to ensure the continued promulgation of the white supremacist agenda (Althusser, 1971; Leonardo, 2009).

Media is one of the most affective and, therefore, effective ideological state apparatuses. Ultra-conservative voices like DiIulio (1995) along with a host of other conservative "pundits" have vilified Black boys born to single mothers in impoverished communities for decades. This ethos is captured in DiIulio's (1995) "Superpredator" theory. Scholarship in the vein of DiIulio's tenuous theory serve to promulgate fear, racial profiling, and a deadly reification of negative, Black male stereotypes. Therefore, purported claims of fear for one's life, when face to face with an unarmed Black man, in the minds of people who accept these problematic stereotypes, somehow, allows for juridically sanctioned murder of unarmed Black boys and men. This negative reification of Blackness is convenient for white supremacy's capitalistic endeavors as well: Black males are sadistically over-represented in the multi-billion-dollar prison industrial complex (Alexander, 2010). This is Chattel Slavery, reformulated. According to Sabol, West, and Cooper (2010), the Bureau of Justice statistics data showed "an estimated 4.8% of Black men were in prison or jail, compared to 1.9% of Hispanic men and .7% white men." The incarceration rates of Black people have been on the decline from 41.3 percent in 2000 to 38.6 percent in 2006 (Sabol et al., 2010); however, this is not the popular narrative because this narrative has the potential to begin unraveling the web of inconsistencies that white supremacy necessitates for its continued existence and prominence. Still, Black males are more than six times as likely as White males to be incarcerated in this country (Alexander, 2010). So, either Black men and boys are innately and intrinsically prone to criminality, or, more accurately, there is a carceral system in place that was instituted to police, imprison, and exploit the bodies of Black males (Alexander, 2010).

Behind the mask: Uncovering whiteness

What is whiteness? Whiteness is, first and foremost, the power to control language. Moreover, it is the power to define, to classify, to categorize, to shun, to eschew, etcetera. Whiteness validates the standard and derisively invalidates any and everything it considers non-standard. It is interpellational and accusatory, yet malleable. Moreover, whiteness positions itself as the "universal equivalent"(per

Marxist terminology); that is, it is positioned as the determiner of both use and exchange value, and thus, value and, ultimately, worth. Whiteness determines the value of other commodities, in this case of other cultural commodities. It is also able to determine what qualifies as valuable and invaluable. In our society, whiteness has the power to determine what does and what does not count as currency, as capital, by either recognizing or ignoring forms of cultural capital based on their proximity to whiteness. This power of valuation is not limited to material goods. It has been extended to encompass cultural value as well. Cultures that are commensurate with Europocentric values of "democracy," meritocracy, free trade, often Judeo-Christian and or Protestant aesthetics are of much more value than cultures that are incommensurate with these Europocentric, heteronormative, patriarchal ideals. Culture that is different from or perceived to be in opposition to whiteness is dismissed, denigrated, and sometimes destroyed (see the panoply of African and Indigenous cultures destroyed throughout our history) with only palatable vestiges left to be appropriated and exploited.

Racist depictions of African Americans—that have been reified and commodified through mass media vehicles like Blackface Minstrelsy, and concretized through various conscious and unconscious racist institutions and practices—have not simply disappeared. Imagery that depicts African Americans as unintelligent, bestial sub-humans, who speak a vulgar, corrupt form of English are still pervasive (though subtler), and are deeply ingrained in the collective American psyche (Lott, 1993). Even our Nation's former leader, and arguably the most powerful man in the world, President Barack Obama, was not exempt. Despite his academic pedigree, Obama, a graduate of Columbia University and Harvard Law School, where he was the president of the Harvard Law Review and where he received a juris doctorate in law, was still fodder for the New York Post editor who in 2010 ran a cartoon likening the author of the stimulus bill in question (presumably President Obama) to a dead ape. Still, overt racist attacks like this one are much less prevalent than they once were, though, following the election of the 45th President of the United Sates, there has been an uptick in hate crimes. Nevertheless, they are just as powerful. These types of attacks have transmogrified and are now recapitulated through deficit model thinking and the policy that it catalyzes. No longer is it explicitly stated (and widely accepted) that African Americans have intrinsic, biological deficiencies; now, the deficiencies are attributed to more abstract conceptions like culture. To this point Foucault (1977) writes: the second mode for turning human beings into objectified subjects [i.e., "others"] is related to, but independent from, the first. Let us call it "scientific classification." "It arises from the modes of inquiry which give themselves the status of sciences;

for example, the objectivizing of the speaking subject in grammaire generale, philology, and linguistics…" (Foucault, 1977, p. 78).

The classificatory nature of our society, though problematic in my opinion, is not what I am addressing per se; rather, I am addressing for the sake of analysis the way/s that ideological predispositions inform the classificatory process. This is important because these classifications determine the ways in which people are perceived in racialized and gendered terms, among others. These perceptions, then, inform the opportunities that different people are afforded. This, in large part, is the impetus for much of the struggles that Black boys, the focal group of this book, face in STEM in particular and in school more generally (Mahiri & Sims, 2016). As I mentioned before, though a lack of opportunity is perhaps the most reliable determinant of Black male success in STEM (Darling-Hammond, 2010), Black boys and their families and even their culture is often blamed for their struggles in STEM. According to Steele (2010), Black boys then begin to internalize the negative stereotypes that have been made to seem endemic, intrinsic, and innate. To this point Fanon writes:

> Every colonized people—in other words every people in whose soul an inferiority complex has been created by the death and burial of its local and cultural originality—finds itself face to face with the language of the civilizing nation; that is…The colonized is elevated above his jungle status in proportion to his adoption of the [colonial] mother country's cultural standards. He becomes Whiter as he renounces his Blackness, his jungle. (Fanon, 1968, p. 14)

The promulgation of anti-Black rhetoric, policies, and laws via both ideological and juridical sanctions, is, in large part to blame for the cultural misidentification that many Black boys are forced to confront. According to Gramsci (1971), this type of self-devaluation is the result of a deeply embedded (cultural) hegemony: Over time, the oppressed are repeatedly indoctrinated and, consequently, they are "duped" into becoming complicit in their oppression (Gramsci, 1971; Hall, 1996; Marx, 1977). Poor marginalized students who come from under-resourced, underfunded schools—children who are tracked into classes with low expectations—become resistant to and alienated from school culture (Delpit, 2012; Kozol, 2005). Black students are far less likely to go to graduate high school and/or go to college than their white or Asian counterparts (Steele, 2010). It cannot simply be because they are inherently less capable—this assumption often couched in colloquial language is racist and erroneous; yet it is in circulation. Therefore, the more likely explanation for the continued underrepresentation of Black students in STEM is not aptitude or interest. On the contrary, it is the lack of equitable educational opportunities that this Nation's White supremacist based educational ideology and practice engenders (Althusser, 1971; Foucault, 1977).

Althusser (1971) names two discrete State deployed controlling mechanisms, Ideological State Apparatuses (ISA's) and Repressive State Apparatuses (RSA's), respectively. For Althusser, RSA's ensure domination by force whereas ISA's are employed to coerce complicity even to one's own detriment. This is hegemony. More precisely, whereas issues of domination operate from the outside, e.g., direct threat of force by police, militia, posse, etcetera—hegemony, on the other hand, operates from within. Often the dominant group employs ISA's to indoctrinate and condition the oppressed; for Althusser, ISA's are "certain number of realities which present themselves to the immediate observer in the form of distinct specialized institutions" (p. 143). Any number of ISA's can be made to work in concert to produce and preserve a distinctly Westernized White reality. Schooling is a normalizing enterprise. In Althusser's terms, schools are Ideological State Apparatuses that work to normalize or in more specific terms, standardize, the values, encoded language, aesthetics, and sensibilities of students of color so that if even if students of colors' ideologies are not in lockstep with White supremacy, at the very least they are not a threat to it.

Playing with house money: Whiteness commoditized

Whiteness is pervasive: it is licentious and seductive; it cruelly beckons non-whites because it becomes the ultimate instantiation of capital "C" culture and high class. It is excess, success. However, it is a tease, a ruse. It seduces, but in truth has not the slightest inkling to widen its aperture to allow for the inclusion of people bereft of the most necessary commodity in this toxic relationship, whiteness. This fact, though, it hides well. Therefore, racial minorities still, perhaps unwittingly, measure their success by their proximity to this elusive whiteness (Fanon, 1968. Hence, it is a fetishization of privilege akin to a fetishism of commodities, because it is precisely that: a commodity. Whiteness, the universal equivalent, is imbued with mystical, god-like powers of creation. Therefore, it cannot be pinned down because it, unlike, say, Blackness or Mexican-ness cannot or more specifically will not be reduced to simple physiognomy. Whiteness is the default nationality: it is just "American" here in the states. Whiteness carries with it the power to delimit levels or degrees of specificity; whiteness can compartmentalize and marginalize. Because it is ubiquitous, it seems almost phantasmal or in the least nebulous and unidentifiable. However, it is pervasive and suffocating. It is purposely opaque.

According to Roediger it is "nothing but false and oppressive"; yet, it is "constructed from real, predictable, repeated patterns of life (Roediger, 1994)." (In the preceding quote Roediger is speaking of race in general, but his analysis extends to whiteness proper as well.) Thus, Roediger argues that only the abolition of whiteness will begin to remedy the injustices and inequalities that it foments. This view though desirable, is possibly too expansive to ever become realizable. More specifically, whether whiteness is abolished, committed educators that work alongside students marginalized, persecuted, and oppressed by white supremacy must continue to press forward even if white supremacy is not yet eradicated. We must conduct guerrilla warfare—that is, we must fight the injustice catalyzed and ensured by white supremacy wherever we are whether it be in our classroom, at the organizing level, in the policy sphere; it must be in whatever sphere of service we occupy. We must continue to call out and address the wages of white supremacy that we see as well as the wages that our students identify, even if we do not see because whiteness has historically and frustratingly dodged blame for the injustices that it catalyzes and later institutionalizes. Instead of whiteness being put on trial, marginalized oppressed people's moral compass, language, even their culture writ large is tried (and often, convicted) for their own precarious lived realities. This dissimulation affords a space for whiteness to function in the interest of whiteness, albeit, without making whiteness manifest. This has much to do with whiteness' control of language, which is why whiteness does and must continue to repudiate and or castigate all languages it deems non-standard, i.e., non-white. Attitudinally, whiteness is utopist and dismissive: that is, it envisions a world where whiteness is the standard; where whiteness is privileged; where whiteness is the goal (much like the one we currently inhabit) to perpetuity.

So, then, to disallow whiteness from exculpating itself yet again, we must say, rightly, that it is the root cause of the nihilistic threat discussed earlier. Whiteness would have it that the inequalities and injustices that marginalized groups are confronted with seem natural, even ordered. Whiteness is renowned (by itself) for its work ethic, which allows for arguments regarding structural injustices to be reducible to an insignificant and patently false discourse on meritocracy. The main tenets of this argument go something like this: non-whites, that is those who do not enjoy/experience whiteness, are deficient in some way, whether it is morally, culturally, linguistically, educationally, etc. Therefore, they are unable to secure for themselves the tools, the capital, to earn/purchase merit. Whiteness prefers to speak in individual generalities, which also serve, paradoxically, as essentialisms. In this way, whiteness makes a habit of accusing the accuser: if someone claims that structural and/or institutional racism is to blame for her or his condition, whiteness points an accusatory finger right back at the accuser. The accuser's class, culture, language or even their race comes under fire. It is in this way that whiteness extricates itself from blame. It becomes the accuser's own "deficiencies" that best describe her or his oppressed condition, not white supremacy. (In truth, the term deficiency is just a colloquialism that describes ones' distances from or to whiteness.) Because whiteness controls the legitimation of language and therefore the legitimation of thought, it can determine who is and who is not deficient. For much of our history here in the United States, whiteness has defined itself vis-à-vis another abstraction: Blackness.

The construction of "Whiteness" vis-à-vis "Blackness"

Whiteness is an assumed patriarchal positionality: the founding fathers are just that, fathers; they are men. Consequently, they are the exemplars of whiteness. Every non-white, then, is an infant of sorts. More precisely, every non-white is infantilized by whiteness to maintain whiteness' requisite patriarchal structure. What is more, whiteness is married to fantasy of the American past. This is problematic because the good ole' days involve, inextricably, the institution of slavery. Plantation nostalgia relies on these images—the two, slavery and plantation lore are inseparable (Sharpe, 2016). Depictions of the contented Black slave, a perpetual infant, and the benevolent white slave owner/patriarch are mainstays of the "good old days" myth. For this reason, the notion of "whiteness" in the United States is forever tethered to the notion of "blackness"; the first form of mass entertainment, Blackface Minstrelsy was a vehicle that promulgated and later reified notions of difference. Whites' recognize themselves as well as other whites through, firstly, differentiation (e.g., that they are white and not Black) and later through identification, either knowingly or unknowingly, with the privilege that accompanies their "whiteness." (Whiteness here is meant to be analogous to superiority; this whiteness is predicated, by and large, on the conformity of non-whites to the role of the subservient "other" in order to complete these unequal dyads.) Ernest (1998) illuminates the egocentric and ethnocentric racist motivation behind the forced capitulation of black males, by that of white males, in the face of slavery. He writes:

> In this complex and tenuous performance of social identity, the security of selfhood is challenge constantly by the presence of others who, either overtly or implicitly, remind one than one is in fact playing a role. One's self-consciousness about the artifice of one's identity [...] leads one to force others into roles that complete one's own identity. (Ernest, 1998, p. 1111)

Psychological consequences of othering, ideological inculcation and cultural misidentification

The Eurocentric domination of reality and therefore of history has left the African American relatively devoid of historicity (Fanon, 1968). This lack comports them in a very peculiar way; that is, in a Hegelian sense, they are always in the stage of *being-for-others*, as opposed to the more agential stage of a being *in-itself-and-for-itself*. As far as this, Fanon (1968) writes:

> As long as he [the Black male] has not been effectively recognized by the other [the White Patriarch], that other will remain the theme of his actions. It is on that other being, that his own human worth and reality depend. It is that other being in whom the meaning of his life is condensed. (p. 217)

Further, Fanon argues that it is this type of reality that leads the oppressed to adopt (condescending) "White masks." The oppressed begin to see themselves and their culture, including if not especially their language, through the eyes of the oppressor. Fanon goes on to write: "There is a fact: White men consider themselves superior to Black men. There is another fact: Black men want to prove to White men, at all costs, the richness of their thought, the equal value of their intellect" (Fanon, 1968). (Fanon speaks almost exclusively of the Black male experience partially because as a wartime psychologist, the clear majority of his patients, both Black and white, were male.) According to Fanon and his contemporary Sartre (1984), it is this type of *neurosis* that causes the Black man to abdicate, even deride, his own mother tongue in favor of one that is more palatable and thereby more acceptable to Whites. This is seemingly a stipulation in a racist, psychological contract, a contract which is based on an empty promise: "The colonized is elevated above his jungle status in proportion to his adoption of the [colonial] mother country's cultural standards. He becomes Whiter as he renounces his Blackness, his jungle" (Fanon, 1968, p. 84). Furthermore, Fanon, elucidating what he later re-terms as a *phobogenic* neurosis (which he argues is deeply embedded within the Negro psyche), writes:

> When the Negro makes contact with the White world, a certain sensitizing action takes place. If his psychic structure is weak, one observers the collapse of the ego...The goal of his behavior will be the Other (in the guise of the White man), for the Other alone can give him worth. (Fanon, 1968, p. 17)

Next, Fanon discusses what he diagnoses as a phobogenic neurosis, which haunts, conditions, and configures all current and former colonized peoples. Fanon's framework is especially enlightening because of his work as a clinical psychiatrist; his observations are based on more than 400 case studies. Furthermore, Fanon is widely regarded as one of the foremost third world, anti-colonial thinkers of our time. Beyond that, while others have hinted at the psychological phenomenon that is present within the African American, Fanon names it (see above). His particular psychoanalytic framework affords us a clearer view into the conflicted psyche, the double-consciousness (Dubois, 1903) that Black people, including middle school Black boys, must wrestle with. We saw this firsthand when we asked each new cohort of MAN UP Scholars to draw a STEM professional.

Pre and post STEM identification surveys. A pre-survey was administered during the program's first session in September of 2013, and a post-survey with the same questions plus additional ones on cohorts' satisfaction with the program was administered during the final academic session in May of 2014. The first prompt on these surveys asked students to "Please draw a scientist, technologist, engineer and/or a mathematician. (Please label your drawing)." On the pre-survey 14 of the 17 focal students drew a balding, bearded, middle-aged European American male in a white lab coat. None of the respondents drew a person of color. One student drew a European American woman, and the remaining two drew extra-terrestrial aliens. On the post surveys, 16 of the 17 focal students drew STEM professionals that were clearly African-American males. Only one student drew a picture of a balding, bearded, middle-aged European American male in a white lab coat. In fact, eight of the students drew pictures of themselves. This is quite significant, because when alloyed with the data that demonstrates students' aspirational shifts regarding their desire to pursue STEM majors and STEM careers, these data suggest that this process was both concomitant and even, perhaps, linear. More specifically, this data, in the form of revisionist drawings, seemed to suggest that members of the focal cohort that began exhibiting growths in their STEM identities by pictographically "becoming" applied STEM practitioners.

By drawing themselves or people who looked like them, they were beginning to re-envisage the role that they could play in STEM and the multiple roles that STEM could potentially play in their futures. This re-positioning was based on the focal cohorts' confidence in applying STEM to issues that they deemed important as well as their expressed desires to pursue both STEM majors, and ultimately, STEM careers. Initially, STEM was limited to middle-aged white men. These revised pictographic representations of STEM professionals clearly demonstrated the focal cohorts' work to challenge the stereotypes that, initially, caused them to limit their own entry into STEM while, simultaneously, devising ways to break down the real barriers to STEM access they face. By changing the face of STEM, these young men created spaces in STEM that they could fill. This is poignantly captured by one member of the focal cohorts' response to why he changed his drawing:

> Well, at first, I kinda felt like only white men could be scientists. That's all I ever see— even on cartoons. I now know that there's a reason for that—that those types [of representations] are based on and support stereotypes. I changed my drawing to a picture of me in order to challenge the stereotypes that say I can't be a STEM professional or be a STEM major. I know I can. That's why I changed my [drawing] to a self-portrait.

The pre-survey also asked students whether they saw themselves as future STEM professionals, and only three of the 17 students from the focal class agreed. On the post-survey, 16 of 17 agreed that they saw themselves potentially as STEM professionals. For example, they indicated considerable increases in their aspirations for pursuing STEM in high school, college, and careers in the post-survey in contrast to the pre-survey. This shift was evidenced by the fact that during the pre-identification survey, only three members of the focal cohort agreed or strongly agreed that they wanted to pursue STEM as a career. Conversely, as mentioned above, during the post-identification survey all but one of the members agreed or strongly agreed that not only could they see themselves as STEM professionals but that they also wanted to pursue STEM in college as well as for a future career. Clearly, as evidenced by the focal cohorts' initial renderings of their conceptions of STEM professional, the focal students initially held rigid conceptions of what STEM practitioners looked like, but over the course of the program, their perceptions dramatically changed to seeing people who looked like them, including picturing themselves as STEM practitioners. In addition to this survey, which was geared specifically to assess students' shifts in STEM identification, the Yearend Program Satisfaction Survey (YPSS), which sought to elicit students' feedback on the overall efficacy of MAN UP, provided valuable data regarding the focal cohorts' shifts in STEM identity.

It's not just about White privilege: Whiteness must be abolished

The term, white privilege (McIntosh, 1988), describes the phenomena of unearned benefits being conferred on people of European ancestry simply by virtue of their pigmentation. This term seems to be more popular than ever in today's political climate. However, for me, this term is insufficient precisely because it does not account for the genesis of the benefits unduly conferred on "White" people. In its current conception, it is as though these benefits, the benefits conferred on White people without merit, are simply pulled from some unknown storehouse of benefits. But, of course, this is not the case. The benefits of white privilege are created by the appropriation and exploitation of non-whites. More simply put, the benefits of white privilege are built on the backs of people of color (Leonardo, 2009). What is more, the notion of privilege suggests that were it not for these privileges, the playing field would be otherwise equal. This is simply not the case. This is precisely why I do not spend a great deal of time deconstructing white privilege; for me, white privilege should not be the focus of critical, emancipatory work because it is but a mere symptom of a much larger, much more deleterious disease: white supremacy.

Roediger (1994) argues that whites must actively dis-identify with whiteness so that whiteness can be abolished. He postulates that rejection of whiteness, by whites, will catalyze a "process that gives rise to...attacks on racism..." (Roediger, 1994, p. 13). He argues that the dissolution of whiteness will not only free oppressed racial minorities, but whites as well—whites who are "burdened by whiteness" (Roediger, 1994, p. 17). Likewise, we know that repeated inculcation at the hands of whiteness' Ideological State Apparatuses in particular (e.g., schools, media, church, etc.) results in coercion; however, this coercion is packaged as complicity. And, arguably, later it does indeed cause a kind of "real" complicity for non-whites. All the while, whiteness positions itself as a kind of non-entity; that is, it makes believe that it does not exist. More precisely, it exculpates itself from blame by relying on a rhetoric of cultural deficiency, linguistic deprivation, and culture of poverty.

To be clear, there is a distinction between Whiteness, which the systemic progeny of white supremacy and people from Scandinavian, European, and Nordic descent/ancestry, among others. I am in no way arguing for the abolition of the actual corporeal bodies of people that consider themselves to be white. What I am arguing for, however, is the abolition of the system of whiteness that pays for and confers unearned benefit to "white" people on the backs of people of color (Leonardo, 2009).

Though differentiating between the abolition of whiteness and the abolition of white people is complicated, it must take place to move this exigent conversation forward. Roediger's plan necessitates a realization of Marxist universal consciousness to be achieved for oppressor and oppressed, for real change to take place. Obviously, this is something of an oversimplification of Roediger's argument; however, the fact remains that he is calling for white people to renounce and reject the privilege that their whiteness ensures them. To be clear, this means that they would, in effect, be acting against their own best interest, at least materially. If our Nation's history is any indication, this is a hard sell.

Ultimately, I agree with Roediger that there must be a thorough uncovering of whiteness before any talk of abolition is to progress—the "enemy" and its many manifestations must be identified. Moreover, there must be a rubric, a legend or key that helps whites to recognize the machinations of whiteness, which is the intent of Whiteness Studies. White supremacy must not be allowed to remain hidden, to maintain its position as the secret puppeteer that animates society for its own interest and advancement, just beyond consciousness or sight. The pervasiveness of White supremacy must be taken to task. To do that, there must be more theory, more discourse, and more discussions that aid in the identification of white supremacy, not only for people of color, but for whites as well. White supremacy is a disease, a cancer; but before we can go about the work of curing it, that is abolishing it, we must understand what triggers it, and where it thrives; we must uncover and ultimately disrupt its teleology.

I am arguing for a tactical, precise, albeit continued progress toward the eradication of white supremacy by calling out and deconstructing the pernicious effects of whiteness on people of color. One of the most dangerous effects of white supremacy on Black boys is that it has cast them as threats.

The transmogrification of Black Males: Thugs and threats

The word "thug" has become synonymous with African-American male. There is no discernible difference in either words usage by many of the people who report on the murders of unarmed Black males. For them, the two words seem to be interchangeable. This, of course, is an issue of framing. During slavery, the Negro was depicted as a happy-go-lucky pickaninny, who was wholly reliant on the slave master to provide for him; this was a justification for the peculiar institution of American chattel slavery (Fanon, 1968). This image changed during Jim Crow (Alexander, 2010): the happy-go-lucky Negro was transmogrified into the Black brute (as a new justification for the abject violence that was visited upon African-Americans by whites, and a justification for segregation). This is illustrated by the willful discursive shift from the term Negro to that of the dreaded nigger. No longer was the Negro a peaceful, God-fearing oaf akin to a farm animal; instead, he became a rapacious, licentious nigger who was only interested in defiling the "virginal" white woman (Lott, 1993).

This is the imagery, with the requisite caricatures, that has won the day now. And, because of this, Black males have been permanently positioned as threats. And, violent (over)reactions to them are based on this positioning. Homicide becomes "justifiable" when one feels as though their life is in danger and that there is no way to avoid bodily injury. Based on the deaths of Michael Brown and Tamir Rice, to name two, clearly the notion of justifiable homicide, when exercised on a Black male—armed or not, requires decidedly less justification. Sharpe (2016) describes this as an aspect of (anti)Blackness in the wake of the peculiar institution of American Chattel Slavery. In this paradigm, theoretically, and in practice as evidenced, microcosmically, but the abovementioned murders of Blackness, the wake of Slavery has positioned Blackness as an irredeemable threat worthy only of violent death.

So, it follows that if society has been duped into becoming complicit in imagining all Black males as threats, irrespective of who they are individually, then, the rationale for justifiable homicide and the burden of proof for justifiable homicide is much lower (or nonexistent). This is the result of the masses having been coerced into believing that all African-American males represent a real and present danger—a threat. This is not only true of police officers, this is also true of the people who would serve as jurors on a potential grand jury or any case that brings charges against an officer who has been charged with violating an African-American male's civil rights.

And, the sad reality is for many Americans is that this makes perfect sense. These travesties of justice, when unarmed Black men, women, and children are gunned down in interactions with law enforcement, are viewed as instances of justifiable homicide precisely because Black people have been positioned as the instantiation of terror, though we have been terrorized ever since the first African forcibly set their emaciated, shackled feet in the new world (Sharpe, 2016). Now to be clear, this is not a recrimination of police. Most police officers, White police officers, do not kill unarmed Black males. That is not something to be applauded, mind you—but it is true. The fact that that this statement needs to be uttered, or in this case written down, speaks volumes. But, I believe instances of police shooting unarmed Black males like Michael Brown and Tamir Rice (a twelve-year old child, playing with a toy gun in an open-carry state) is informed by both the non-conscious and conscious (erroneous) conflation of Black male and threat. What is more, undercover Black male police officers are more than twice as likely to be gunned down by their fellow officers in cases of "friendly fire" than their European American counterparts. This problematic (and patently false) association on the one hand informs police officers interactions with Black males and, simultaneously, supersedes any one interaction between white police officers and Black males. The idea that all Black males are threats and must be subdued is present whether a particular Black male is in fact a threat (Miller, 2011). This is true in our school system as well (Ferguson, 2001).

The 21st century urban colonized

There have been many permutations of popular Black male imagery. Early on characters created and popularized by Blackface Minstrelsy cast the negro as a buffoon only interested in maintaining his obsequiousness while indulging, ad nausea, in licentious behavior and watermelon. Eventually, the antebellum Negro became—during Jim Crow—the dreaded nigger (Lott, 1993. The main character from Wright's (1940) novel, Native Son, Bigger Thomas was the epitome of this newly concocted caricature. Another shift, in the 1990's, was arguably catalyzed by a tragic event in Chicago, Illinois. A shocking murder took place in the Ida B. Wells housing projects: a five-year-old boy was thrown to his death, from a fourteenth story window. The age of the victim as well as the ages of the accused murders, both 10 years old, sent shock-waves reverberating throughout Chicago. This tragedy made national headlines. The public outcry, once the news broke, prompted then-President Bill Clinton to openly address the rampant violence that plagued Chicago's south side. News of this type of depraved, genocidal violence took many Americans by surprise. Many Americans were taken aback by the accounts of the abject violence featured in our America; these Americans did not live in southside Chicago, or East Saint Louis, Missouri, or Gary, Indiana, or Oakland, and Richmond, California. For poor people living in places like Chicago's south side, this kind of violence did not invoke disbelief. In Richmond, California, we already knew stuff was this bad. I remember that when I was in the first-grade, body parts of a third grader were found in the elementary school directly across the street from my house. Police had been looking for a missing young man for a few days. They were alerted to his dismembered corpse because another elementary school student found an ear. Purportedly, this 9-year-old was the casualty of a drug deal gone bad.

Nevertheless, the abject conditions of life in the Ida B. Wells Projects, in Southside Chicago, was met with obdurate disbelief by many white Americans who do not deal with these daily realities. They could not accept that living conditions, here in the Land of Promise, could be so deleterious, so utterly hopeless. West (1993), commenting on the ubiquity of disenfranchisement, low expectations, and violence that pervades inner-city (urban) neighborhoods, argues that a "nihilistic threat" has "infected" the Black community. This ominous threat serves as an explanation, though not exculpation, of many of the social ills (i.e., symptoms) that plague urban ghettos throughout America, e.g., wanton fratricide, misogyny, patriarchal absenteeism; and, disproportionately high rates of crime, under-education, incarceration, out of wedlock births, etc. West defines the nihilistic treat as: a severe apathy that disenfranchises and incarcerates an individual until said individual repudiates the reality of existence, the reality of life, to the point where life itself no longer has value. As I recounted in Chapter One, this was my reality, too. Fanon (1968) in his illuminating anti-colonial treatise, "The Wretched of the Earth" describes behavior by that of the colonized people throughout the Third World that is indecipherable from that of the perceived lumpenproletariat that inhabit the poor, substandard, inequitable living conditions here in the United States. The commonalities that exist in both contexts, colonized and ghettoized, respectively, are too numerous and too persistent to ignore. For example, both groups have become, in essence, domestic expatriates; they are ostracized and separated; consequently, they are made to live on the outside, as the "other" even though they are within their own country. This is because they, colonies and urban ghettos, respectively, are one and the same to the racist white apparatus that instituted both slavery and colonization.

These urban-colonies constitute what Harrington (1962) refers to as the "Other America." Harrington argues that there may be up to 50 million people who are impoverished physically and spiritually. According to Harrington, these people are part of the "other" America. Harrington's work sought to reveal this population, which was either naively overlooked, or purposely ignored. The nihilistic threat is the byproduct of this very same racist, purposeful non-recognition. This problem is widespread, which is why educators, especially urban educators, must be trained to account for the post and persistent-traumatic stress that racism, via neo-colonization, exacts on the urban-colonized; however, this must not be done in an infantilizing way, but in a way that is compassionate, efficacious, and genuine. I am confident that most if not all prior successful teaching of the urban-colonized has, at some point, accounted for these psychosocial, psychosomatic injuries.

The archenemy of hope: The nihilistic threat

Jacobi (https://plato.stanford.edu/entries/friedrich-jacobi/) introduced the concept of nihilism into philosophical discourse. Jacobi was skeptical of rationalism, especially the form of rationalism proffered by Immanuel Kant, which states that, in the end, all rationalism is reducible to nihilism, i.e., to nothingness. For Jacobi, Kant's view is too pessimistic; therefore, he felt that it should be circumvented in favor of a doctrine that, unlike Kant's offering, does not obviate a higher power (God). Nietzsche (2006), who himself was disenchanted and disenfranchised with the over-arching absolutist, religious hyper-morality that characterized his time, redefined nihilism yet again: for him, it was as emptying of the world where values, meanings, purposes, and truth were nonexistent. It is Nietzsche's definition that West (1993) builds on. For West, a person that is tormented by a pervasive nihilism feels as though life is not worth living; what is more, the life that he or she does live is at best illusionary. Nihilism oftentimes results in the creation of a psychopathic behavior. For West, it is the hopelessness that this nihilistic threat produces that is most damaging; to this point he writes, "…the major enemy of Black survival in America has been and is neither oppression nor exploitation but rather the nihilistic threat— that is, loss of hope and absence of meaning (West, 1993, p. 15)." This is precisely because, "…as long as hope remains, and meaning is preserved, the possibility of overcoming oppression stays alive (West, 1993, p. 15)." However, without hope and meaning, West, like Noguera's quote early on in Chapter One, warns that the future of Black America is in grave peril. This is due to a near total disregard of life that characterizes this threat; moreover, a person who is trapped in this kind of snare has a certain predisposition toward suicidal and or homicidal behavior (West, 1993).

Evidence of these violent tendencies is provided by Hutchinson, in an article entitled "Black-on-Black Violence":

> In the 25 years of homicide records from 1976 to 2002 by the Bureau of Justice Statistics, blacks are six times more likely to be murdered than whites, and seven times more likely to kill than whites. (http://www.blacknla.com/news/Articles/EHNOKillings.asp)

This type of destructive behavior is not a new phenomenon: under Imperialistic rule, colonized (Black) African people have historically exhibited eerily similar behavior. Fanon (1968) attributes this type of behavior to a neurosis: "With the exception of a few misfits within a closed environment, we can say that every neurosis, every abnormal manifestation, every affective erythrism in an Antillean is the product of his cultural situation (Fanon, 1968, p. 152)." Fanon, through-out his work, makes no special distinction between the Antillean and all other subjugated colonized people. In this quote the Antillean is representative of all who share their struggle, be it American Blacks, Africans, Indigenous Peoples or "brothers and sisters in Latin America."

This "neurosis" is not happenstantial, nor is it the result of faulty intrinsic wiring or a lack of non-Christian morality (as has been argued). Rather, it is a result of the forced exteriority ("otherness") via the White-supremacist conception of race (in the guise of Western tradition), that Blacks—irrespective of physical locale—through slavery, colonization, and other such atrocities have been made to symbolize. It is the compulsory designation (and subsequent lived reality) as the "other" that creates the nihilistic threat that West described. Consequently, I feel that it is necessary to provide an overview of the (oppressive) progression from slavery to the present, which has created and subsequently reified the notion of Blackness to cast it, forever, in the role of the "other."

The other and "otherness"

Sartre (1984) argues that we perceive ourselves being perceived and subsequently, we come to objectify ourselves in the same way we are being objectified. This is what he terms the look (and later, the gaze). This process exacerbates the urban-colonized's suffering; that is, the oppressor's gaze objectifies the oppressed to the point where the objectified begins to view him or herself in the same way. In this context, regarding the Black man, the objectifying gaze is Eurocentric; it is imbued with the omnipotent power to grant or deny agency at its capricious whim. This was present in our MAN UP scholars. During our first session together, we asked the MAN UP scholars to draw a scientist, technologist, engineer, or mathematician—nearly all the scholars drew pictures that were hetero and Anglo-normative, i.e., all but one drew a picture of a white male. (A more detailed description of this exercise can be found in Chapter Three.) To this point, Fanon writes: "For the Negro there is a myth to be faced. A solidly established myth. The Negro is unaware of it as long as his existence is limited to his own environment; but the first encounter with a white man oppresses him with the whole weight of his blackness" (Fanon, 1968, p. 150). With slavery and colonization especially, white-supremacists exert dominance through violence; their dogma is one that calls for unquestioned adherence to their dictates through the all-too-real threat of death, (both social and actual/physical). Domination differs from the hegemony, which now characterizes present day colonies/ghettos. Hegemony is every bit as coercive as domination, albeit sans the explicit threat of force: it functions on both the subconscious and non-conscious level. It forces pseudo-identification with the oppressors through inculcation and indoctrination. This point is crystallized in a pellucid quote by French social theorist, Alexander De Tocqueville,

> The Negro, plunged in this abyss of suffering, scarcely feels his ill fortune; violence had enslaved him, habituation to slavery has given him a slaves thoughts and ambitions; his admiration for his tyrannical masters is even greater than his hatred and his joy and pride reside in his imitation of those who oppress him…for the Negro, slavery coincides with birth…so to speak before he is born. (De Tocqueville, 2000, p. 372)

Fanon, to this point, goes on to say, regarding the propagandistic conditioning that has become an effective weapon in the colonizer's war chest:

> In other words, there is a constellation of postulates, a series of propositions that slowly and subtly—with the help of books, newspapers, schools and their texts, advertisements, films, radio—work their way into one's mind and shape one's view of the world of the group to which one belongs. In the Antilles that view of the world is white because no black voice exists. (Fanon, 1968, p. 152)

In these contexts, domination and hegemony, respectively, Blacks have been cruelly denied any claims of agency or personhood. This is because slavery and colonization necessitate the dehumanizing denial of Blacks' agency; they have to be essentialized and viewed as subhuman, non-agents in order for their maltreatment to be justifiable. According to Sartre, racist institutions like slavery and colonialism, require "…the Other to be falsely seen as an object" (Sartre, 1984, p. 76). Regarding the isolation and subsequent objectification that produces (forced) "otherness," Nast (2000) posits the notion that "… 'black' housing projects were erected across the country [during the 1960's] to resettle impoverished [and displaced] black folks out of [white] middle class view" (Nast, 2000, p. 232). The same argument can be made of the Imperial colonies in the French Antilles, Senegal, and in Kenya. To be colonized is to be forced to the periphery, to be forced to the exterior; what makes the exile so surreal, so psychologically damaging, is that the Africans and African Americans that are excluded from the mainstream (through slavery and colonization, respectively) are not entirely limited spatially. That is, they are still within the world that they are excluded from. This is also true of the multitude of housing projects that house much of America's poor urban Black population: they too are forced to come to terms with their forced separation, their relegation to the exterior. Nast says of her essay: "This paper explores how the black son [in the Oedipal family dynamic] has historically been made to carry the symbolic burden of incest for the white oedipal family, a racialization in keeping with the encoding of incest itself as blackness—a moral abyss" (Nast, 2000, p. 216).

The repudiation of Blackness and by proxy Black agency, by this Nation's White supremacist apparatuses, allows whites to subjectify Black people on the one hand, and to assuage their own fears of interracial penetration (pun intended), on the other. Therefore, legal measures were taken to outlaw miscegenation. Nast extends Freudian psychoanalysis and his conception of the oedipal triad in her work. While Freud's research is limited to the individual, Nast, on the other hand, sets out to diagnose an entire racist ideology. She argues that on a subconscious level, racist Whites have inserted Blacks as the permanent figure of incestuous desire. (Incest in most societies is so serious, so proscribed, that is thought to have the ability to bring down an entire civilization.) Nast writes, "…black men structurally assumed the place of the evil son [in the oedipal triangle] who cannot help his natural inclinations and involution, for he embodies incestuous desire itself (Nast 217)." Precisely because, as Nast puts it: "'Blackness' figured as the negation of the (white) family, white supremacy in the U.S. spoken anxiously through a contrapuntal rhetoric of Black danger and white maternal safety" (Nast, 2000, p. 216). This arrangement, promulgated via mass media, and made manifest materially through racist education, housing, and penal policies have conspired to transmogrify Black people into a group of walking dead. The argument that follows this line of thinking holds that poor Black males are desensitized because they have been conditioned to view themselves through the eyes of the oppressor, as less than human. I do not disagree with this. However, if this argument is not nuanced, it allows for the locus of blame to be placed on Black males while, tacitly, exculpating the White supremacist apparatus that has dehumanized them (us) in the first instance. Specifically, it is our systematic and systemic dehumanization, that results in the inward (psychological), and outward (physical) manifestations of violence within our communities. While theoretically rich, this argument requires a deeper analysis—one in which the psyche of Black males is analyzed vis-à-vis the apparatuses that inflict psychological, emotional, and physical pain on them. According to Alexander (2010), joblessness is the primary determinate for future violent behavior, irrespective of ethnicity. This reality, though, is not a departure from West's conception of the pernicious effects of the nihilistic threat; instead, it supports it.

Black ghettoes: Our "Other" America

Not only are Black people othered psychologically and socio-emotionally, we are also othered spatially as well, which then contributes to a vicious cycle wherein our symbolic othering is legitimized by are spatial othering and vice versa. Harrington's

(1962) work was different from other works on poverty in that it addressed the psyche of ostracized poor people. He illuminated the concentricity that exists between poverty and hopelessness, and hopelessness and a defeatist attitude. He wrote, "…poverty twists and deforms the spirit. The American poor are pessimistic and defeated, and they are victimized by mental suffering to a degree unknown in Suburbia" (Harrington, 1962, p. 3). This suffering, a suffering that is firmly tethered to, even to the point of forming a symbiosis with poverty, leads to, in mild cases, a static ambivalence, and in more serious cases, sheer crippling hopelessness. (This is not to say that rich people are forever excluded from the ranks of the hopeless, or that poor people are evermore relegated to said ranks.) Admittedly, there are no absolutes in this situation; poverty and happiness are no more mutually exclusive than are wealth and sadness. Still, one would be hard pressed to argue that the pervasive nihilism, which is indicative of these areas, is purely imaginary, or worse, non-existent. The effects of penury as well as the poverty of spirit that are indicative of these urban-colonies are, at the core, unhealthy and acrimonious. According to Harrington, "…poverty is constructed to destroy aspiration; it is a system that is designed to be impervious to hope" (Harrington, 1962, p. 10).

Harrington's work served to illuminate the cyclical nature of poverty, not in hopes of immediate redress, per se—(Harrington himself is not prescriptive); rather, he is calling for immediate acknowledgement. He says, "We must perceive passionately, if this blindness is to be lifted from us" (Harrington, 1962, p. 17). To a degree, his book achieved its goal: it helped to bring new attention to the plight of and, simultaneously, open new discourse regarding the long-forgotten others that inhabit the other America. Harrington's book, in no small measure, opened an atmosphere, though still virulent in large part that was, nonetheless, relatively speaking, more accepting of cries for social change. However, the interest and attention that his book garnered for the urban-colonized during the 1960's, was replaced in the ensuing decades by the get-tough, conservative rhetoric of the Regan administration. During this time Black people became the face of poverty, welfare, and the mounting crack epidemic. Again, via mass media, Blacks were recast as the underserving poor, the other.

Still, the question must be asked: How is it that this "otherness" was engendered? During slavery, there was neither film nor radio; moreover, newspapers were not widespread. So, how was this insidious "otherness" promulgated in the first place? How was it so pervasive? It was through America's very first form of mass media/mass entertainment: Blackface Minstrelsy.

Going viral in the 19th century: The minstrel show

Blackface Minstrelsy allowed the New World American white man to exculpate himself, in a sense, from the condescending gaze that he felt the Europeans constantly had fixed upon him. They used Black masks to eschew the behavior thought of as normative or proper by Europeans and higher-class whites as well. The images of these pseudo-Black characters, through misdirection and purposeful misidentification, allowed the white actors, on a conscious level, and native white society, perhaps on a more subconscious level, to throw off the proverbial shackles of propriety, of decorum. In effect, they were no longer themselves while in Blackface; rather, they voluntarily transformed into the uncivilized, American anathema—the Negro. As for the show's format, misunderstanding and confusion constituted much of the humor associated with these sketches; although, this was only a superficial manifestation. These works served as a social commentary of sorts; minstrels functioned as a place outside of reality that still, somehow paradoxically, represented reality. It was a place where patrons could have their socio-political views and values affirmed or substantiated through fantasy. Another reason for the euphoric spell that minstrelsy cast over its audiences was that it provided an unmistakable contrast, which allowed the perceived glory of whiteness to shine even more radiantly vis-à-vis the Black backdrop that the pseudo-Negro characters provided (Lott, 1993).

The actors in these (mis)portrayals wore grotesque smiles on their painted faces. This choice was designed to further dehumanize Africans by making them appear to be non-human creatures and or buffoonish caricatures. These smiles were very significant. The prevailing rhetoric during this time, that slaves were happy with their lot in life, with their forced obsequiousness, early on, was part of white slave-owner doctrine. It served as a simultaneous defense and justification—consciously and unconsciously—for both slavery and the minstrel shows that espoused the dogma of this institution. This absurd belief later became a key component in the plantation lore that fueled the American psyche as well as the minstrel show for decades to come. The white actors who put on these black faces were not after accuracy in their costumes or face paint, though they often tried to make claims of authenticity; on the contrary, they sought only to create or derive comedy from the African American condition. And, more importantly, they sought to cast Blacks as the permanent backdrop for and negation of whiteness.

The primary reason that Black people must be made to occupy the space of the other is so that whiteness can be defined, through differentiation, as that which is not black, and therefore, that which is not heathen, licentious, and animalistic. The notion of "whiteness" in the United States is forever tethered to the notion of "Blackness"; the burnt cork masks of minstrelsy is simultaneously a non-recognition of Blacks' agency, a recognition of whites' agency and perceived superiority. (Though only one part of this dialectic, whiteness, can be seen as positive, because it is at the expense of Blackness). Whites' recognition of themselves as superior in virtue, intellect, and culture, is predicated on the (forced) conformity of Blacks to the role of the subservient "other." Ernest (1998) illuminates the egocentric and ethnocentric racist motivation behind the forced capitulation of Black males, by that of white males in the face of slavery, in his essay, "The Reconstruction of Whiteness: Will Wells Brown's, The Escape; Or, a Leap of Freedom."

He writes:

> In this complex and tenuous performance of social identity, the security of selfhood is challenge constantly by the presence of others who, either overtly or implicitly, remind one than one is in fact playing a role. One's self-consciousness about the artifice of one's identity [...] leads one to force others into roles that complete one's own identity. (Ernest, 1998, p. 1111)

The sentiment of this asymmetrical Black and white juxtaposition is the impetus for a quote that Saxton (1971) included in his book, "The Indispensable Enemy"; "No inferior race can exist in these United States with becoming subordinate to the will of the Anglo-Americans" (Saxton, 1971, p. 43). Whiteness is altogether undecipherable, even indefinable without Blackness and vice versa, although the relationship is, at its core one of hegemony. Further, Lott, strengthens this view; he writes, "In antebellum America, minstrelsy performed a crucial hegemonic function" (Lott, 1993, p. 232).

The hopelessness that is part and parcel of the nihilistic threat haunts the urban colonized. It works to unconsciously control or at the very least forcibly inform the actions and comportment—even the very thought processes—of peoples under its specter. In the case of Black males, according to Fanon (1968), they are always on the ready, muscles coiled, ready to fight or flee. Thus, any misunderstood, misperceived action can be view as an act of aggression (when one is looking for a problem, they can usually find one). This kind of behavior is the result of an ever present, seemingly inescapable threat. Sartre (1984), commensurate with Sharpe's (2016) work on wake work, writes of the recoiled Black man: "this…man knows that his life starts with death he considers himself a potential candidate for death. He will be killed; it is not just that he accepts the risk of being killed, he is certain of it (Sartre, 1984, p. vii)." Fanon (1968), commenting on the bellicosity that results in the fratricidal violence that characterizes the urban-colonized writes, "The colonized subject will first train this aggressiveness sediment in his muscles against his own people. This is the period when black turns on black…" (Fanon, 1968, p. 15). (As evidenced by the aforementioned statistics by provided by the piece by Hutchinson, we are still very much entrenched in this "period.")

Nihilistic threat illustrated in Black literature

To further illustrate the omnipresence of this nihilistic threat, I will turn to popular Black literature to delineate the violent transformations of Wright's (1940) character, Bigger Thomas, and Sethe, from Toni Morrison's novel, *Beloved* (1987). Bigger Thomas, throughout his entire mercurial life, seeks the acknowledgement of his agency by white America, which is a necessary precondition for him to be exculpated from the death sentence that his black skin inevitably guarantees him. Accordingly, Bigger wrestles with two pivotal issues within his consciousness, both of which are derivatives of the continuous torture, at the hands of racist colonization, that Bigger is forced to endure. The two issues are his desire for individual recognition and the fear of death on two distinct levels, psychological, i.e., social death, and physical death. This fear, this nihilistic threat transmogrifies Bigger, he becomes a murderous sociopath: he commits two murders, the first of which is (ostensibly) accidental. He suffocates, in an attempt to avoid the perception of her mother, Mary Dalton, the daughter of his white employer. The second however, of Bessie, his girlfriend, who is Black is intentional, and it is preceded by a violent rape, which is consistent with Fanon's quote. Prior to these murders Bigger accosts and subsequently emasculates his friend Gus, who is also Black. This is especially telling, Bigger attacks Gus because of Gus' accuses Bigger of being afraid to strike out at his true oppressor, the colonizer. Bigger lashes out because he knows, in his heart, that the charge that Gus levels against him is true. Because Bigger is powerless to emasculate his emasculator, he turns inward and attacks Gus, who, like him, is also a colonized victim (Morrison, 1987).

The murders of Mary and Bessie are symptomatic of the coercive force of unmitigated racism which serves to erode Bigger both physically, and psychologically. The weight of this oppressive force is what instigates the turn in Bigger's consciousness. This is evinced by Bigger's declaration, "They wouldn't let me live and I killed" (Wright, 1940, p. 428). Subconsciously, Bigger is fixated by the death drive; early in the novel, he says, "I feel like something awful is going to happen to me (Wright, pp. 21)." As a poor, young Black male—the archetypical "other"—Bigger feels insignificant and hated in the eyes of the dominant class: He is trapped in his black body, which scripts him towards death. Consequently, he becomes a volatile mixture of fear and hatred; he fears death and hates all whom he feels seek to kill him. This flammable amalgam—fomented by his psychological erosion at the hands of racism—eventually explodes. "He felt he had no physical existence at all...he was something he hated, the badge of shame which he knew was attached to a black skin (Wright, pp. 67)." This is the direct result of the otherness that the nihilistic threat ushers in. Bigger feels that he is entombed within a sarcophagus of anonymity; he feels naked and invisible. These visceral feelings are due to Bigger's realization that no matter how hard he strives, he will never be recognized as an individual. There is no way for him to go, his situation is hopeless. Bigger Thomas is representative of the "underprivileged and starving peasant" that Fanon writes about in "The Wretched of the Earth". These peasants, according to Fanon are the "exploited who very soon discovers that only violence pays. For him there is no compromise, no possibility of concession" (Fanon, 1968 p. 23).

I have paid special attention to the Black male predicament because it is the Black male who is, purportedly, more likely to be in jail than in college, it is the Black male that is most likely to die a premature violent death; moreover, it is the Black male that has been called, on numerous occasions, an endangered species. However, I will now shift, in hopes of providing a comprehensive view, to the issue of the Black female via the lens provided by the protagonist of Toni Morrison's novel, Beloved. The most pervasive theme throughout this book is the use of death as the only viable way to resist slavery. Accordingly, death is portrayed as the ultimate act of defiance as well as the only real escape. It represents the only sure way out of the atrocities and injustices suffered by slaves at the hands of their masters locally, and the institution of slavery universally. Many Black students face this kind of psychosocial conundrum: either they must repudiate their personhood with all its constitutive parts in order to assimilate, or, they must fight to maintain their personhood vis-à-vis a system that functions to racialize and subsequent devalue their culture, their abilities, and even their very lives.

The protagonist in Morrison's (1987) novel, Sethe, is a former slave who has, with some help, escaped the plantation—ironically named Sweet Home—where she was kept. She, along with her other compatriots, male slaves: Paul D., Paul A., Paul F., Sixo, and Halle who becomes Sethe's husband, suffered mightily at the hands of slavery. In this novel, racism is symbolized on two speciously disparate levels. Firstly, there is a subversive, almost benevolent type of racism exemplified by the Garners, the plantation owners. They are, ostensibly, kind slave owners; they, especially Mr. Garner, pride themselves on this. Much of the educational reform over the last 50 years reeks of this kind of purportedly altruistic racism. This of course is a false identity; the words "kind" and "slave owner" are incongruous. The second type of racism is exemplified by the character Schoolteacher, who unlike his brother Mr. Garner, is not one to dissemble. He is overtly, maliciously racist; he views Black slaves as subhuman farm equipment akin to cattle. He takes over Sweet Home following Mr. Garner's death and subjects the slaves to sadistic dehumanizing experiments of his own design, all with an aim to constantly remind them of their inherent inferiority. Their castigation, however, is not limited to the psychological realm; on the contrary, upon his arrival, for the first time the slaves at Sweet Home are abused physically as well. They yearn for their freedom (for de-colonization), a freedom that the institutions of slavery, and colonization stand in obstinate opposition to. Sethe, against all odds, escapes the plantation. There, she enjoys freedom for the first time in her life. She is free physically, however, emotionally and psychologically she is still very much in bondage. The suffering that she endured still torments her; she cannot forget, though she tries. She was cognizant of the fact that:

> Anybody white could take your whole self for anything that came to mind. Not just work, kill, or maim you, but dirty you. Dirty you so bad you couldn't like yourself anymore. Dirty you so bad you forget who you were and couldn't think it up. (Morrison, 1987, p. 251)

This reality, the reality that a slave was not their own person, that a slave could be raped, sold, beaten or killed by seemingly any and every white person was a fate that Sethe was not willing to subject her children to. She wanted them to be free, free of the torture and anguish that unrelentingly gripped her, and others like her. The psychological strain that slavery, which like colonization requires Black people to be viewed and positioned as the other, causes her to snap, to become a murder. Like Bigger Thomas, and consistent with Fanon's earlier quote, her aggression is aimed at other Blacks, in this case her children. She tries to destroy what has come to symbolize her badge of shame, the same badge of shame that follows Bigger: Black skin.

Slavery, like colonization presupposes racism and racisms presupposes "otherness"; that is, it is the cornerstone of any justification for either. The truth is: If Black people were considered equal, they would not have been made into slaves. The idea that one could enslave their equal, their neighbor, their brother, et cetera, is preposterous. Furthermore, the institutions of slavery, just like colonization is a calculated endeavor—both attack the site of connection: they function to disallow Black men to be men; therefore, they are unable to be fathers, to be husbands, to be caretakers. Racism seeks to castrate the Black male symbolically, physically, and emotionally. Black women, of course, also suffer mightily at the hands of racism: everything that they care for can be taken away from them in an instant; their husbands, their children, and their lives can all be wiped away without any recourse.

The sad reality is that racism is so pervasive, so omnipresent that physical death, oftentimes, is the only way to be freed from its suffocating grip. Both Wright and Morrison employ this theme—death as, simultaneously, resistance and freedom— to decry the hopelessness and self-hatred that racism engenders, no doubt, in hopes of attenuating the oppressive power that it wields over the urban-colonized. The physical and psychological atrocities that are continually exacted upon the urban-colonized force them to assume the role of the "other"; it is either that role or no role at all. This why a new purview must be first developed and later promulgated if we hope to help the poor, marginalized Black youth that inhabit these modern-day urban colonies. To expand our purview, we must first recognize and admit that these inner city, urban, primarily ethnic minority ghettos are in fact modern-day colonies. If we as educators hope to help these young people thrive, we must view them as such, constantly considering the injurious conditions in which they live. Furthermore, if we hope to ameliorate their sufferings, and to stem and ultimately reverse the tide of underachievement, hopelessness, and worse, violent death, that runs rampant in America's inner-city urban colonies, we must study them through an anti-colonial lens. By borrowing from and applying the work of previous anti-colonial thinkers like Fanon and Paulo Freire, we must acknowledge and account for the damage caused by this nihilistic threat. For, to discount the psychological trauma of colonization, which results in the preponderance and proliferation of the nihilistic threat is to deny these young people any modicum of personhood, one the one hand, and, in so doing, deny that they are indeed suffering, on the other. My intention is not merely to point an accusatory finger; rather, my hope is that by retracing the ontology, and subsequently deconstructing it, piecemeal, the otherness which engenders the disastrous nihilism that inundates many poor, urban Black communities (colonies), can one day, very soon, be eradicated.

I am my brother's keeper: Fratricidal violence in the Black community

Conversations around the protests of police brutality, the killing of unarmed African-American males by white men, especially by white male police officers, often invokes questions as to why the same uproar is not present regarding fratricidal violence within the Black community, i.e., Black on Black violence.

This is, undoubtedly, an exigent matter. Rates of Black on Black violence are heartbreakingly high (Miller, 2011). This is not due to some intrinsic criminality or an innate disregard for lawfulness by African-American males. Rather, it has much more to do with structural and institutionalized inequity that is made manifest by the lack of opportunity for well-paying jobs, academic success, access to health and wellness resources, and the negative effects of pernicious stereotyping (Alexander, 2010). Moreover, what is routinely left out of these conversations is that fratricidal violence is not the exclusive domain of African-American males. The greatest threat to White males, as far as murder is concerned, is other White males; this is also true of Brown (i.e., Latino/Chicano/Hispanic) males.

I am not dismissive when it comes to conversations around fratricidal violence within the Black community. A loss of life is tragic no matter whom the perpetrator is. This is especially true when the lives that are prematurely snuffed out are of preteens and teenagers who irrespective of whatever mistakes they may or may not have made are disallowed the opportunity to learn from them and move on to become more reflective and more thoughtful people.

Conversation around the purported criminality and lack of educational success for Black males is decontextualized. It has become common practice to turn a blind eye to the macro-level problems that catalyze the disproportionate rates of crime in predominately Black communities (Alexander, 2010; Miller, 2011). Instead, conversations about the innate, intrinsic pathology of poor, urban Black communities seems to be the narrative that informs much of the conversations, specifically in mass media (Alexander, 2010), around what happens in predominately Black enclaves throughout this country. Fox News, the number one news outlet in the United States, speaks about the deaths of unarmed Black men as though they happen in an atemporal vacuum. This purposeful framing elides potentially transformative conversations that may serve to demystify the outrage of the Black community when one of its members is murdered, in cold blood, by real or pseudo-agents of law and order (Fanon & Sartre, 1965).

Innocence lost: The adultification of Black males

Black males irrespective of their age are not allowed to make mistakes in the same way that non-Black adolescent males do. That is, there is no presupposed, innate innocence for Black males. I have been alive long enough to know that young people make mistakes. Much of my professional life has been spent working with young people (specifically, Black males), and, sometimes preteens and teenagers do things without weighing the implications or possible consequences of their actions. And while many people know that young people sometimes act on impulse, rather than forethought and planning, Black males are not afforded the same presumption of innocence (Goff, Jackson, Di Leone, Culotta, & Ditomasso, 2014) that non-Black males are, especially vis-à-vis interactions with law enforcement. The abovementioned police interaction that led to the death of Tamir Rice is an instantiation of this. Rice, only 12 years old, was described as a man (waving a gun, which turned out to be a toy gun). This is in no way an exculpation of the officer that took Tamir's life within 3 seconds of finding him, but the officer was told there was a man waving a gun. We can only wonder if his reaction might have been different had he known that the child he was to encounter was a middle schooler—not an adult.

This fatal reaction represents a stark contrast when juxtaposed with a widely-circulated (viral) video of a young man in a police station seen wrestling with several police officers. This video was brought to the fore during the news coverage of the indignation and unrest that the deaths of Michael Brown, Trayvon Martin, and Tamir Rice (among others). The young (European American) male in this video can be seen fighting with police officers for a few minutes, and at one point he was able to grab a police officer's holstered weapon and fire off a shot in the police station, thereby qualifying him as armed and dangerous, i.e., as a real threat. However, this young man, this European American young man, was not shot. When this story broke, this young man was never described as thug. Instead, it was made very clear that this young man was on drugs and was "not himself." We were led to believe that he simply made a mistake, an egregious and dangerously illegal mistake; however, he is still very much alive. The officers involved were lauded for their restraint. As evidenced by Chisulo's story, detailed in the following chapter, Black males are much less likely to receive the protections afforded to people who are perceived as inherently innocent (Goff et al., 2014).

Trayvon Martin and Michael Brown, who were gunned down by a pseudo-law keeper, neighborhood watchmen and an actual law-keeper, respectively, were not characterized as misguided young people possibly making mistakes commensurate with their age. Instead, their respective characters were put on trial to exculpate the men that gunned them down. For all intents and purposes, these two beautiful young men were put on trial for their own murders. Both of their characters were impugned. They were not afforded the benefit of the doubt. But, instead, were depicted as Bigger Thomas-esque (Wright, 1940) thugs who were potential threats that needed to be neutralized, permanently.

This is the reality that many Black males face; and, instead of providing safe haven from these exigent and dangerous realities, schools that are made up of predominately low-income Black students often reproduce these macro and micro-level aggressions (Sue, 2010). This should come as no surprise according to Duncan-Andrade and Morrell (2008): they argue that our national education system was designed to underserve (or in their words, fail) hyper-marginalized students. Racism is far from dead in this country (Leonardo, 2009). If there is doubt, one need look no further than the ever-increasing achievement gap, which is due in large part to racist educational policies (Giroux, 2011; Kozol, 2005; Leonardo, 2009), poorly-prepared urban teachers (Delpit, 2012), and the prevalence and over-determination of deficit-model thinking (Valencia, 1997). The achievement gap is the progeny of the opportunity gap, the opportunity gap is informed by notions of deservedness. Black boys (and men) as evidenced by the preceding review of literature have been deemed unworthy of access to social, legal, educational, and material justice.

However, despite the seemingly immovable obstacles placed in our way, we still succeed. Because even though there is a popular refrain that claims that there are more Black men in jail than in college, this is simply not true. There are nearly twice as many Black men in college than there are in jails (http://www.acenet.edu/the-presidency/columns-and-features/Pages/By-the-Numbers-More-Black-Men-in-Prison-Than-in-College-Think-Again-.aspx). That said, we are still grossly over-represented in jails, which speaks to the abject failure of our educational, juridical, and civil systems to provide viable educational and employment opportunities for the marginalized of the marginalized. Again, this points back to the aforementioned opportunity gap. In the following chapter, I will discuss the opportunity gap regarding access to rigorous STEM instruction, which is, perhaps, the most pronounced and easily most obdurate gap in the education of Black boys.

Chapter 2 review: Considerations and questions

Consideration:

In this chapter, I discussed the undeniable role that White supremacy, racism and whiteness play in informing the prevailing imagery of Black people, generally, and Black boys, specifically. In working through this material, my goal is to help readers understand that the academic struggles that Black boys experience, albeit at a disproportionate rate, are not a direct reflection of their ability, aptitude, and or desire to succeed, though this line of thinking is seemingly axiomatic now. Rather, there are white supremacist based mechanisms and apparatuses positioned to delimit our individual and collective ability to reach our full personal and communal potential. So, we have to work; that much is true. Nevertheless, we have to do so knowing that our work is not always valued in the same way that other people's work is. This is unfair and inequitable; however, we have, and we will continue to succeed in the face of the obstacles placed in our way.

Just know that despite the troubling statistics covered in this chapter, we still rise. We're still here. We still succeed. This is important to note: for all of the Black males that may be reading this book, just know that while these statistics paint a bleak picture, they are in no way your (our) destiny. We have continued to make a way in an inhospitable, and downright inimical educational system; and, we will continue to succeed. You are brilliant.

Questions for students:

1. This chapter spoke in detail about many of the negative effects of White supremacy on the ways that Black people are portrayed and on how we sometimes view ourselves as the result of these portrayals. These portrayals or images are false. They were created to cause us to think less of our abilities and ourselves. How will you work to debunk these portrayals in your life in and out of school; and, how will you help other family/community members actively fight against these stereotypical depictions?
2. Why do you think that there has been such an all-out attack on the image, character, psyche, ability, and physical body of Black males in this country?
3. How are you going to use your understanding about white supremacy to make sure that other Black males as well as other marginalized students are no longer negatively impacted by these lies about their ability?

Consideration:

The presupposition of this chapter is this: Whiteness is a system that upholds white supremacy, and that white supremacy is ubiquitous and deleteriously pernicious, especially for Black boys and men. If this is true, it is incumbent upon critically committed educators from all walks of life to actively combat white supremacy inside and outside of their classrooms. In this chapter there is little to no mention of white privilege, or what is now simply referred to as privilege because the modifier "White" was too painful for "white" people as it invoked feelings of white guilt.

Questions for educators:

1. How do you actively work to mitigate the deleterious effects of white supremacy in your work with Black boys and other hyper-marginalized students of color?
2. If you are a person that identifies as European American, how do you work in the best interests of Black boys and other students of color while repudiating the wages of whiteness and maintaining your whole self?
3. How will you create spaces for students, especially Black males, to interrogate and deconstruct white supremacy in the work that they do without patronizingly over-determining the role that it consciously plays in their life?
4. If there is indeed value in thinking through ways to revolutionize, even at the micro-level, your pedagogy—what can you/will you do differently to carve out sustainable spaces for Black males to participate in the meaning-making and knowledge-creating processes that take place in your class?

Keywords:

Blackness, whiteness, stereotype threat, transmogrification, racism, white supremacy, inequity, STEM, violence, adultification

References

Alexander, M. (2010). *The new Jim Crow: Mass incarceration in the age of colorblindness.* New York, NY: The New Press.

Althusser, L. (1971). *Lenin and philosophy and other essays.* New York, NY: New Left Books.

Darling-Hammond, L. (2010). *The flat world and education: How America's commitment to equity will determine our future.* New York, NY: Teachers College Press.

Delpit, L. (2012). *Multiplication is for White people: Raising expectations for other people's children.* New York, NY: The New Press.

De Tocqueville, A. (2000). *Democracy in America.* New York, NY: Perennial Classics.

DiIulio, J. (1995). Broken bottles: Liquor, disorder, and crime. *Wisconsin Policy.*

Dubois, W. E. B. (1903). *The souls of Black folk.* Digireads.Com Publishing.

Duncan-Andrade, J., & Morrell, E. (2008). *The art of critical pedagogy: Possibilities for moving from theory to practice in urban schools.* New York, NY: Peter Lang.

Ernest, J. (1998). The reconstruction of whiteness: William Wells Brown's the escape; or, a leap for freedom. *PMLA, 113*(5), 1108–1121.

Fanon, F. (1968). *Black skin, white masks.* New York, NY: Grove Press.

Fanon, F., & Sartre, J. (1965). *The wretched of the earth*. New York, NY: Grove Press.

Ferguson, A. A. (2001). *Bad boys: Public schools in the making of Black masculinity*. Ann Arbor, MI: University of Michigan Press.

Foucault, M. (1977). *Discipline and Punishment*. London: Tavistock.

Giroux, H. A. (2011). *On critical pedagogy*. New York, NY: Continuum Books.

Goff, P. A., Jackson, M. C., Di Leone, B. A., Culotta, C. M., & Ditomasso, N. A. (2014). The essence of innocence: Consequences of dehumanizing Black children. *Journal of Personal and Social Psychology, 106*(4), 526–545.

Gramsci, A., In Hoare, Q., & Nowell-Smith, G. (1971). *Selections from the prison notebooks of Antonio Gramsci*. New York, NY: International Publishers.

Hall, S. (1996). *Critical dialogues in cultural studies*. New York, NY: Routledge.

Harrington, M. (1962). *The other America*. Portland, OR: Book News.

Kozol, J. (2005). Still separate, still unequal: America's educational apartheid. *Harper's Magazine, 311*(1864), 41–54.

Leonardo, Z. (2009. *Race, whiteness, and education* (Kindle ed.). New York and London: Routledge.

Lott, E. (1993). *Love and theft: Blackface minstrelsy and the American working class*. New York, NY: Oxford University Press.

Mahiri, J. (2017). Deconstructing race: Multicultural education beyond the color-bind. New York, NY: Teachers College Press.

Mahiri, J., & Conner, E. (2003). Black youth violence has a bad rap. *Journal of Social Issues, 59*(1), 121–140.

Mahiri, J., & Sims, J. J. (2016). Engineering equity: A critical pedagogical approach to language and curriculum change for African American males in STEM (55–70). Z. Babaci-Wilhite (ed.), In *Curriculum change in language and STEM subjects as a right in education*. Rotterdam: Sense Publishing.

Marx, K. (1977). *Capital: A critique of political economy, volume one*. New York, NY: Vintage Books.

McIntosh, P. (1988). White privilege and male privilege: A personal account of coming to see correspondences through work in women's studies. Wellesley, MA: Wellesley College, Center for Research on Women.

McLaren, P. (2015). *Pedagogy of insurrection: From resurrection to revolution*. New York, NY: Perter Lang Publishers.

Miller, J. G. (2011). *Search and destroy: African-American males in the criminal justice system* (2nd ed.) New York, NY: Cambridge University Press.

Morrison, T. (1987). *Beloved*. Atlanta, GA: Atlanta Book Company.

Nast, H. J. (2000). Mapping the "unconscious": Racism and the oedipal family. *Annals of the Association of American Geographers, 90*(2), 215–255.

Nietzsche, F. W., Ansell-Pearson, K., & Large, D. (2006). *The Nietzsche reader*. Malden, MA: Blackwell Pub.

Roberts, D. (2011). *Fatal invention: How science, politics, and big business re-create race in the twenty-first century*. New York, NY: The New Press.

Roediger, D. (1994). *Towards the abolition of Whiteness: Essays on Race, Class and Politics*. London, UK and New York: Verso Books.

Sabol, W. J., West, H. C., & Cooper, M. (2010). *Bureau of justice statistics bulletin: Prisoners in 2008*. Washington, DC: U.S. Department of Justice.

Sartre, J.-P. (1984). *Being and nothingness*. New York, NY: Gallimard.

Saxton, A. P. (1971). *The indispensable enemy: Labor and the anti-Chinese movement in California*. Berkeley, Ca: University of California Press.

Sharpe, C. (2016). *In the wake: On Blackness and being* (Kindle ed.). Durham, NC: Duke University Press.

Steele, C. (2010). *Whistling Vivaldi: And other clues to how stereotypes affect us*. New York, NY: W. W. Norton.

Sue, D. W. (2010). *Microaggressions in everyday life: Race, gender, and sexual orientation*. Hoboken, NJ: Wiley.

Valencia, R. R. (1997). *The evolution of deficit thinking: Educational thought and practice*. London: Falmer Press.

West, C. (1993). *Race matters*. Boston, MA: Beacon Press.

Wright, R. (1940). *Native son*. New York, NY: Harper & Bros.

Standing in the gap

Black boys and STEM

"Mr. J, I'm gonna keep it one-hundred with you: black boys just aren't good at math. Chinese kids are good at math. But, we're not. It's is what it is." This excerpt is part of a conversation that I had with Desmond, an 8th grade student at MAN UP. He was explaining away, just I had done 20 some years early, the struggles that he was experiencing in math. Many of the young men that we served in MAN UP were doing extremely well in math. However, this was not the case for all of our scholars. There was a group, made up almost exclusively of 8th graders, that struggled in math and that had, erroneously, determined that they were doomed to struggle with math in perpetuity. One of the primary objectives of the MAN UP program was to create spaces for Desmond and students like him to situate themselves vis-à-vis STEM. Our goal was to create nutritive educational opportunities where our "scholars" could immediately apply their newfound STEM knowledge to issues that they deemed important. We wanted their STEM learning to be contextualized; we wanted it to be useful in their immediate context—not simply for future use. This approach is very different from the realities that most Black males face in their STEM classes/course. For most of us, STEM is positioned as apolitical and therefore culturally neutral. However, the ways that STEM curriculum and concomitant pedagogy is designed and applied here in the U.S., intentionally values and legitimizes a very particular Europocentric episteme (Bang & Medin, 2010) and in so doing devalues and delegitimizes non-Europocentric contributions to the fields represented by the overarching STEM umbrella. Therefore, we were careful to include the contributions of Black people and other people of color to

STEM in addition to the brilliant yet now stock characters like George Washington Carver, Daniel Hale Williams and now Ben Carson.

Where we at, though? Black males' conspicuous absence in STEM spaces

To be clear, STEM barriers are not unique to Black males. The United States produces fewer White STEM professionals compared to past years. In addition, other traditionally marginalized groups like women and Latinos continue to lag European-American men regarding STEM degrees, and consequently STEM careers, according to the National Center for Education Statistics. That said, the situation is far more pronounced, and far more exigent for Black males. According to the National Center for Education Statistics (http://www.huffingtonpost.com/2011/10/24/stem-education-and-jobs-d_n_1028998.html):

- Black people are 12 percent of the U.S. population and 11 percent of all students beyond high school. In 2009, they received just 7 percent of all STEM bachelor's degrees, 4 percent of master's degrees, and 2 percent of PhDs, according to the National Center for Education Statistics.
- From community college through PhD level, the percentage of STEM degrees received by Blacks in 2009 was 7.5 percent, down from 8.1 percent in 2001.
- The numbers are striking in certain fields. In 2009, African-Americans received 1 percent of degrees in science technologies, and 4 percent of degrees in math and statistics. Out of 5,048 PhDs awarded in the physical sciences, such as chemistry and physics, 89 went to African-Americans—less than 2 percent. (National Science Board report, 2010, http://1.usa.gov/nwHbku).

According to the article that the above-mentioned data comes from "several factors are cited by scientists, educators and students" that shine light on why this gap has remained persistent. One is a self-defeating perception that STEM is too hard, which can be attributed to, among other things, racist stereotyping and stereotype threat (Steele, 2010). Also mentioned is a lack of role models and mentors, which delimits these students' ability to fully develop a STEM identity as well as socioeconomic pressure to earn money quickly because of impoverished living conditions, and discouraging academic environments, like inequitable, subpar schooling.

These "discouraging academic environments," according to Freire (1997) are the direct result of the alienating, disempowering, and stultifying banking model of education. The counter to the banking model of education, which is purposely anti-critical, is critical, emancipatory pedagogical practices that center students' real-life experiences (Gutstein, 2005). The oppressive pedagogical practices that Freire wants to disrupt still exist; in fact, these oppressive practices, buoyed and legitimized by oppressive polices, have become ubiquitous and deeply entrenched for Black males. Moreover, instead of addressing the disease that produces the policy that makes way for these pedagogical practices, Black males are recrimi- nated and blamed for their academic struggles due to their race-based, perceived academic/cognitive deficiencies and their purported penchant for criminality.

Criminal minds? The criminalization of Black males

One of the young men that participated in MAN UP, already a star football player, found out early on that his Blackness carried an innate sanction. This young man had an incredibly powerful Afrocentric name. In this book, I use the pseudonym, Chisulo, which in Ibo means: strong as steel. And, even though he was only in the 8th grade, Chisulo was nearly six feet tall and a heavily-muscled 190 pounds. For most, he cast a Bigger Thomas-esque presence (Wright, 1940). He is a brilliant young man. He is taciturn; but when he spoke, the other scholars always listened intently to him. Nevertheless, the inescapable Blackness of his "presence" came to the fore in an incident he had at his junior high school. Chisulo recounted a then recent incident where, in class, after incorrectly answering a question when called upon by his teacher, this teacher berated him for his lack of preparedness. Embarrassed, Chisulo spoke up to vindicate himself. However, this teacher was having none of it. He told Chisulo to "sit down and shut up," and when he did not, the teacher hurled more insults at him—eventually calling him "stupid." This, for Chisulo, was the proverbial straw that broke the camel's back. Chisulo rose up out of his chair:

Mr. J: What was going through your head when this was going on?
Chisulo: I was mad; I was embarrassed. But this stuff wasn't new. Mr. Blank just didn't like me. I was the only Black kid in his class. He always had something to say; or, he would just like at me like I did something to him.

Mr. J:	But, he never called you stupid or dumb before, right?
Chisulo:	No, but he went out of his way to make me feel dumb—that's for sure.
Mr. J:	What do you mean?
Chisulo:	Class participation is a big part of our grade. So, I try to participate. But, sometimes I participate by asking question because I'm kinda lost. Anytime, well, most of the time, when I ask a question, he'll say something like: well, if you read the material, or, you should have asked this question a long time ago and you wouldn't be lost now. It's like, man, I can't even ask a question without him belittling me.
Mr. J:	So, when you got up what were you thinking?
Chisulo:	[tears streaming down his face] I'm not sure. I just knew that I couldn't sit there anymore. I had to go. I wasn't even really thinking about him. I just wanted the? attack to stop. He tried to say I threw a desk at him.
Mr. J:	I heard. That's crazy.
Chisulo:	Yeah, the desk was nowhere near him. He lied. But, I had to get out of that class.

Understandably, Chisulo could no longer endure this adult's malicious verbal attack. When he stood up, his desk toppled over. He made no effort to advance toward the teacher, who, according to Chisulo was at least 20 feet away at the time. Still, once Chisulo removed himself for this toxic environment, he and his parents were informed that he was expected at an expulsion hearing and that he was being charged with attempted assault for allegedly "throwing" a desk at his teacher. At this very moment this young man, this thoughtful, caring brilliant young man had been transmogrified into a thug. For this teacher and the institution that was supposed to support him, Chisulo's innocence (if he was ever afforded any to begin with) was gone.

As a young adult, I too went through an experience that had the potential to be life changing. My mom was off work and decided to pick me up from school. This was a rarity because as a latch-key kid, I was responsible for getting myself to and from school since grade school. She dropped me off at home on her way to the supermarket. Not more than five minutes elapsed when I heard a loud knock on the door: "open up!" Startled and admittedly angry, I open the door with disdain on my face. On the other side of the door, to my surprise and utter dismay, were five detectives and three uniformed police officers. The lead detective, aggressively, told me step aside so that he could search our family apartment. In a moment of feigned bravado, I asked him if he had a search warrant. He pushed right past me as he told me that he did not need one. When he emerged from our small two-bedroom apartment, he ordered that I be handcuffed. He looked me in the eye and asked: "how come you didn't tell me you had a gun in there?" Of course, there was no gun; and, I knew that—but I also knew that it was my word against his, and that my word vis-à-vis his was completely powerless. I asked why this interaction was even taking place. No one answered.

More than 45 minutes passed since the initial knock on the door. By this time at least five more uniformed officers were on the scene. I had no idea, whatsoever, as to why I was forced out of my home, handcuffed, and paraded throughout my building. No one provided any explanation. After conferring with the other detectives on site, the lead detective directed one of the uniformed officers to walk me through the parking lot to the sidewalk. It was at this point, more than an hour into this ordeal, that someone finally explained to me what was going on. Earlier that day a woman had been robbed at gunpoint at a nearby supermarket. I was being marched to the street's edge so that the victim could inform the officers as to whether I was the perpetrator. The police car drove by and I could see that this woman was visibly shaken, though she was trying desperately to hide her face. She shook her head, signaling "no." I felt an immediate rush of relief, albeit momentarily. My mind began to wander: What if she was unsure and in her distraught state mistakenly identified me as the perpetrator of this heinous crime? Even if I was exonerated, eventually, at that very moment I would have been incarcerated, forthwith, and left to rely on the acumen of my county's public defender to prove my innocence. I, too, would have been transmogrified into a thug irrespective of the reality that I had no actual involvement with this crime.

These are not isolated incidents; they are systemic precisely because Black maleness has been conflated with criminality in this country. In contradistinction to the ethos of our judicial system, Black men are not considered innocent until proven guilty. Rather, we are considered guilty because, purportedly, we are innately predisposed to criminality (Bennett, 2005; DiIulio, 1995). No more than three minutes into this ordeal, the police officers that I encountered handcuffed me. It was clear that they were uncomfortable with allowing me to be unshackled because for these officers my Blackness made me a threat. For them, my Blackness meant that I was predisposed to thuggery, and despite my innocence, they treated me accordingly. This is (but) one of the unmistakable wages of whiteness (Roediger, 1994). Therefore, my call for a critical-reality pedagogical approach for Black boys in STEM is a call to holistically address the wages of whiteness exacted on this group while encouraging, empowering, and equipping Black boys to call out and address these wages themselves for their individual benefit as well as the collective benefit for oppressed people all over. For, me this is part and parcel of *keeping it 100*.

Where I come from, this approach is called keeping it 100

The idea of "keeping it one-hundred (percent)" is synonymous with keeping it real and not pulling punches. When participants begin a dialogue by first agreeing to keep it 100, this means that, for better or worse, this dialogue is going to cut straight the truth. More simply put, this rhetorical move instantiates the ratification of a pseudo-contractual speech-act that ensures that the ensuing conversation will be authentic and, potentially, painfully honest. We know that authenticity is crucial in forming relationships with youth (Emdin, 2016) irrespective of their race, class, and/or socioeconomic status. That said, I would argue that this is especially true for Black males because schooling for them has traditionally been reductive and oppressive. So, in this chapter, I am going to keep in "one-hundred" by illuminating the source of Black males' disproportional struggles in STEM. Spoiler alert: it is not due to innate, intrinsic deficiencies that are in any way endemic to Black males as Herrnstein, R. J., & Murray (1996) would have us believe. Something systemically pernicious, and perniciously systematic has been and still is taking place.

The ensuing section represents a review of extant literature on the educational plight of Black males in this country. That said, it must be noted that while there is a corpus of literature on education and Black males, from many different vantage points, literature that investigates middle school Black males shifts in STEM learning, STEM identity, and socially just applications of STEM vis-a-vis a critical-reality pedagogical approach to teaching and learning is scant to say the least. Therefore, to form the conceptual frame and theoretical positionality that undergirds this work, this literature review borrows from several theoretical traditions to provide a coherent frame from which to understand the nature and scope of the work that this book, simultaneously, chronicled, illuminated, and analyzed.

Much has been written about the problems of a digital divide between Blacks and others, and similar considerations attend to STEM disparities. In this chapter, however, after an analysis of the issues that contribute the above-mentioned scholastic divides, I will highlight scholarship that offers prospects for better understanding the structural issues that Black males face so that we can begin ameliorating these issues through more comprehensive understandings of effective ways to build on the cultural and intellectual assets of Black youth. These understandings come from a broad swath of research and scholarship from the social sciences, from multicultural education, and from critical pedagogy. In combination, they offer much-needed counter considerations to the pathological framing of Black males in education, in society, and in the media.

Academic performances of Blacks and other marginalized groups can be characterized in terms of opportunity gaps rather than achievement gaps. Like many of the students MAN UP served, I, too, know this reality firsthand. I attended an under-resourced, urban school in one of Northern California's most dangerous neighborhoods. Unlike my primarily Asian American, middle class peers that I know from my church youth group, my school offered no after school programming—other than detention. There was no "math club," English, or geography club at my school. My school was almost entirely Latino, Black, and South East Asian (specifically Laotian, Cambodian, and Hmong). We were not lacking enthusiasm, because I remember the school-wide celebrations that our successful test results garnered. For those of us that excelled on standardized testing, it was as though we had the keys to the school, so to speak. However, we never had the opportunity to go further than whatever was necessary to pass the standardized tests that our perceived worth was being measured against. Therefore, again, we were not bereft of enthusiasm, but we were violently bereft of opportunity for academic enrichment, especially where STEM was concerned.

However, since opportunities in a society are selectively constructed and socially structured, they can be re-constructed through a more culturally connected language of instruction and designs of curriculum that make educational achievement a right for all students. In line with this, scholarship reviewed in this section will work to shed light on the ways that Black students develop identities with and competencies in STEM subjects when exposed to pedagogies that are linguistically and culturally relevant and that connect STEM learning to socially beneficial applications. More simply put, when Black male students, like most hyper-marginalized student groups, are encouraged and empowered to fully participate with their whole-selves—or to keep it *one-hundred*—they are, then, equipped to actively debunk the deleterious stereotypes that have been sutured to their identities by succeeding in STEM for themselves, for their families, and for their communities. This must be the goal of critical-reality pedagogy.

Identifying the educational gap in STEM

In today's hyper-competitive, technological economy, graduating from high school and subsequently obtaining a postsecondary degree can mean the difference between a lifetime of poverty and a secure economic future. However, in the United States, high school graduation and college-readiness rates are alarmingly low, particularly among students of color. The numbers for African-American male students are especially disheartening: less than 47 percent of African-American male students graduate from high school within four years; and of the ones that do, fewer still are adequately prepared with the necessary skills needed for college admission (and ultimately, college success).

Many researchers have investigated and theorized the root causes of the long-standing "educational gap" between poor minority students, especially Black and Latino students and higher socio-economic status Whites and Asians, respectively. Despite the corpus of research and subsequent reforms and policy changes that purportedly seek to bridge this gap, very little has changed (Darling-Hammond, 2010). Poor Brown and Black students still do far worse on standardized testing; also, Brown and Black students continue to be grossly underrepresented in college enrollment and alarmingly overrepresented in our Nation's multi-billion-dollar prison industrial complex. To this point, Steele (2010) argues that year after year, Black students fall further behind their European American counterparts.

This is especially true regarding outcomes in STEM, where there are pronounced inequities in educational attainment: By the 6th grade, only 35 percent of African-American students in California performed at grade level in mathematics, compared to 67 percent of White students and 80 percent of Asian students (Scott, 2010). Just 16 percent of African-American students enroll in Algebra II, which is required to meet eligibility guidelines to apply to attend a public university in California. Of the students who enroll in Algebra II, only 14 percent of African-American students mastered the content and reached proficiency. In 2009, only 1,551 African-American students were enrolled in a STEM discipline across all UC campuses. This represents just 2 percent of all STEM undergraduates (2010). However, seven of the top ten fastest-growing occupations over the next ten years are in STEM fields (Bureau of Labor Statistics, 2009), which, again is a consideration, but is not, necessarily, the impetus for this program. The impetus of this program was to provide low-income Black male middle schoolers with the opportunity to learn and excel in STEM while carving out a STEM identity as young people who are encouraged, equipped, and empowered to use their STEM knowledge to uplift their communities.

Pedagogy that oppresses: Exclusionary nature of traditional STEM education

For Black males, particularly, STEM pedagogical practices in K–12 education continue to be characterized by what Freire (1997) termed the banking model of education. This troublesome model positions students as empty receptacles equipped only to receive the (deposited) knowledge that their benevolent teachers see fit to bestow upon them. Linn and Eylon (2011) later termed this stultifying, anti-critical educational paradigm the absorption model of education.

The adage that likens children to sponges is the byproduct of this educational paradigm. This approach is problematic because it obviates consideration of what students bring to their respective classrooms precisely because the ability to create knowledge, in the form of rote, decontextualized facts (Gutstein, 2005), is viewed as the exclusive domain of the adult knower. This top-down pedagogical approach does not allow students to question the knowledge they receive. And, it disallows them from devising ways to critically contextualize and therefore connect and apply STEM to their own lives in a meaningful way (Brown, 2006; Gutstein, 2005). So, then, STEM—for many of these students— is decontextualized.

Emdin (2010), Nasir's (2011), and Gutstien's (2006) respective work demonstrates the clear benefits of connecting students' lives outside of the classroom to STEM course content. However, for most low-income, underrepresented students of color, the opportunity to engage in rigorous, relevant STEM course work is scant (Scott, 2010). Overwhelmingly, these students are forced to endure STEM course work that is decontextualized, disempowering and, perhaps, worse yet delivered by under-qualified or even wholly unqualified teachers (Darling-Hammond, 2010). And, according to Leonardo (2010) this form of structural and institutionalized inequity works to recriminate its victims by making it appear that their academic struggles are endemic due to their ethnicity, culture and or socio-economic status. This is especially true where low-income Black males are concerned. This is an exigent issue because the access to viable opportunities to receive and engage in quality, critical STEM education is the most reliable predictor of STEM educational attainment (Darling-Hammond, 2010)—not intrinsic and or innate drive, intelligence, and ability, as the term achievement connotes.

Minding the opportunity gap

According to Duncan-Andrade and Morrell (2008) this is not a nation of opportunity in the truest sense, which has caused many to rename the long-standing achievement gap, replacing it with the appellation: the opportunity gap. In truth, outcomes are rigged; they have been for a long time. Schools are, according to Althusser (1971), ideological state apparatuses that function to inculcate and repress perceived threats to the status quo. In this sense, schools are not failing— if Althusser is correct, they are an overwhelming success. According to Gramsci (1971) proletariat education should endeavor to make students critical consumers and co-creators of the information that they receive so that they are equipped to become critical producers of counter-narratives and counter-measures. MAN UP was developed with this goal in mind. We hoped to position our students to interrogate and disrupt problematic metanarratives around Black male academic struggles by equipping them to use their STEM knowledge to challenge their forced subaltern positionality. However, most Black males do not receive this kind of critical STEM education (Darder, 1998). Instead, we have a problematic one size fits all educational approach. This approach assumes that all students learn in the same way. They do not. Educators, as much as possible, need to be sensitive to differential learning styles. Instead of questioning our own ideological predispositions or cultural understanding, far too often, we unknowingly subscribe to hegemonic, stereotypical associations that inform the ways in which we interact with students that come from cultures different than our own. This is incredibly challenging precisely because hegemony naturalizes the process by which mainstream inequity is made to appear normal, endemic, or worse, innate due to the purported intrinsic deficiencies of marginalized people (Althusser, 1971; Leonardo, 2010).

Because of unchallenged stereotypes, hegemonic depictions of Black males position them in an uphill, life-or-death struggle for not only recognition of their personhood, potential, and talent—but for their very freedom. In fact, Toldson and Snitman (2010) found that "All of the problems related to the school-to-prison pipeline disproportionately affect black males" (2010, p. 2). Likewise, in a 2008 study of "4, 164 black, white, and Hispanic males" the authors found that "59 percent of black males reported that they had been suspended or expelled from school, compared to 42 percent of Hispanic males, and 26 percent of White males [respectively]" (2010, p. 5). This is especially challenging because the same study, unsurprisingly, revealed "disciplinary referrals are [...] associated with negative attitudes and dispositions toward school [...]" (2010, p. 5). This is significant because students that are disproportionately and inequitably disciplined may begin to internalize and perform the negative stereotypes that have been sutured to them due to their race, ethnicity, and or socio-economic status (Burrell, 2010).

Real talk: Demystifying stereotype threat

Steele's (2010) work confirms that traditionally marginalized Black boys do, in fact, internalize the troubling narrative that they are intrinsically unable to excel in STEM due to supposedly innate cognitive and or cultural deficiencies. Philip (2011a) argues that because of its seemingly endless promulgation, this pernicious lie has reached axiomatic status. This is obviously disconcerting on many levels, as is the overall lack of response to the exigency of Black males' absence of access to equitable educational opportunities. Make no mistake: poor Black males are in a crisis in this country (Noguera, 2008). However, instead of addressing the structural and institutional inequities that catalyze the problems that Black males face, our society has committed an egregious non-sequitur. Rather than working to create culturally sustaining (Paris & Alim, 2017) educational spaces that encourage, empower, and equip Black males, which should be the logical response, our Nation has created entire prison industries out of Black male misery (Alexander, 2010). Moreover, instead of working to ameliorate inequitable educational policies and practices that lead to Black male academic underperformance, the response has been to create jails to house young men who were, essentially, pushed out of school as the result of racist, oppressive structural and institutionalized inequity. And, if despite all this, many Black males do stay in school and succeed; though, by and large, they must do so in the face of widespread (erroneous) negative stereotypes regarding their inherent intelligence, culture, drive, work ethic, and family life. This inequitable educational reality results in cyclical, psychological violence because students that feel that they are being negatively stereotyped, traditionally, perform poorly on standardized tests. This is important because standardized testing metrics are designed to determine inherent ability. So, Black males struggles with standardized testing are then used to justify White supremacist notions of Black peoples' intrinsic intellectual inferiority. According to Steele (2010), these lies can and often do become self-fulfilling prophecies for negatively-stereotyped students:

> Since the publication of our initial report [on stereotype threat] a decade ago, nearly 100 studies on stereotype threat have been conducted, both by us and by researchers around the world, showing that stereotype threat is a significant factor in the achievement gap [...]. These studies shed considerable light on how stereotypes suppress the performance, motivation, and learning of students who have to contend with them.
> (http://www.ascd.org/publications/educational-leadership/nov04/vol62/num03/The-Threat-of-Stereotype.aspx)

Working to disconfirm pernicious stereotypes, even at the non-conscious level, for many bright Black students robs them of their full cognitive ability because they must continually use far too much of their computational power to focus on non-essential tasks like refuting stereotypes (Aronson, Fried, & Good, 2002). According to Aronson (2004):

> Research indicates that Blacks are well aware of their group's negative reputation. Indeed, some research suggests a tendency for Blacks to be hyperaware of the negative expectations about their group and to considerably overestimate the extent to which the mainstream sees them as less intelligent and more likely to commit crimes and live off welfare [...]. Thus, when black students are in an evaluative situation—being called on in class, for example, or taking a test—they experience an additional degree of risk not experienced by non-stereotyped students.
> (http://www.ascd.org/publications/educational-leadership/nov04/vol62/num03/The-Threat-of-Stereotype.aspx)

Undoubtedly, much needs to be done around the overall, holistic social welfare of the urban poor; and, this is perhaps especially true in poor, predominately Black enclaves that are besieged by abject rates of unemployment (Alexander, 2010), wanton violence, inequitable access to quality health care and quality education. Access to quality education is a key component for upward mobility for hyper-marginalized people (Wacquant, 2008). According to the Intercultural Development Research Association's (IDRA) website:

> Education has been and is a way out of poverty, especially for minority students. Students with a college degree have fared far better (even during the last recession) than those who either left school before graduation or earned only a high school diploma.
> (http://www.idra.org/IDRA_Newsletter/January_2013_Fair_Funding/Education_as_Pathway_Out_of_Poverty/#sthash.CHg6x1DW.dpuf)

Of course, conceptions of quality education differ throughout K12 education. What is understood, however, is that whatever conceptualization of education ultimately becomes normative (i.e., standardized), STEM education will take center-stage. So, then, it follows that conversations about STEM education hold the potential to be sites of potentially transformative dialogues. These conversations hold the potential to shift extant educational paradigms towards a pedagogical approach that centers critical-reality pedagogy and is impelled by notions of social justice.

As I discuss below, the banking model of education (Freire, 1997) that characterizes our current educational milieu in test-centric, under-resourced urban schools has made the (so-called) achievement gap even more protracted for hyper-marginalized Black male students. Therefore, it behooves equity-minded educators, especially those interested in the plight of Black males, to begin participating in conversations around STEM education by center it as an issue of social justice.

Getting it right: STEM education can and should center criticality

Moses and Cobb's (2001) work in the Algebra Project served to position access to quality math instruction as a civil rights issue. We know from Brown V. The Board of Education (Bell, 2004) that access to equitable educational opportunity is in fact a civil right, with deeply political implications. Moses and Cobb's work acknowledges this whilst simultaneously narrowing the level of specificity by perspicaciously identifying math, and algebra as an educational bulwark that has been used to serve the interest of and maintain a hegemonic (Gramsci, 1971) status quo. This status quo relies, in part, on an oppressive educational approach to perpetuate and ensure its continued dominance (Drew, 2011). Ultimately, what Moses was up against was the pedagogy of the oppressed, which is built upon the repressive, numbing banking model of education (Freire, 1997). For Freire (1997), the pedagogy of the oppressed is built on a false dichotomy. According to Freire, oppressive pedagogy juxtaposes teachers, diametrically, vis-a-vis the students that they serve. The result of this false binary is an awkward teacher student relationship, where teachers are the knowers and the students are positioned as unknowing blank slates, with little or nothing to contribute. To counter this Freire (1997) argued for a universal consciousness, or what he termed, conscientization, wherein the oppressed could be re-positioned so that they could begin questioning the apparatuses, institutions, and structures that are responsible for their oppression. For Freire, this called for a move away from an oppressive pedagogy to an emancipatory pedagogy, founded on problem-posing.

Freire argued that a problem-posing pedagogy will equip oppressed people to realize their ontological vocation: that is, to be fully human. Freire called for the problem posing educational model in contradistinction to the banking model precisely because he contended that the banking model (1997) was designed to further vitiate the already waning spirits of the oppressed. In the banking model, marginalized peoples are "taught" to acquiesce. Freire writes, "The 'humanism' of the banking approach masks the effort to turn women and men into automatons—the very negation of their ontological vocation to be more fully human" (1997, p. 55). While Freire's work has been immensely influential in many educational circles, the oppressive pedagogy he sought to deconstruct and ultimately eradicate is still the rule and, sadly, not the exception. The ever-increasing achievement gap for Black males proves that this model of education is still as damaging and pernicious as it was in Freire's day.

It is worth mentioning that Freire was writing, primarily, about literacy education. Like the work of Eric Gutstein (2005), which applied Freirean conceptions of emancipatory education to math instruction—in the same spirit—this study applies Freirean conceptions of emancipatory education to aspects of science, technology, engineering and math. According to Gutstein (2005), instead of a math pedagogy that empowers students to use math as a tool for equity, students are, instead, made to anti-critically ingest and then regurgitate the information their teachers feed them. Students' measured ability to employ rote memorization techniques to regurgitate the information that is deposited into them is purported to be proof of their ability to not only succeed academically, but also to learn. Linn and Eylon (2011) term this model of science education the absorption model of education.

Furthermore, students are often made to feel as though their lives outside of their "sanitized" classrooms spaces hold no value and are therefore taboo in the educational spaces they spend most their waking hours within. This is especially true of STEM content. Criticality, if allowed, is often relegated to the humanities or the "soft" sciences (Giroux, 2011). Indeed, there are spaces where youth's epistemological curiosities regarding STEM content are stoked, developed, and curated. However, Black males, arguably as much as or more than any other group, have been traditionally and routinely disallowed to participate in these kinds of critical, empowering educational milieus (Darder, 1998). According to Freire (1997), "When teachers engage students in reading and writing the world regardless of the subject they are enacting problem posing pedagogy's" (1997, p. 48). Freire wanted to move is beyond a pedagogy that stultifies hyper-marginalized students, by positioning them as empty receptacles suitable only to be filled by knowledgeable teachers, precisely because they are viewed as devoid of agency, expertise and valuable input. This is not happenstance. The pedagogy of the oppressed serves to delimit the possibilities for hyper-marginalized (Freire, 1997) students because it disallows students to question, critique, and ultimately challenge the systemic forces that catalyze and ensure their oppression. Instead, far too often, these students are duped into believing that they are innately and intrinsically (as well as culturally) unable to excel in school in general, and in STEM (Leonardo, 2010).

Therefore, in response to this and to create a safe space for urban, low-income middle school Black males to develop their STEM identities, while becoming more competent in STEM and in applying STEM for social justice, MAN UP instructors devised ways to employ many aspects of culturally relevant teaching (Ladson-Billings, 1995):

1. *Identity Development:* MAN UP Students are encouraged to explore and employ STEM as urban, middle school Black males. They are not forced to, explicitly or implicitly, repudiate their identity to become fledgling STEM practitioners. Quite the obverse is true: MAN UP students are encouraged to connect STEM to their lived experiences as Black males by using their STEM mastery to address inequity within their own respective communities.

2. *Equity and Excellence:* MAN UP Instructors are unwavering in their belief that all students can learn, and more acutely, that all MAN UP students will learn. We will not settle for less.

3. *Teaching the Whole Child:* MAN UP centers the lived experiences of middle school Black males in STEM, and in doing so, we focus not only on the intellectual development of our students, but their psychosocial development as well.

4. *Student Teacher Relationships:* MAN UP instructors, via their own experiences alloyed with eight hours of professional development on critical pedagogy, realize that the teacher-student dichotomy that permeates K-12 education here in the United States (Freire & Macedo, 1987) is patently false.

My goal as the founding director of this program was to encourage the STEM instructors to remain malleable by reinforcing the fact that in addition to being facilitators of learning (Ballou, 2012), knowledge creation, and meaning co-construction, we were students as well. Nevertheless, while the above stated principals of CRT proved invaluable in developing MAN UP's curricular approach and pedagogical frame, it was my belief that CRT as a pedagogical approach lacked one crucial element: a focus on activism. CRT, when properly employed, undoubtedly contributes to a more equitable and inviting educative space, which is phenomenal and necessary for marginalized students. However, for me sans the activist focus that critical pedagogy is predicated on, it can potentially fail to foment real agentive, transformative societal change *by* students—not just *for* students. In CRT, educative spaces are transformed for students by benevolent teachers and/or administrative staff. The curriculum becomes culturally diverse and therefore more inviting. However, it is not the students themselves who are necessarily working to transform their educational reality, or, to re-create their respective worlds (Fanon, 1968). Developing a thorough understanding of culturally responsive/relevant pedagogy is indispensable to the work that each of us do in the service of our students. And, while this is most assuredly true, there seems to be something of a paradigm shift afoot in the field regarding inclusive, empowering teaching and learning theory and practice (i.e., praxis). Culturally sustaining pedagogy has been building momentum for a few years now, based largely on the work of Professor Django Paris.

Paris and others argue that a conceptual/terminological/pedagogical shift is necessary to truly benefit hyper-marginalized students. They argue that responsivity and relevance are not enough because, traditionally, they have not been used as levers to challenge the intrinsically inequitable structure of schooling in this country. Instead, they are conceived of as ways to create safe spaces within an unsafe environment, which is necessary; however, they fail to adequately challenge the oppressive structures that make safe spaces exigent in the first place. Culturally sustaining pedagogy (CSP), on the other hand, argues that the very structure of schooling with all concomitant curricular, content-based, and pedagogical considerations should be re-imagined in a way that does not merely respond to cultural dissonance, but instead works to integrate the language, culture, and ways of being of hyper-marginalized students into the very fabric of their schooling experiences. The authors define culturally sustain pedagogy thusly:

> Culturally sustaining pedagogy seeks to perpetuate and foster—to sustain—linguistic, literate, and cultural pluralism as part of the democratic project of schooling. In the face of current policies and practices that have the explicit goal of creating a monocultural and monolingual society, research and practice need equally explicit resistances that embrace cultural pluralism and cultural equality. (Paris, 2012, p. 1)

MAN UP students were encouraged to be agentive and to mandate and even provide cultural sustenance for themselves as well as other marginalized peoples. Our goal was to prepare to these young men to demand positive social change, not by simply marching or more overt forms of protest, but also by deconstructing the stereotypes that have caused them to internalize both educational and STEM failure, and, by doing (applying) STEM to address problems that they themselves identified. I wanted MAN UP students to not only feel comfortable in their classes because there were pictures of Reverend Dr. Martin Luther King, Jr., on the wall. While this is important, I also wanted them to know that there is much work to be done and STEM is, perhaps, the primary medium in which they could begin to repair the broken neighborhoods and cities that they hail from. Critical pedagogy is founded on just this type of transformative action (Duncan-Andrade & Morrell, 2008).

Shifting the paradigm: Critical-reality pedagogy in STEM education

Clearly, there is room for criticality in STEM. Students should be encouraged to question naturalized axioms (Philip, 2011a) as well as their own positionality and subjectivity within their specific socio-political, socio-historical, and socioeconomic realities (Freire, 1997). Therefore, the MAN UP instructional team sought to implement components of critical pedagogy in our instructional practices. Critical pedagogy is decidedly Marxist in that it is concerned with alienation and exploitation (Freire, 1997; Giroux, 2011) and, it is simultaneously postmodern precisely because its ontological vocation is deconstruction (Derrida & Caputo, 1997). Critical pedagogy seeks to re-empower traditionally oppressed students by presenting them with the necessary tools to come to consciousness so that they can begin to exercise their power to deconstruct the ideological and juridical bulwarks of inequity that wreak havoc on and in their lives. More specifically, it works to provide students the means to think meta-cognitively about their own ideological predispositions (Althusser, 1971; Apple, 2004; Leonardo, 2010) as well as the unmistakably Eurocentric, Western-centric ideology that pervades their social reality (Fanon, 1968; Leonardo, 2010). The goal of this kind of critical interrogation is that students would begin to question the assumptions and limitations that they have placed on themselves because of the sadistic ubiquity and proliferation of the negative stereotypes, which have been sutured to their identities as urban Black males.

The impetus of critical pedagogy (Duncan-Andrade & Morrell, 2008; Giroux, 2011), then, according to proponents and practitioners is to equip oppressed students with a critical framework that will afford them the means to extricate themselves from a pedagogy that has continuously repressed and oppressed them, educationally, socially, and consequently culturally (Baugh, 1996; Freire, 1997). Furthermore, critical pedagogy seeks to facilitate this transformation by encouraging, equipping, and empowering students to develop their agentive voices so that they can begin to transform their worlds by deconstructing the seemingly axiomatic Eurocentric meta-narratives that animate Western culture (Philip, 2011a), both nationally and globally. By centering critical pedagogy, the goal of MAN UP's curricular approach was to emancipate students from STEM education that is predicated on uncritical, rote memorization and regurgitation. We have to break away from this stultifying STEM educational approach so that students would begin to identify as change agents capable of breaking this cyclical educational inequity by making STEM their own, by contextualizing, appropriating, and subsequently applying STEM in the remediation of societal issues that are important to them. More simply put, MAN UP students were encouraged to be critical producers of STEM, not merely passive consumers of it. Freire's work was indispensable in conceptualizing the way that MAN UP sought to alloy critical pedagogy and STEM education. Reality pedagogy (Emdin, 2010, 2016) argues that students' lived-experiences need to be valued and incorporated, not unlike critical pedagogy; however, Emdin (2010), in defining reality pedagogy, argues that it is perhaps most useful specifically within STEM educational context. Thus, the pedagogical approach that MAN UP instantiated was a combination of critical-reality pedagogy because I felt that this approach provided the optimum way to engage MAN UP students as individuals full of potential, promise, concerns, and expertise vis-à-vis the rigorous STEM work that this program featured.

According to Freire (1997), the pedagogy of the oppressed disallows intellectual discourse between the student and teacher, teacher and student, in favor of a monologue, or worse, dictation. Furthermore, Freire contends that the pedagogy of the oppressed functions to maintain the hegemony that exists in a given oppressive society. He writes: "If people, as historical beings necessarily engaged with other people in a movement of inquiry, did not control that movement, it would be (and is) a violation of their humanity" (1997, p. 66). He goes on to write, albeit, in much more pointed words, "Any situation in which some individuals prevent others from engaging in the process of inquiry is one of violence…to alienate human beings from their own decision-making is to change them into objects" (Freire, 1997, p. 66). To this point, I feel a pellucid quote from Fanon (1968), reflects perfectly Freire's own polemic against the oppressive nature of the banking of education that educational humanism espouses:

> In capitalist societies, education, whether secular or religious, the teaching of moral reflexes handed down from father to son, the exemplary integrity of workers decorated after fifty years of loyal service, the fostering of love for harmony and wisdom, those aesthetic forms of respect for the status quo, instill in the exploited a mood of submission and inhibition which considerably eases the task of the agents of law and order. (Fanon, 1968, p. 3)

The "agents of law and order," the elites, are the ones who determine what knowledge is, and, what knowledge should be disseminated. Consequently, what is taught concretizes the social arrangement that educational humanism simultaneously presupposes and promotes: i.e., that there is a knower, who by her or his knowledge is societal elite, and one who does not know, who, conversely, is marginalized due to her or his lack of knowledge. For much of our Nation's history, Black people and more specifically Black males have been forced to assume this obsequious position—the non-knower (Leonardo, 2010). As Fanon (1968) writes, this inequitable, White supremacist based positioning makes the maintenance of the status quo, speciously, in the name of "order," much easier to infuse and indoctrinate into the subordinate class, i.e., the oppressed. What is more, this hegemonic relationship purposely leaves no room for critical inquiry: the knower knows, and his knowledge is unquestioned.

This is how STEM is positioned in K–12 education (Emdin, 2010). If these conditions are accepted, criticality is discouraged in the student. If Fanon is correct, this is a controlling mechanism. The marginalized groups "learn" or more precisely, they are inculcated with the "virtue" of living out a subservient existence according to the auspices of the "social institutions...that embody the fruits of civilization" (Fanon, 1968, p. 31). Freire warns that any attempt to re-order this dynamic will greeted with bitter opposition: "to resolve the teacher-student contradiction, to exchange the role of depositor, prescriber, domesticator, for the role of the student among students would be to undermine the power of the oppressor..." (1997, p. 56). However, this ambitious and potentially contentious goal was the goal that impelled the development of MAN UP's pedagogical approach.

Deconstructing this reality was (and is) crucial precisely because the persistence of the hackneyed banking model of education (Freire, 1997), in general and in STEM education specifically, continues to oppress and stultify Black males. According to the traditional model of STEM education, mastery necessitates a kind of rote, passive acceptance. MAN UP was designed to move away from this anti-critical model to reinvigorate the tension between criticality and STEM. The curricular approach if the MAN UP program was intended to first encourages, empowers, and equips, then, requires students to critically (and meta-cognitively) interrogate and subsequently employ STEM in order to better not only their own lives but also the lives of members from their local, national, and global community/ies. For the MAN UP instructional team, this is a matter of social justice.

Ring the alarm: Social justice and STEM education

Gutstein's (2005) analysis of math education is a microcosm of STEM education writ large in that math has, traditionally, been viewed as a gatekeeper that wards off hyper-marginalized students and precludes them from achieving academic success at comparable rates to their European American and Asian American peers (Gutstein, 2005; Moses & Cobb, 2001). Gutstein argues for a version of math education that affords hyper-marginalized students a nutritive educational space where they can not only learn math, in the canonical sense, but also where they can agentively apply math to issues that inform and affect their sociopolitical and socioeconomic realities. He argues that this has not been the impetus of math education, traditionally:

> The goal of increasing equity within mathematics education does not explicitly position teachers and students as having the transformative power to rectify fundamental structural inequalities through their participation in civil society, both within and outside of educational remiss. In this sense, it does not connect school into the larger sociopolitical context of society. (Gutstein, 2005, p. 31)

Furthermore, Gutstein (2005) argues that by canonizing a form of depoliticized math education that serves to maintain an inequitable status quo, the National Council of Teaching Mathematics is contributing to an exploitative capitalist endeavor that necessitates the positioning of the poor and uneducated as mechanistic workers upon whose backs capital can be accrued:

> Thus, in analyzing the sociopolitical context of mathematics education, my contention is that (a) mathematical literacy, as a form of functional literacy distinct from critical literacy, serves the needs of capital accumulation in the United States; (B) the NCTM, as the major organizational force within the mathematics education community, has frame mathematical literacy largely from the perspective of US economic competitor to this in the global order and has avoided discussions of whose interest is served; and (C) mathematical literacy from various groups of students in a stratified labor market, unfortunately, has divergent meanings for different social groups. A reconceptualization of the purpose of mathematics education is needed—one that includes envisioning mathematical literacy as critical literacy for the purpose of transforming society, in its entirety, from the bottom up toward equity and justice, for all students whether from dominant or oppressed groups. (Gutstein, 2005, p. 281)

To this point Barton (2001) writes: "…marriages between capitalism and education and capitalism and science have created a foundation for science education that emphasizes corporate values at the expense of social justice and human dignity" (2001, p. 847). She goes on to argue that this dynamic is especially prevalent and especially pernicious in urban educational settings. Thus, the MAN UP approach sought to immerse students in STEM education and curriculum that encouraged them to make connections between STEM and their real lives so that they could transform the seemingly static bulwarks of structuralized race-based inequity that inform their lived-experiences as low-income, urban, Black males.

In order to position them as young people who were attuned to the varied manifestation of social injustice that characterized their lives as urban, (predominately) low-income Black males course content inhered around and was derived from matters of social justice and social injustice.

Social justice, as an educational framework (Giroux, 2011; Gorski, Zenkov, Osei-Kofi, Sapp, & Stovall, 2013; McLaren, 1994; Smyth, 2011), functions to empower, encourage, and equip hyper-marginalized students to use their agentive voices so that they are armed with and have the propensity to employ critical theoretical lenses, which are necessary to disrupt the inequitable milieus that students are forced to navigate. These milieus can be social, political, civic, and/or educational. In MAN UP, we were especially interested in the educational spaces where social justice is routinely enacted. However, this is not to say that we turned a blind eye to the other areas that inform MAN UP students' lived-experience as Black males within a National milieu that has been (and continues to be) inhospitable and traditionally fearful of Black males (Noguera, 2008). According to Gutstein emancipatory, critical math education should disambiguate: "underlying ideologies and begin to understand how mathematics can be used to reveal or hide injustice" by using "statistical examples that draw students' attention to social inequalities such as how poor people pay taxes they cannot afford while the rich use loopholes to avoid taxes" (Gutstein, 2005, p. 3). One of the goals of an emancipatory, critical math education should be to ensure that "students understand mathematics and the political nature of knowledge whose knowledge is, and is not, valued, as well as how mathematics is often used to hide social realities" (Darder, 1998, p. 24).

There is, unequivocally, a certain degree of plasticity regarding working definition of social justice. However, in developing the MAN UP pedagogical approach, I along with the STEM instructors, Mr. K and M.S, adhered to a straightforward criterion that we agreed our particular social justice frame must adhere to: (1) It has to work to disambiguate false metanarratives (e.g., meritocracy, melting pot metaphor, etc.); (2), In addition to this, it must work to disrupt the banking model of education (Freire & Macedo, 1987); and, contiguously, (3), if it is to be an efficacious social justice oriented frame (and curriculum), it must be vitally concerned with empowering agents to exercise self-determination and realize their full potential; and, (4) it must seek to equip students to deconstruct oversimplified explanations for societal injustice and inequity; (5), and, it must seek fair (re)distribution of resources, opportunities, and responsibilities, while (6), building social solidarity and community capacity for collaborative action.

The (peculiar) institution of compulsory, K–12 public education, from its inception here in the United States, has been a tool or ideological state apparatus (Althusser, 1971) that has been employed to mechanically reproduce a certain type of purportedly normative student (Giroux, 2011). To be more precise, schooling here in the United States is, essentially, a factory that reproduces a definite Eurocentric, middle class aesthetic (Leonardo, 2010). This is why our schools have failed many Black male students (Duncan-Andrade & Morrell, 2008; Noguera, 2008). The reality is that, according to Toldson and Snitman (2010), 80 percent of America's teaching force self-identifies as European American (this term is interchangeable with white in this study). And, what is more, more that 65 percent of all teachers are in fact European American women. Make no mistake: I am not arguing that these statistics are not inherently problematic. European American teachers, whether female or male, are not unable or incapable of teaching Black males simply because of their differential ethnicity. Nevertheless, the reality for the clear majority of Black male students is that they will encounter very few teachers who come from where they come from, and very few teachers who look like them (Ladson-Billings, 1995) in their respective educational careers.

Reasonably, many instances of cultural dissonance arise because of this dynamic. This program, MAN UP, was created as a space where the issues that spring out of this cultural (and gendered) mismatch can be addressed, and ultimately redressed. I was convinced, in developing the pedagogical plan for this program, that a focus on critical-reality pedagogy, as the pedagogic and curricular vehicle, held the potential to begin ameliorating this mismatch—precisely because a critical education is, in fact, a matter of social justice (Smyth, 2011). And, practically, it should work to prepare MAN UP students to begin thinking through ways to use STEM for societal uplift. Far too many hyper-marginalized students, especially poor, urban Black males are not exposed to critical, socially just, relevant curricular material in school, much less in their STEM coursework (Delpit, 2012). This is perhaps more pronounced concerning STEM education, precisely because STEM education, according to scholars like Barton (2001) and Gutstein (2005), is routinely taught in a depoliticized and decontextualized manner that functions to further strengthen the United States' multibillion-dollar Military Industrial Complex. According to Gutstein (2005), this anti-critical approach to STEM education runs counter to a social justice educational agenda:

> From a social justice perspective, there is a significant problem with framing mathematical literacy from the perspective of economic competition. In essence, this positioning places the maximization of corporate profits above all else. This is fundamentally in

opposition to social justice agenda that instead places the material, social, psychological, spiritual, and emotional needs of human beings, as well as other species of the planet, before capital's needs. (Gutstein, 2005, p. 24)

The goal of the MAN UP pedagogical approach involved a constant unveiling of reality, which strived for the emergence of conscious, critical contextualization of STEM by MAN UP students. In this study, I define the critical contextualization of STEM thusly: The critical contextualization of STEM is evidenced by students beginning to appropriate and critically apply STEM as a tool to redress issues or problems, which are connected to students' lives that inhere around notions of equity/inequity and or social justice. This approach sought to increase the opportunities for MAN UP students to critically interrogate and intervene for socially just individual and collective outcomes. In order to create opportunities for our scholars to become proficient and adroit in applying their STEM knowledge for social justice, we had to create a safe, nutritive educational environment by simultaneously fighting against the negativity that has been sutured to their culture while welcoming their language and culture into the various educative spaces that the MAN UP program represented.

We are what we speak: Dissin' Black English and the correlation between language skills and scholastic expectations

Low expectations are often sutured to (perceived) linguistic aptitude or more specifically, students' proximity to or distance from mastery of Standard English. This point can be evidence by the disproportionate number of Black students in special education/special needs courses Nationwide (http://www.emstac.org/registered/topics/disproportionality/intro.htm). Obviously, there are other confounding variables that contribute to the alienation of marginalized students, but, linguistic differentiation cannot be overlooked. Look no further than the creation of English Second Language (ESL) classrooms. These special courses separate out students who have the greatest distance from the mastery of Standard English; this is also true of special education classrooms. Greene and Walker (2004) write, "The arrival of desegregation brought to light the issues of having to deal with Black English in the classroom" (2004, p. 437). Furthermore they continue, "Black and non-Black teachers alike ridiculed the use of Black English suggesting instead that students should abandon the pattern in order to blend into American [white] culture with few observable differences as possible" (2004, p. 437). To this point Wofford (1979) writes:

> The consequences of teachers' attitudes toward dialect are profound. For example, attitudes can affect teachers' initial judgment about how intelligent children are likely to be, or how they are grouped for instruction, how their contributions in class will be treated, and the like.

This phenomenon can be further elucidated via a distinctly Marxist economic model in that usefulness, specifically the usefulness of a varied linguistic inventory, is replaced by the notion of exchange-value. This perversion (or what Marx refers to as fetishism), then, devalues the use-value of Black English by viewing only its perceived exchangeability on the linguistic market, where sociocultural capital is king. One can reasonably argue that in very specific contexts, for example, a job interview or an inquiry as to the availability of a living space (outside of the hood), to speak in Black English it to one's detriment. However, this type of thinking is narrow and fails to take into consideration the psychosocial benefits and usefulness of BE's valuation both educational and socially. Language and culture are inextricably tied. The widespread dismissal of Black English in educational spaces is analogous to and precipitated the widespread dismissal of what is perceived as non-standard, Black culture.

More, Green and Walker (2004) argue that "Black English functions as more than a tool for communication. It reflects individual and group identity as well as promotes group solidarity" (p. 17). But, what is the result of the ongoing devaluation of Black English? Green and Walker, to this point write, "Teachers should realize that students reflect their [the teachers'] negative attitudes toward Black English" (p. 18). Students begin to view themselves the same way that some educators do, based primarily on their language use. That is to say, BE speakers begin to subscribe to the theory that that very little can be expected of them because like their teachers, they too believe that language use is in one-to-one correlation with intelligence. The defeatist, nihilistic mentality that marginalization (and alienation) engenders is readily apparent via depressing statistics of Black youth incarceration, incidence of AIDS, teen pregnancy, drop-out rates, and underrepresentation in higher education. Of course, our Nation's political, educational, fiscal, judiciary, penal, and monetary systems, which serve the interest of white supremacy, produce, promulgate, and reify pathological narratives that center the depressing statistics that I mentioned above strictly at the feet of Black people.

It should come as no surprise, then, that in an analysis of research over a 20-year period, Denbo (1986) found that study after study demonstrated that both low and high teacher expectations greatly affect student's performances. Likewise, Schilling and Schilling (1999) capture clearly the broad idea that expectations are vital to education:

> Expectations are also shaped by teacher and student perceptions of the reasons for successes and failures. Teachers may attribute successes and failures to factors such as ability, effort, task difficulty, and luck. Teachers often project high expectations for the future if they believe that a student's success is due to her high ability, and will attribute a high achiever's failure to bad luck. When a student's failure is attributed to low ability, a teacher will begin to expect less in the future. Subsequent "lucky" successes of such a student are unlikely to be taken as evidence that the low ability label should be changed. (Schilling & Schilling, 1989)

Correspondingly, Steele (2010) notes that with each successive year, Black students fall farther behind their White counterparts; this has to do with the overall design of schooling here in the States: schools were made to cater to and consequently reproduce a distinctly middle class, mainstream aesthetic, persona, and value system.

Flipping the script: Connecting cultural-linguistic identities and STEM competencies

Because there is a plethora of both teaching and learning styles, identifying one as the exemplar is impossible. Undoubtedly, teaching and learning styles reflect the richness of cultural diversity and individual differences. However, the reality is that there are inequities in representation. That is to say, certain ideological configurations are privileged over others thereby demarcating the boundaries of mainstream and non-mainstream. Black history is not required; however, a very Eurocentric leaning account of history is. This creates a serious problem precisely because learners whose cultures and learning styles are elided in the culture, content and organization of the classroom are less likely to be highly motivated and benefit from instruction that they feel fails to recognize their personhood. Therefore, paradigm-shifting pedagogy both within and without STEM education is exigent. The way an educator facilitates knowledge creation either serves as a catalyst for learning or, on the negative end, a blunt instrument that further bludgeons traditionally marginalized students into an anti-critical submission via a decontextualized, stultifying pedagogical approach (Mahiri & Sims, 2016).

Further exacerbating the problem according to Hale-Benson (1982) is the fact that "formal education has not worked for many Black youth because it has not employed teaching styles that correspond with students' learning styles." She goes further, "Many Black youth have barely mastered the norms of their own culture when they are confronted with teaching styles that are incompatible with their accepted learning patterns" (p. 27). An incongruity between teaching and learning styles causes Black children specifically to become less motivated and much more likely to question their own self-worth. This can and often times do lead to disenfranchisement.

Furthermore, Hale-Benson (1982) argues that "Before teachers can understand and appreciate the learning styles preferred by students, it is important to understand the role culture plays in shaping learning styles. It shapes cognitive development, children's approach to academic tasks and their behavior in traditional academic settings." We have to get away from the notion that "Blessed are those who expect nothing ... for they shall not be disappointed"; according to Denbo (1986) "Too frequently, parents and teachers protect themselves by adhering to this quotation." Murnane (1975) found that as teachers increase their expectations of Black youth, their behavior toward these youths undergoes a change. That is to say, when high expectations are evident, teachers provide more support and, subsequently, the youths in question feel more positive about their ability and self-worth. Obviously, we cannot simply begin to just expect more of students and hope for the best. To do this without properly equipping them would be irresponsible and would potentially be more damaging than helpful, no matter how well-intentioned.

Steele's (2010) work on individual and group stereotype threat provides an expansive lens for viewing how identity contingencies and other socially constructed obstacles work to mitigate the academic achievement of Black Students. Stereotype threats are felt in specific situations in which stereotypes associated with one's individual or group identity are prevalent. Mere awareness of the stereotype can be distracting enough to negatively affect a person's performance in the domain connected to it. Negative stereotypes of Blacks' academic achievement in STEM subjects can be debilitating, but their affects can also be circumvented by a variety of interventions. One mitigating approach that has been identified is providing critical feedback along with opportunities for analysis of the larger societal context and structures that motivate stereotypes (Steele, 2010). In this regard, research is also beginning to show how some Black students are achieving in STEM by developing abilities to better manage or "flip" the negative impacts of stereotype threat .Another approach extends from how teachers can work to foster feelings of identity safety in how classroom discourse and culture are constructed to access rigorous curriculum content (Mahiri and Sims, 2016). Additionally, important research (Emdin, 2010; Gutstein, 2005; Nasir, 2011) argues that there is indispensable value in incorporating students' authentic lived-experiences into the overall learning of STEM. These approaches, (have in common a valuation and integration of marginalized students' individuality, culture, language, and real-life experiences in and out of school), represent a necessary paradigm shift in the way that teaching and learning in and of STEM, especially for hyper-marginalized students, must be reformulated.

Many scholars have shown the importance of connecting positive academic identities to the cultural-linguistic identities and lived experiences of students. For example, Nasir (2011) and Tate (1995) demonstrated ways that positive academic identity development is at the root of academic success in math for Black students. Nasir's (2011) research found a positive reciprocal correlation between positive academic and cultural identity development and increased math performance for Black students. Lee (2005) illustrated the importance of attending to specific English dialects of urban students to directly build on their cultural-linguistic competence for learning curriculum content. Lee (2005) further showed the significance of accessing cultural identity to effectively teach Black students by synthesizing findings from numerous research studies supporting critical connections between language, identity, and learning.

Essentially, linking learning to students' cultural-linguistic diversity and competences is the cornerstone of approaches to multicultural education and culturally relevant pedagogy (Ladson-Billings, 1995). Banks (et al.) noted, "The more we know about a student's level of identification with a particular group and the extent to which socialization has taken place within that group, the more accurately we can predict, explain, and understand the student's behavior in the classroom" (2004, p. 27). Similarly, the central idea of culturally relevant pedagogy is that if learning structures and stimuli are grounded in a cultural-linguistic context that is familiar to students, there will be greater potential for cognitive expansion and knowledge growth (Allen & Boykin, 1992; Ladson-Billings, 1995). Delpit (2012) expanded upon the framework of culturally relevant pedagogy by delineating methods of culturally responsive teaching that specifically used cultural characteristics, experiences, and perspectives of ethnically diverse students to increase their learning. Five essential components of this approach are developing a knowledge base about cultural diversity, including diverse curriculum content, demonstrating caring and building learning communities, cross-cultural communication, and cultural congruity in instruction. In working to build the Black middle schoolers' identification with STEM, the MAN UP instructors employed each of these components throughout the program.

Bridge building over troubled waters: Connecting STEM learning and social justice

Social justice as an educational framework is integral to critical pedagogical approaches to teaching and learning (Duncan-Andrade & Morrell, 2008; Giroux, 2011; Gorski et al., 2013; Smyth, 2011). These approaches attempt to equip marginalized students with the theoretical lenses necessary to disrupt the inequitable conditions they face and work to navigate. Extending from the work of Freire (1997) and further informed by scholars like Giroux (1983/2001) and McLaren (1994), critical pedagogy seeks to facilitate this transformation by empowering students to locate and develop their own critical, agentive voices and productive capabilities. A central goal of critical pedagogy is to disrupt the "banking model" of education—the positioning of learners as empty vessels to be filled with ideas and information that continues their oppression.

Limitations of the banking model outlined by Freire have been addressed in STEM subjects as the "absorption" model. Linn and Eylon (2011) noted hallmarks of the absorption approach in science instruction as requiring students to listen to lectures, read textbooks and complete exercises, and conduct experiments or investigations following step-by-step procedures. Fundamental aspects of the absorption approach do not build on individual interests and intuitions or cultural-linguistic backgrounds and competencies of learners. Linn and Eylon argued that when these constraints are circumvented by a more active and agentive knowledge integration approach, then "everybody can learn science" (p. ix).

Proponents of critical pedagogy argue, however, that opening access to STEM subjects and careers to everybody, by itself, is not enough. They feel that though access to high quality STEM instruction is a civil and human right, a larger critique of the positioning and roles of STEM in the very processes of oppression and marginalization must accompany increasing access to STEM content. They argue against attempts to limit these kinds of critiques to the social sciences and humanities and advocate that these perspectives are just as imperative to the learning of STEM subjects. Blikstein (2008), for example, suggested that knowledge and use of digital technology, and particularly the design of new digital devices, derived from math and science are necessary tools for fulfilling Freire's vision of humanization and societal transformation.

Studies conducted in after school contexts (Vakil, 2014) and within school contexts (Norris, 2014) found significant ways that critical pedagogical approaches enhanced Black and Latino middle school students' social justice perspectives in conjunction with their learning STEM subjects. Moses and Cobb's (2001) work with the Algebra Project earlier connected these kinds of efforts to the socio-political implications of how math (and algebra specifically) is both a gateway to and gatekeeper of STEM content and careers.

Black males more than any of group have been marginalized the most by these systemic forces in education generally and in the learning of math specifically (Darder, 1998). To counter this, Gutstein's (2005) argued for a version of math education that affords hyper-marginalized students a nutritive educational space where they can not only learn math, but also where they can learn to apply math to issues that inform and affect their socio-political and socio-economic realities in the larger societal context. In this regard, Gutstein noted, "mathematical literacy, as a form of functional literacy distinct from critical literacy, serves the needs of capital accumulation in the United States" and further that "A reconceptualization of the purpose of mathematics education is needed—one that includes envisioning mathematical literacy as critical literacy for the purpose of transforming society, in its entirety, from the bottom up toward equity and justice, for all students whether from dominant or oppressed groups" (2005, p. 28).

The first premise of MAN UP was: it is vitally important that students begin to apply STEM for issues that are germane to their lived-experiences as urban Black males, for outcomes that they deem important. To this point, Freire (1997) pointed out: "problem posing education does not and cannot serve the interests of the oppressor. No oppressive order to permit the oppressed to begin to question" (1997, p. 67). To be clear, the MAN UP instructional team was not simply interested in identifying and talking through problems that we felt students should be made aware of; rather, we used the students' interests as points of connection for larger discussion of socially just, humanitarian issues that have the potential to be redressed (at least in some small measure) by our students' applications of STEM. Of course, this approach made curriculum development more difficult for instructors, precisely because, students' lived-experiences functioned as anchors for our curricular focus instead of a preformed scope and sequence of content topics. Thus, instructors could not come in with a one-size-fits-all curricular approach. Instead, instructors had to be willing to be flexible, to be malleable, and to, most importantly, participate in co-generative dialogic and co-constructed meaning making alongside the students being served (Emdin, 2010).

More specifically, we sought to position students vis-à-vis STEM in a way that would positively affect their self-image and would, consequently, help them re-envisage themselves as potential STEM majors and STEM professionals, by first engendering a space for positive academic identity development. Of course, these are middle school students whose self-images will change numerous times. So, we were not seeking to pigeon hole them. Black males in STEM are a rarity. This is significant because our economy is positioned toward technological and infor-mational technology, which means the best paying jobs will be STEM focused. Nevertheless, the goal of MAN UP was never to merely work towards producing a group of Black male technocrats that un-problematically adhere to our Nation's technocratic, capitalist ethos (Gutstein, 2005). This was not the measure of suc-cess for this program; rather, we were interested in facilitating the development of Black males who applied STEM not only for base gain, but also for the overall improvement of their respective communities. Our goal was commensurate with Tate's (1995 view of mathematics pedagogy; she argues that the primary purpose of math pedagogy should be: "…to empower students to critique society and [to] seek changes based on their reflective analysis" (1997, p. 169). In order to work towards this goal, we employed a critical-reality pedagogical approach, which was possible because of the (socio-academic synergistic) environment that we inten-tionally and painstakingly created while, simultaneously holding our scholars to high scholastic, behavioral, and collaborative expectations. By taking this inno-vative approach, we were convinced that these students would begin to identify as (social justice oriented) applied STEM practitioners, who because of their new STEM identities, would begin to grow more competent in the STEM subjects covered and in their critical applications of STEM for social justice.

Greater than hope: Insisting on high expectations for Black boys

Surely, the earnest hope of all educators is that each and every child that crosses their path will do well both educationally and humanly. That is, that students will pass through primary through secondary school educated and properly socialized, and, that the young people that they teach will ultimately go on to earn a college degree. However, I believe that there is a striking difference between hopes, ear-nest or otherwise, and that of expectations; more specifically, there is a striking difference in both the theoretical and practical pedagogy and praxis of educators who expect, rather than just hope, that the traditionally marginalized students of color they encounter will buck the trend of low scholastic achievement, which has been a persistent, pejorative characteristic of low socio-economic, marginalized minorities. To this point Halpin (2001) writes,

> [H]opefulness, as experienced by those who have it, entails both anticipating future happiness and trusting in present help to come to it. This is something any good teacher would quickly be able to identify with, in the sense that being such a person entails having both high *expectations* of a pupil's potential as well as the faith that the educational process will help realize it. (Halpin, 2001, p. 394)

It is not my position that hopes and expectations are mutually exclusive. However, it is my position that hopes without expectations are potentially misleading and ephemeral. The notion that for marginalized minority groups, hope is all we have, in my estimation, is crippling. We have to go beyond mere hope and begin to expect great things of ourselves, even if no one else does. Of course, this is no small feat; and, I do not pretend to know the way to reach this end. I do know, however, that something has to be done.

In my experience, when I began to expect things of myself, to hold myself accountable, my teachers soon followed suit. Prior to transferring to the University of California as an undergraduate, I had struggled in community college, off and on, for nearly a decade. At one point in my community college journey, I was dismissed from a local community college because my G.P.A was 1.1 for consecutive semesters. I grew up in low-income housing. In order to maintain low-income status reduced rent, upon turning 18, I had to enroll in school full time. However, I did not have to complete my coursework; I simply had to sign up for it. I routinely signed up for classes; however, as soon as I ran into difficulty, I would simply stop attending classes without ever officially dropping the courses. It was unclear as to whether the Housing Authority expected me and other young people from neighborhoods just like mine to succeed; what was clear, however, was they simply did not care if we succeeded or not. I did not expect much from myself. Undoubtedly, the system I was under was not conducive to my scholastic success. Nevertheless, I was an adult at this time and the onus was on me to take charge of my educational trajectory. To be clear, I want to be careful so that I do not seem to be saying that the onus lies exclusively with young people. That would be unfair and untrue. What is true, however, is that for all students, but especially for poor, hyper-marginalized students' low expectations are deleterious.

The consequence of low expectations

One of the most problematic, albeit pervasive features of our pul̲ ̲
tion system for marginalized students of color is the fact that often the̲
expected to do well scholastically. Moreover, it is well documented that Bla̲
general and Black males specifically (and especially) are haunted by the specter of
low expectations. What do expectations have to do with scholastic performance?
According to Schilling and Schilling (1989):

> The literature on motivation and school performance in younger school children suggests
> that expectations shape the learning experience very powerfully. For example, classic stud-
> ies in the psychology literature have found that merely stating an expectation results in
> enhanced performance, that higher expectations result in higher performance, and that
> persons with high expectations perform at a higher level than those with low expecta-
> tions, even though their measured abilities are equal. (Schilling & Schilling, 1989, p. 22)

Thankfully, there is a somewhat extensive body of literature that bemoans
(rightly) the negative effects of low expectations for Black students, and, furthermore, just how these lowered expectations exacerbate preexisting poverty-induced
problems—problems that can be traced back to long-standing institutional and
structural racism. However, simply identifying the problem, though helpful, is not
far-reaching enough. Educators need work alongside young people to empower,
encourage, and equip them to succeed in the face of these problems rather than
allow structural and/or institutional racism to claim more and more victims.
At MAN UP we insisted that our expectations remain high while also considering where each student was in relation to competency, engagement and interest
precisely because high expectations without adequate supports is not helpful,
rather it is burdensome for students. So, the rigor that we insisted on was always
informed by our understanding of how a given student wanted to meaningfully
engage with the curricular material we developed. As a result, this paradigm shift
in pedagogy, for us, necessitated a reimaged and reinvigorated conception of rigor.

Out with the old: (Re)Conceptualizing rigor

Webster's Dictionary defines rigor thusly: extremely thorough, exhaustive, or
accurate (https://www.merriam-webster.com/dictionary/rigor?utm_campaign=s
d&utm_medium=serp&utm_source=jsonld). This definition needs re-articulation.
Therefore, the instructional team at MAN UP (Mr. K, Mr. S, and myself) worked

to define rigor differently, and we argued, more expansively. The goal of the MAN UP pedagogical approach, which centered a blend of critical-reality pedagogy, was to define rigor by situating it within students' diverse socio-political contexts. This is an age-old problem, which, despite many passionate, intelligent, and careful ameliorative attempts, continues to grow at an alarming rate. Surely, this problem necessitates rigorous analysis in attempts to begin to eradicate it. Inequity, based on race, socioeconomic status, gender, etc., will not be remedied simply. Therefore, MAN UP's pedagogical approach, which was anchored by MAN UP students' real lives, was designed to help our students begin identifying paradigm-shifting questions, and perhaps solutions, for issues or problems that were important to them.

Traditional conceptions of rigor necessitate a divorce between students' real-life experiences and the purported objective truths of STEM (Gutstein, 2005). Traditional conceptions of rigor require students to accept the de-contextualization of STEM as normal and even axiomatic (Philip, 2011b), such that it becomes incredibly difficult (or abnormal) for students to situate their learning within a STEM context (Bang & Medin, 2010). This delimits (and sometimes disallows) students' ability to identify as critical, applied STEM practitioners. Research (Nasir, 2011) supports the argument that positive STEM identity development is necessary, especially for hyper-marginalized students, for their academic success in STEM to increase. My presupposition is in line with Nasir's findings: that is, when students are encouraged to apply STEM, critically, to issues that they deem important—as opposed to passively receiving and regurgitating decontextualized facts—their ability to shift their critical, contextual understanding and application of STEM increases such that their identification with, understanding of, and competency in STEM also increase. This situated, contextualized approach to STEM pedagogy is far more rigorous than its obverse: decontextualized, rote memorization and regurgitation of STEM-based facts, precisely because it requires students to apply STEM critically and rigorously to long-standing, seemingly intractable social conundrums.

So then, the goals of the MAN UP pedagogical approach were to encourage, empower, and equip MAN UP students to:

- Situate their STEM learning within a larger socio-political context based on solidarity with other MAN UP students as well as other hyper-marginalized people locally, nationally, and globally.
- Develop ways to situate students' STEM learning within real-life (socially just) sociopolitical context.

- Help students make tangible connections between students' lives—outside of the classroom—and STEM course content.
- Re-conceptualize rigor and situate rigorous STEM learning within a larger socio-political context so that students' conceptual understanding of STEM in application increases.
- Facilitate students' growth regarding the development of student's identities as critical, applied STEM practitioners.
- Invite students to co-create meaning with them within their shared classroom.

More simply put, the MAN UP pedagogical approach was arguing for a conception of rigor that incorporated and intertwined content and process. (For example, critical dialogic discussions about the sociopolitical context of mathematics.) Rigor is much ballyhooed in STEM educative circles, however, though necessary, it is not the solitary goal; instead it is but one constitutive part of a critical and empowering educational triumvirate (i.e., relationships, relevance, and rigor). This three-pronged approach, which was built upon a cornerstone of respectful, reciprocal and empowering relationships between students and educators, was integral. When alloyed with curricular material that demonstrates relevance to students' lived-experiences, this approach should encourage, empower, and equip students to learn and apply STEM critically and agentively to begin to deconstruct and, hopefully, redress social inequity.

During the second year of this program, I decided to formally study the impact of this critical pedagogical approach for learning and making identity connections to STEM for the young Black male participants during the 2013–14 academic year. Although MAN UP served a total of 43 students in 6th, 7th, and 8th grades, I focused on the 17 students in the first year of MAN UP (fourteen 6th graders and three 7th graders) to capture how they responded to and developed through the program during their first year of participation. Therefore, the guiding question for this study was:

> What are the impacts of a critical-reality pedagogical approach to the learning of STEM subjects on 6th and 7th Grade Black male students' competency in, identity with, and understanding and development of socially just applications of STEM?

Data collected on the first year MAN UP cohort included pre and post surveys, individual and focus group interviews with the students; interviews with the instructors of the science/technology and math classes; participant observation, video recordings, and field notes on class activities and field trips.

Circling back to one of the primary tenets of MAN UP, which was to afford students a space to be who they are, urban middle school Black males, this program was impelled by a curricular focus that was aligned with course content that encouraged MAN UP students to do STEM just as they were by connecting STEM to issues that were in some cases specific and in others simply important to them as urban Black males (Ladson-Billings, 1995). One of the goals of this approach was to help MAN UP students develop and strengthen their own academic identities. Nasir's (2011) research on the vicissitudes of Black students vis-à-vis math education has underscored the importance of positive academic identity development as a constitutive part of academic success for traditionally marginalized Black students. Studies find that there is a positive reciprocal correlation between positive academic and cultural identity development and increased math performance (Gutstein, 2005; Nasir, 2011).

Because of this MAN UP's curricular and pedagogical approaches sought to equip, encourage, and empower (Anzaldua, 1987) middle school Blacks boys to disrupt the negative stereotypes that have been sutured to them (Sims, Hotep, & James, in press), so that they can forge new available identities as critical, socially just scientists, technologists, engineers, and/or mathematicians.

Because I am aware of the psychological vicissitudes that many urban Black males face simply by virtue of the families that they were born into, the core tenets of MAN UP reflected my desire to provide Black male students with a robust, critical, STEM-focused educative environment. And, in doing so, my goal was and continues to be to disrupt subtractive schooling practices that produce a false binary between urban non-white students and students of color. Because of this ubiquitous yet altogether false dichotomy, Black males must either choose to stay true to their home environ, identity, etc., or opt to get out (Fordham & Ogbu, 1986). This is a difficult proposition for adults: just imagine how it can weigh on a young person. This difficult proposition becomes unbearably arduous, according to Steele (2010), when marginalized students are faced with course material, especially STEM material, which has been stereotypically (and erroneously) positioned as beyond the scope of their cognitive abilities.

In the face of the myriad issues Black males face in our educational system, I, along with the MAN UP Instructional Team, worked to create a nutritive educational atmosphere impelled by love. All of the work that we did, the innovative critical-reality pedagogical work, was the direct result of our love for justice and equity and, especially, our love for traditionally marginalized young people. Love is indispensable for emancipatory educational work. According to Freire (1997), "…love is an act of courage, not of fear, love is a commitment to others. No matter where the oppressed are found, the act of love is commitment to their cause--the cause of liberation" (p. 117). Not only this, according to Freire, love holds the potentiality, the power, to incite student knowledge-creating precisely because love creates a learning atmosphere where students are valued, encouraged, and safe. This kind of environment, where relationships, relevance, and rigor coalesce creates opportunities for students to challenge themselves precisely because failure is no longer indicative of ability—instead, it is simply part and parcel of a learning experience that encourages students to work towards their fullest potential.

Therefore, we structured this program so that love, care, and consideration was evident in our curricular focus as well as our critical-reality pedagogical approach to teaching and learning. Both out curricular foci and pedagogical approach centered the live-experiences of our scholars.

As I discuss in detail in subsequent chapters, our curricular foci and concomitant critical-reality pedagogical approach set the stage for students to being critically contextualizing STEM. In the following subsection, I discuss the research design as well as data collection and data analysis procedures.

Does this approach work: Data analysis procedures

To assess the efficacy of the critical-reality pedagogical approach to STEM education at MAN UP, I used qualitative methods for collecting and analyzing data guided by the work of Denzin and Lincoln (2003). I also utilized the work of Spradley (1979) with respect to conducting interviews with the students and their instructors. In addition to interviews, I made audio/video recordings, and took field notes on the study participations' various learning activities during their Saturday classes and fieldtrips. I also provided opportunities for the first-year cohort to express considerations about their learning and social experiences as Black males in STEM.

The pedagogical approach of MAN UP represents a union between discrete, yet similar educational approaches. This amalgamated pedagogical approach alloys critical pedagogy with reality pedagogy, henceforth critical-reality pedagogy. Critical Pedagogy (Giroux, 2011) takes the first position that education should tool not only for upward mobility but also for emancipation from the oppressive pedagogical practices that many hyper-marginalized students are continuously subjected to. Reality pedagogy (Emdin, 2010) argues that students' lived experiences need to be valued and incorporated, specifically within STEM educational context in order to position students as real-world problem solvers. This conjoined pedagogical approach was designed to engage the focal students in rigorous STEM content such that their learning of, identification with, and competency in developing socially just applications of the STEM significantly increased. I collected and analyzed data on the 17 Black students in their first year of MAN UP. The study followed the focal students for an entire academic year, from September 2013 until June 2014. In this study I was seeking to iden- tify instances when students begin to (re)envisage themselves as applied, criti- cal STEM practitioners, capable of using their STEM learning to affect positive, socially just societal outcomes by wielding STEM as a tool for change. It was my presupposition that the MAN UP pedagogical approach to STEM education should encourage, equip, and empower students to demonstrate, through rigor- ous, comprehensive socially just applications of STEM, a positive shift in their learning regarding the STEM subjects taught at MAN UP as well as with regard to the ways in which they either identified or dis-identified with STEM.

Site: MAN UP: It was 8:20 a.m. as a mixed stream of bright-eyed and sleepy- faced young men began filing into the charter school that housed the MAN UP program. Exuberant conversations about anything and everything reached a fevered-pitch in a matter of seconds as the young men began greeting each other. Because MAN UP met every other Saturday, there was time for the young men that did not go to school together to miss each other. There was a lot of catching up taking place. As each student entered they were greeted with a handshake, hug or a combination thereof that we in the Black community fondly refer to as "dap." We established this ritualistic welcome early on. Each young man needed to know that we saw them, that we were happy that they were with us, and that we cared for them. This ritual was the first step in establishing an environment that could support the varied psycho-social, socio-emotional, and cognitive learning needs and epistemological curiosities of the young men that we were blessed to serve.

During this study, MAN UP served a total of 43 Black male students divided by each of the three grade levels of middle school. Although every student attends a middle school in the general area of the site for the program, it met in a rented space of a local middle school. However, there was no formalized affiliation with the middle school site. Instead, MAN UP is part of a larger non-profit organi- zation. The program took place every other Saturday from September 2013 to June 2014 for a total of 22 sessions. Once for each of the two semesters, there was an additional Saturday session devoted to a field trip. Each session was a five- hour block from 9:30 a.m. to 2:30 p.m. in which the cohort had a total of three classes, each about 75 minutes in length: Computer Science (CS), Math, and the Rhetorical Analysis of Manhood (RAM). Infused in the content, each class incorporated social justice applications for the learning. The three courses took place simultaneously. For example, when 6th graders were in Rhetorical Analysis of Manhood from 10:00 a.m.to 11:10 a.m. on a given Saturday, 7th Graders were in Math, and 8th graders were in Mobile Applications so that during the course of each Saturday session the 6th graders, 7th graders, and 8th graders received instruction from the teachers of each of the classes.

The focal cohort: Although there were 43 students in the program across the three grade levels, the focal cohort for this study were the 17 students in their first year of the MAN UP program grade along with their instructors. The first-year cohort was selected to explore the impact of the program during their first year of participation. A key demographic characteristic of these 17 first year students was that 80 percent qualified for free or reduced lunch and thus considered to be from low-income families. Eighty percent also attended Title 1 public schools. Sixty percent were from single parent homes, and 60 percent had parents or guardians that did not have a college degree. The average GPA of cohort was 2.99 because the program's selection process focused on students who were already achieving some measure of success in school.

The instructors for the three Saturday classes were men. The MAN UP scholars referred to me as Mr. J. In addition to teaching the Rhetorical Analysis of manhood, (RAM) classes, I also held the title of Founding Director. At the time of this study, I was also a doctoral student in education. I now serve as the Director of Equity for the College of San Mateo. The instructor for the Computer Science and Mobile Apps (CS) classes, who the students called Mr. S, is Iranian and, at the time was a doctoral student in education. Mr. S., is now an associated professor at the largest public University in the country. Additionally, he had a master's degree in engineering. The instructor for the math classes, who the students called Mr. K, is a Black male who was a public-school math teacher at the time of this study is now a Math Professor at a large Bay Area Community College.

The focal class for this research was students in their first year in the program. Their demographic breakdown was as follows:

> Eighty percent of the focal class qualified for Free and/or Reduced Lunch and are thus considered low-income.
> Sixty percent of the focal cohort is from single-family homes.
> Eighty percent of focal cohort attend Title 1 public schools.
> Average CST Math score for focal group is 400/600 (Proficient).
> Average GPA for focal group was 2.99.
> Sixty-six percent of focal cohort' parent/guardian's do NOT have a college degree.

Shakers, makers, and takers

From the pre-survey, which asked MAN UP' students to answer questions pertaining to why they wanted to join this STEM focused program; I identified three discrete categories of participation. The three archetypes that became manifest were: students whose answers seemed to suggest that they were desirous to use STEM to benefit either their respective local communities and/or their macro-level identificatory groups, primarily, young and/or urban Black males. This group, which I identified as the "Shakers", represented the ideal because their answers on the pre-survey suggested that they were interested in shaking up the current, inequitable status quo by using STEM as a tool for equity. The students involved were unaware of this appellation.

Data collection procedures: For the 10 months that data was collected from September 2013 to June 2014, there were 22 sessions of the program. There were two sessions per month except for October 2013 and March 2014 when there was a third session designated for a field trip. In addition, the final month of June 2014 featured only the year-end celebration in which students presented their final group projects. The following data collection procedures were implemented during the specific months and sessions noted below across the two semesters of this research project. Data included pre-post surveys, pre-post concept inventories, pre and post focus group interviews, pre and post individual interviews, participant observation, and audio-video recording of the entire focal class as for at least one of the two regular sessions each month. Additional data included: reflective online journals and videotapes of students' project presentations from all three classes. Finally, data collection completed with the sixth-grade math assessments and interviews with the remaining two STEM instructors.

Across all data sources, I looked for evidence of the focal cohorts' developing identification with, competencies in, and critical application of key aspects of STEM that were taught in their three courses and the other activities of the MAN UP program. When these three components congeal, it is the realization of what I have termed the critical contextualization of STEM. Consequently, the fundamental approach of this study was to analyze the entire range of data sources through the overlay of these three categories of identification, competencies, and critical applications. Since I wanted to see the students' initial and on-going development in these three categories with respect to STEM, I analyzed for each category through the various data sources collected during the first and second semesters. Therefore, I was able to identify, code, and analyze evidence of development of the focal cohort in all three classes across the entire academic year of the study.

Reevaluating competency: Identification and socially just applications of STEM

Competency was determined by pre/posttests and/or concept inventories in each course offering. Additionally, though not assessed in the same way as the pre-post concept inventories, students (audio-video recorded) ability to create ways to apply STEM in the amelioration of social injustice was also considered demonstrative of their competency in not only understanding the concepts of the STEM courses they took, but also, perhaps, going one step further to critically apply their STEM learning for societal uplift. This data is derived from individual and focus group interviews, classroom observations and interviews with their STEM instructors. I was also looking for the focal participants' demonstrated ability to shift their socio-political understanding or context such that they could begin to address societal issues that bear some similarity to, but were not identical with an issue that they themselves have faced and/or addressed. In other words, I was looking for the extent to which the students could extend their context and reveal and even operationalize abstract terms like equity/inequity, equality/inequality, justice/injustice and the role that STEM can be made to play in addressing and/or redressing the very same issues that they identified. Additionally, student shifts in identification were determined by students' pre-post identification surveys answers as well as individual and focus group interviews, the yearend program satisfaction survey (YPSS) and via their participation in their final projects, and classroom observations, and participant observation. STEM instructors were also asked to speak to any shifts in identification they witnessed taking place in the focal cohort of students in one-on-one interviews. These analytical procedures were designed to illuminate my primary research goals, i.e., to identify instances of critical contextualization of STEM as evidenced by the focal cohorts increases in STEM identity conjoined with increases in both STEM competency as well as their demonstrated ability to apply STEM for social justice, and to gauge the role it may have played in students' learning of and identification with the STEM subjects taught in MAN UP.

Chapter 3 review: Considerations and questions

Consideration:

In this chapter, I discussed literature that speaks to the root causes of underperformance in STEM for Black males: white supremacist-centered notions of Black inferiority and the, related, pedagogical practices that are predicated on the erroneous, stereotypical depictions of Black males. These negative stereo-types have been normalized through mass media such that they are accepted as fact in far too many educational circles. This chapter also spoke in greater detail about the many of the negative stereotypes are associated with us, Black males, and how these stereotypes are part and parcel of a larger systematic push to blame us for our academic struggles instead of identifying the real culprit: race-based, structural inequity. However, let me keep it 100 right now. These stereotypes are false. There is nothing innately inferior or deficient about any Black male or any other student from a non-dominant group. We all have the same capacity to realize our fullest potential, because intelligence grows over time; it does not remain static.

Questions for students:

1. Now that you know that stereotypes are part of a larger, systemic push to devalue us (Black males) so that we fail to reach our full potential in STEM and beyond, how do you plan to actively combat and deconstruct these stereotypes in your academic and daily life so that more and more people begin to realize that these stereotypes are untrue?

2. This chapter also spoke about the benefits of inviting our language and culture into educational spaces: how often does this happen for you? And if it doesn't happen, what are you willing to do to make sure that your real-life experiences are part of your educational experience?

3. What does it mean to use STEM as a tool for social justice? And, what can/does this look like in real life? More specifically, how will you use STEM to improve your life and/or the lives of your family and community?

4. Do you think that your race, ethnicity, and/or culture impacts the way that your teachers view your academic potential (please explain)?

Consideration:

Part Two of this chapter detailed my research methodology. Positioning teachers as researchers carries benefits in that it positions them to interrogate their peda-gogical practices in a reflective/reflexive manner. This approach also repositions students in that as "research subjects" there bring something to the educative space and are, therefore, no longer viewed as mere blank slates in need of inscrip-tion or repositories in need of filling.

Questions for educators:

1. Arguably, one of the benefits of teachers/educators viewing themselves as researchers is that it creates opportunities for students to co-construct knowledge alongside the educators that work with them. This repositioning, then, allows for greater development of student voice—do you do this in your work currently?
2. Building from question 1, if you do not currently create opportunities for students to co-construct meaning in your class, how will you create these kinds of opportunities moving forward?
3. This chapter also spoke about the benefits of inviting the language and culture of Black males, specifically, and traditionally marginalized people, generally, into educational spaces: do you feel comfortable attempting to do this?
4. And if it you don't—at least right now—what are you willing to do to make sure that your create opportunities for your Black male students to bring their real-life experiences, concerns, issues, joys, triumphs, etc., into your classroom space?
5. If you are a STEM educator, do you discuss what it means to use STEM as a tool for social justice?

Keywords:

Stereotype threat, AAVE, social justice, opportunity gap, education gap, critical-reality pedagogy, culturally relevant pedagogy, culturally sustaining pedagogy

References

Alexander, M. (2010). *The new Jim Crow: Mass incarceration in the age of colorblindness*. New York, NY: The New Press.

Allen, B. A., & Boykin, D. (1992). African-American children and the educational process: Alleviating cultural discontinuity through prescriptive pedagogy. *School Psychology Review, 21*, 586–596.

Althusser, L. (1971). *Lenin and philosophy and other essays*. New York, NY: New Left Books.

Anzaldua, G. (1987). How to tame a wild tongue. In *Borderlands/La Frontera: The new mestiza* (pp. 53–64). San Francisco, CA: Spinsters/Aunt Lute.

Apple, M. W. (2004). *Ideology and curriculum*. New York, NY: Routledge Flamer.

Aronson, J. (2004). *The effects of conceiving ability as fixed or improvable on responses to stereotype threat*. Unpublished manuscript, New York University.

Aronson, J., Fried, C., & Good, C. (2002). Reducing the effects of stereotype threat on Black college students by shaping theories of intelligence. *Journal of Experimental Social Psychology, 38*, 113–125.

Ballou, J. (2012). *Reshaping how educators view student STEM (Science, technology, engineering, and mathematics) learning: Assessment of the SENCER experience*. Retrieved from http://www.sencer.net/About/projectoverview.cfm

Bang, M., & Medin, D. (2010). Cultural processes in science education: Supporting the navigation of multiple epistemologies. *Science Education, 94*(6), 1008–1026.

Barton, A. C. (2001). Capitalism, critical pedagogy, and urban science education: Interview with Peter McLaren. Journal of Research in Science Teaching, 38(8), 847–859.Baugh, J. (1996). Dimensions of a theory of econolinguistics. In G. Guy, C. Feagin, D. Schiffrin, & J. Baugh (Eds.), *A social science of language* (pp. 397–419). Philadelphia, PA: John Benjamins.

Bell, D. (2004). *Silent covenants: Brown v. Board of education and the unfulfilled hopes for racial reform*. Boston, MA: Oxford University Press.

Blikstein, P. (2008). Travels in Troy with Freire: technology as an agent for emancipation. *In P. Noguera and C. A. Torres (Eds.), Social Justice Education for Teachers: Paulo Freire and the possible dream* (pp. 205–244). Rotterdam, Netherlands: Sense.

Brown, B. (2006). "It isn't no slang that can be said about this stuff": Language, identity, and appropriating science discourse. *Journal of Research in Science Teaching, 43*(1), 96–126. Retrieved from http://www3.interscience.wiley.com/journal/112159296/abstract?CRETRY=1&SRETRY=0

Burrell, T. (2010). *Brainwashed: Challenging the myth of Black inferiority*. New York, NY: Smiley Books.

Darder, A. (1998). *Schooling as a contested terrain*. Claremont, CA: Institute for Cultural Studies in Education.

Darling-Hammond, L. (2010). *The flat world and education: How America's commitment to equity will determine our future*. New York, NY: Teachers College Press.

Delpit, L. (2012). *Multiplication is for White people: Raising expectations for other people's children*. New York, NY: The New Press.

Denbo, S. (1986). Improving minority student achievement: Focus on the classroom. Washington, DC, Mid-Atlantic Equity Center Series.

Denzin, N. K., & Lincoln, Y. S. (Eds.). (2003). *Collecting and interpreting qualitative materials* (2nd ed.). Thousand Oaks, CA: Sage.

Derrida, J., & Caputo, J. D. (1997). *Deconstruction in a nutshell: A conversation with Jacques Derrida* (2nd ed./auth). New York, NY: Fordham University Press.

DiIulio, J. (1995). Broken bottles: Liquor, disorder, and crime. *Wisconsin Policy Research, 8*(4–5).

Drew, D. E. (2011). *STEM the tide: Reforming science, technology, engineering and math education in America*. Baltimore, MD: The Johns Hopkins University Press.

Duncan-Andrade, J., & Morrell, E. (2008). *The art of critical pedagogy: Possibilities for moving from theory to practice in urban schools*. New York, NY: Peter Lang.

Emdin, C. (2010). *Urban science education for the hip-hop generation: Essential tools for the urban science educator and researcher*. Ithaca, NY: Columbia University Press.

Emdin, C. (2016). *For white folks who teach in the hood … and the rest of y'all too: Reality pedagogy and urban education*. Boston, MA: Beacon Press.

Fanon, F. (1968). *Black skin, white masks.* New York, NY: Grove Press.

Fordham, S., & Ogbu, J. U. (1986). Black students' school success: Coping with the "burden of 'acting white'." *The Urban Review, 18*(3), 176–206. doi:10.1007/BF01112192

Freire, P. (1997). *Pedagogy of the oppressed* (20th century anniversary ed.) (Myra Bergman Ramos, Trans.). New York, NY: Continuum Publishing.

Freire, P., & Macedo, D. (1987). *Literacy: Reading the word & the world.* New York, NY: Continuum Publishing.

Giroux, H. A. (1983/2001). *Theory and resistance in education: Toward a pedagogy for the opposition* (rev. ed.). Westport, CT: Bergin & Garvey.

Giroux, H. A. (2011). *On critical pedagogy.* New York, NY: Continuum Books.

Gorski, P. C., Zenkov, K., Osei-Kofi, N., Sapp, J., & Stovall, D. (2013). *Cultivating social justice teachers: How teacher educators have helped students overcome cognitive bottlenecks and learn social justice concepts.* Sterling, VA: Stylus Publishing.

Gramsci, A., In Hoare, Q., & Nowell-Smith, G. (1971). *Selections from the prison notebooks of Antonio Gramsci.* New York, NY: International Publishers.

Greene, D., & Walker, F. (2004). Recommendations to public speaking instructors for the negotiation of code-switching practices among Black English-speaking African American students. *The Journal of Negro Education, 73*(4), 435.

Gutstein, E. (2005). *Reading and writing the world with mathematics: Toward a pedagogy for social justice* (Critical Social Thought). New York, NY: Routledge.

Hale-Benson, J. (1982). *Black children: Their roots, culture, and learning styles.* Baltimore, MD: Johns Hopkins University Press.

Halpin, D. (2001). Utopianism and education: The legacy of Thomas More. *British Journal of Educational Studies, 49*(3), 299–315.

Herrnstein, R. J., & Murray, C. A. (1996). *The bell curve: Intelligence and class structure in American life.* New York, NY: Simon & Schuster.

Ladson-Billings, G. (1995). Toward a theory of culturally relevant pedagogy. *American Educational Research Journal, 32,* 465–491.

Lee, C. D. (2005). Culture and language: Bi-dialectical issues in literacy. In P. Anders & J. Flood (Eds.), *The literacy development of students in urban schools.* International Reading Association.

Leonardo, Z. (2010). *Race, whiteness, and education* (Kindle ed.).

Linn, M. C., & Eylon, B. S. (2011). *Science learning and instruction: Taking advantage of technology to promote knowledge integration.* New York, NY: Routledge.

Mahiri, J., & Sims, J. J. (2016). Engineering equity: A critical pedagogical approach to language and curriculum change for African American males in STEM (55–70). Z. Babaci-Wilhite (ed.), In *Curriculum change in language and STEM subjects as a right in education.* Rotterdam: Sense Publishing.

McLaren, P. (1994). *Life in schools: An introduction to critical pedagogy and the foundations of education.* New York, NY: Longman.

Moses, R. P., & Cobb, C. E. (2001). *Radical equations: Civil rights from Mississippi to the Algebra Project.* Boston, MA: Beacon Press.

Murnane, R. J. (1975). *The impact of school resources on the learning of inner city children.* Cambridge, MA; Ballinger Publishing.

Nasir, N. S. (2011). *Racialized identities: Race and achievement among Black youth.* Stanford, CA: Stanford University Press.

National Science Board. (2010). Preparing the next generation of STEM innovators: Identifying and developing our Nation's human capital. (National Science Board report, 2010, http://1. usa.gov/nwHbku).

Noguera, P. (2008). *The trouble with Black boys: And other reflections on race, equity, and the future of public education.* San Francisco, CA: Jossey-Bass.

Norris, A. (2014). Make-her-spaces as hybrid places: Designing and resisting self-construction in urban classrooms. *Journal of Equity & Excellence in Education, 47*(1), 63–77.

Paris, D. (2012). Culturally sustaining pedagogy: A needed change in stance, terminology, and practice. *Educational Researcher, 41*(3), 93–97.

Paris, D., & Alim, H. S. (2017). *Culturally sustaining pedagogies: Teaching and learning for justice in a changing world.* New York, NY: Teachers College Press.

Philip, T. M. (2011a). An "ideology in pieces" approach to studying change in teachers' sense-making about race, racism and racial justice. *Cognition and Instruction, 29*(3), 297–329.

Philip, T. M. (2011b). Moving beyond our progressive lenses: Recognizing and building on the strengths of teachers of color. *Journal of Teacher Education, 62*(4), 356–366.

Twenty-First Century. New York, NY: The New Press.

Roediger, D. (1994). *Towards the abolition of Whiteness: Essays on Race, Class and Politics.* London, UK and New York: Verso Books.

Schilling, K. M., & Schilling, K. L. (1999, May–June). Increasing expectations for student effort. *About Campus, 4*(2), 4–10.

Scott, A. L. (2010). *Dissecting the data: The STEM education opportunity gap in California.* Retrieved from http://www.lpfi.org/sites/default/files/dissecting_the_data_-_STEM_ed_opportunity_gap_lpfi_report.pdf

Smyth, J. (2011). *Critical pedagogy for social justice.* New York, NY: Continuum.

Spradley. J. P. (1979). The ethnographic interview. Belmont, CA: Wadsworth.

Steele, C. (2010). *Whistling Vivaldi: And other clues to how stereotypes affect us.* New York, NY: W. W. Norton.

Tate, W. F. (1995). Returning to the root: A culturally relevant approach to mathematics pedagogy. *Theory into Practice, 34*(3), 166–173.

Toldson, I. A., & Snitman, A. (2010). Education parity and economic disparities: Correcting education-attainment discrepancies among Black people in the United States. *Journal of Negro Education, 79*(1), 1–5.

Vakil, S. (2014). A critical pedagogy approach of engaging urban youth in mobile app development in an after-school program. *Equity & Excellence in Education, 47*(1), 31–45.

Wacquant, L. (2008). *Urban outcasts: A comparative sociology of advanced marginality.* Cambridge: Polity.

Wofford, J. (1979). A legitimate system of oral communication. *Journal of Black Studies, 9,* 367–382.

Wright, R. (1940). *Native son.* New York, NY: Harper & Bros.

Changing the game

The role of critical contextualization and socio-academic synergy in developing STEM identities

STEM education has been reliant on axioms and purported facts that have been delivered in a banking or absorption model that is, arguably, anti-critical. Unsurprisingly, this pedagogical approach to STEM education has failed large segments of students; and, this is especially true of Black males. This study investigated the potential inroads and vistas of a Saturday Science, Technology, Engineering and Math (STEM) program, Male Aptitudes Nurtured for Unlimited Potential (MAN UP), designed to foster interest and competence in STEM subjects by middle school Black males. Critical pedagogical perspectives were central to the program's design and implementation as was the intent to increase their STEM competency in conjunction with developing STEM identities that are informed by social justice perspectives. Data collection covered the implementation of this program with first year MAN UP students for two or three Saturdays per month for a full academic year. Data included pre and post and focus group interviews with the entire first year cohort, participant observation in a focal class, classroom observations of the cohort's two additional STEM classes, video tapes of cohort students' project presentations, their online reflective journals, as well as interviews with their STEM instructors along with the instructors' online learning designs and reflections. This study significantly illuminates and documents viable approaches to increasing the interest in, competence with, and potential for socially just applications of science, technology, engineering, and math by students who are often marginalized in these subjects.

MAN UP's curricular focus and pedagogical approach was built on a foundation that emphasizes critical-reality based pedagogical approach to teaching STEM. The goal of this approach, in the first instance, was to create a space (both philosophical and actual) for students to begin critically contextualizing STEM: that is, to bring STEM into their real life concerns, issues, struggles, aspirations, etc., by applying their STEM knowledge to address issues that are important to them. The term "the critical contextualization of STEM" arose out of a need to adequately describe the focal cohorts' shifts in positive STEM identity, STEM competency, and subsequent socially just applications of STEM. This term was created partially in response to a common complaint that MAN UP students shared regarding the STEM instruction they routinely received at their home schools: i.e., that it was disconnected from their lives, or decontextualized. The concomitant pedagogical and curricular aim of MAN UP was to do the obverse, that is, to create a space where Black middle school males could critically connect (i.e., contextualize) STEM to their lived-experiences as individuals and justice-oriented community members. The goal of analyzing this phenomenon was to assess whether the critical contextualization of STEM was taking place. If so, the question was whether and how it informed students' levels of competency (as measured by pre-post course concept inventories) in, understanding of (confidence in applying STEM to difficult social realities), and identity (i.e., instances where students began to re-envisage themselves applied STEM practitioners and, perhaps, later as potential STEM majors and STEM professionals) with STEM.

To achieve this goal, the MAN UP curriculum and parallel pedagogical approach sought to both create an atmosphere where students could not only learn STEM, but also begin to appropriate STEM, make it their own, and as they saw fit apply it to situations that they felt they had the power to address. This is what I termed: socio-academic synergy. Socio-academic synergy is a symbiotic relationship between students' lives outside of educational settings and the curricular goals, course content offered at MAN UP, and the pedagogical approach employed by MAN UP instructors. Curating a positive, educationally-nutritive, and empowering atmosphere—which included an emphasis on building positive and trusting relationships between instructors and students—was integral to this endeavor. We provided examples of STEM being applied for socially just causes both locally and nationally, and even globally on occasion. We challenged students to think through ways that they could apply STEM to age-old, complex societal problems in, perhaps, novel ways. The intended message was that even though they were only 11 years old, they had the power within them to appropriate STEM and apply it to ameliorate the myriad issues they faced based on their skin color and socioeconomic status. This is what I termed the critical contextualization of STEM. So, to be precise the goal of socio-academic synergy was to create an educative space where these students felt encouraged, equipped, and empowered to begin developing their positive STEM identities, growing more competent in STEM, and devising ways to apply STEM for social justice, which is the manifestation of the critical contextualization of STEM. The critical contextualization of STEM should result in, for MAN UP students, the realization that they had the power to affect positive change for themselves, for their community, and potentially, for the world.

Critical contextualization explicated

The definition of critical contextualization is as follows: critical contextualization is the process in which students understand and critically analyze the sociopolitical and socio-historical dynamism of their given context such that they are equipped and empowered to competently extend their critical contextual understanding to both familiar and/or altogether new social milieus.

Constitutive Phases of Critical Contextualization: These three phases are not necessarily incremental. In fact, they can happen both concurrently and/or simultaneously. These phases are both mutually constitutive and mutually beneficial. The delineation below is an ideal rollout of each of the three contiguous phases.

- **Phase 1:** During Phase 1, intentional work must be done to engender, ensure and curate a positive, critical and empowering educative atmosphere by inviting students to co-create and co-develop the behavior, cognitive, and affective norms of the given educational space.
- **Phase 2:** Predicated on and contiguous to Phase 1, during Phase 2 work to develop supportive relationships, which are centered on student input and student voice, must be the primary focus. These relationships must be emancipatory and liberatory in nature. They must be dialogic as opposed to monologic; and, they must seek to build a community of co-constructive meaning makers.
- **Phase 3:** During phase 3, content should be interwoven into the atmosphere. This content must be anchored. It must connect to students lived experiences. And, it must be germane to them in some way. The best way to ensure relevancy is to consult students, have them participate in the meaning making process, and afford them space to comment on the way that the content is delivered space (i.e., pedagogy).

This triumvirate must coalesce, eventually becoming triune, i.e., three in one. The "one" in this study is MAN UP the program, which is made up of the abovementioned constitutive phases. Each of these independent phases required intentional and purposeful cultivation. This is key. The atmosphere, in many ways, is directly informed by the relationships; and, the inverse is also true. Essentially, the way that pedagogy and content are received is wholly dependent on both the atmosphere and the relationships between community members.

The Critical Contextualization of STEM: is the process in which students understand and critically analyze the sociopolitical and socio-historical dynamism of their given context such that they are encouraged, empowered, and equipped to competently extend their critical contextual understanding to both familiar and/or altogether new social milieus as demonstrated by their ability to apply their STEM knowledge in the interest of amelioration of socially unjust milieus. The critical contextualization of STEM was evidenced by students beginning to appropriate and critically apply STEM as a tool to redress issues or problems, which were connected to students' lives d that inhered around notions of equity/inequity and or social justice.

Ultimately, the critical contextualization of STEM in an educational program, like MAN UP, should begin to resemble and even function as a fluid, dynamic concentric circle:

Figure 4.1: Socio-academic Synergy

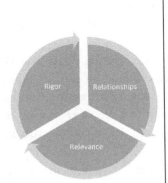

Socio-Academic Synergy:
Connecting the Course Content to The lived-experiences of our Scholars

- This term (perhaps a neologism) ***denotes a concomitant relationship between the academic programming and the politicized, racialized lived-experiences of our scholars.***
- Scholars were never asked to repudiate their identities as urban African American males; instead, they were ***encouraged to explore, traverse, and apply STEM as urban African American males.***
- ***We sought to meet our scholars where they were*** so that they began to see themselves as co-constructors of and contributors to the meaning making process
- ***We created spaces for them to contextualize and therefore connect material from each course offering,*** meta-cognitively, so that they could begin to determine the role/s that this newfound knowledge could (potentially) play in their lives as young men and, later, as adults.

Source: Author

The work that was going on at MAN UP necessitated the creation of these two terms to adequately describe both the atmosphere and pedagogical aim of this program. In working through these definitions, I came to realize that the term "rigor" needed analysis as well precisely because its standard definition did not quite capture the critical work that these young applied STEM practitioners were endeavoring to do. To identify instances of critical contextualization of STEM, I coded for instances where students' critical contextualized understanding and applications of STEM became apparent.

Emerging critical contextualization

- Demonstrated a working knowledge of socio-historical, socio-political, and socio-economic processes as they relate to critical global and local issues and how they inform societal injustices.
- Used understanding of equity, inequity, and justice as a frame when discussing and/or writing about one's lived experience as an urban Black male in the United States, and used their lived experiences as a catalyst to higher level empathy when discussing the plight of other marginalized groups both locally and globally.
- Could reassess, reorganize and restructure assumptions, ideological predispositions and knowledge based on new information (metacognitive).
- Critically and comprehensively analyzed new information, taking into account the cultural context, implicit and explicit motivations, and underlying assumptions of the source.
- Demonstrated an understanding of the usages of the design process and how to use it to understand and potentially redress societal injustices.

Evidence of emergent critical contextualization of STEM

- Could see himself as a current or emergent change agent, equipped to use STEM for socially just outcomes.
- Used STEM as a tool to address injustice in their own communities and beyond.
- Proposed ways to use STEM in novel ways or in ways that are new to the students.

- Began to see themselves or speak of themselves as applied STEM practitioners.
- Demonstrated understanding of STEM education as inherently political.
- Began to think of ways to use STEM as a tool to address issues that are important to a given student or group of students.
- Shifted their "frame of reference" to critically analyze problems and perspectives; and, can conceptualize ways to use STEM to address the problems identified.

It was entirely possible for students to understand and demonstrate evidence of critical contextualization without also developing and or demonstrating evidence of the critical contextualization of STEM. In most cases, critical contextualization preceded the critical contextualization of STEM, but this was not always the case. Some students developed and demonstrated elements of both conceptions, simultaneously, while others developed and demonstrated understandings of these two conceptions independently or in the obverse order. However, when students began to demonstrate competency in designing and, subsequently, developing social justice oriented STEM applications, this meant that they were functioning as shakers (i.e., applied STEM practitioners), ready, willing, and able to apply their STEM knowledge for local, national and even global equity.

Manning UP: Shifts in students' STEM identities

The findings on the focal students in the MAN UP program are reported in the three central categories that were delineated in the research question for this study. Over the course of the 2013–14 academic year, I found that the focal cohort had developed significant increases in their personal identification with STEM subjects and careers as well as increases in key STEM competencies. Additionally, the data uncovered substantial increases in their understanding and implementation of socially just applications of STEM. Evidence for these findings came from all of the data sources. The five sources were the pre and post identification and program satisfaction surveys, the pre and post concept inventories, focal group interviews, interviews with the math and CS instructors, and the participants' work on final projects in each of their three classes that was documented with videos. In addition to these five sources, I assess the focal students along the lines of three categories of participation that emerged to further illuminate the shifts made by the students over the course of this study.

Remixing identity: Developing identification with STEM

The MAN UP instructional team felt that creating a space for the students to develop a positive STEM identity was not only exigent, but also a prerequisite for increases in STEM competencies. And while opportunities for positive STEM development were intentionally created in all three courses, the Rhetorical Analysis of manhood (RAM) course was a primary space for conversations around African-American male identities vis-à-vis STEM education. So, in conjunction with the data sources noted above, I used the manhood course both to develop and assess shifts in the focal students' identification with STEM as evidenced in part by their confidence in applying STEM to important issues, their expressed desires to major in STEM, and, ultimately, their increased interest in pursuing STEM careers. I also indicate how these young men began seeing themselves as capable of using STEM for social amelioration. The groundwork for my analysis of the focal cohorts' shifts in STEM identity began with the pre-post STEM identification survey.

Yearend program satisfaction survey (YPSS): In response to survey questions regarding the overall satisfaction with the program, 15 of the 17 members of the focal cohort indicated that their abilities to identify with STEM subjects and careers was highly impacted by having instructors who were themselves role models of STEM practitioners. For example, one student responded, "I benefited mentally seeing role models of my color skin." Another noted how important it was "getting help from teachers who inspired me and were my role models." A third respondent wrote on his post-survey that "they helped me see myself as someone who could do well in math and science." The focal cohort also indicated satisfaction with their own perceptions of having increased their identification with STEM through completion of the program and "getting together with kids my age and race to do this work." According to the yearend program satisfaction survey (YPSS), 16 of 17 students from the focal cohort agreed or strongly agreed that they are confident that they could use their STEM knowledge to make their local, national, and global communities more equitable. The realization, for them, that they were becoming or in fact had become applied STEM practitioners was predicated on and indicative of their developing STEM identities. They were not just as young men who were becoming more competent in STEM—but, perhaps more importantly, they were identifying as young men who were also competent in applying STEM for equitable societal change (i.e., for social justice). The sentiment expressed by the focal cohort on the YPSS was echoed by the MAN UP instructors during the STEM Instructor Interviews.

STEM instructor interviews: The two STEM instructors were interviewed on two separate occasions: at the midpoint of the academic year (late December 2013) and at the end of the academic year (June 2014). The instructors further reinforced the focal cohorts' identification with STEM by intentionally calling them "applied STEM practitioners" throughout the program. Interviews with Mr. S, the CS instructor, and Mr. K, the Math instructor were conducted by Mr. J at the close of the 2013–14 academic-year. Mr. K felt that positioning and referring to the cohort as applied STEM practitioners was important to their identity shifts. "I feel like this approach worked," he said in his interview. "They responded to it and tried to own up to the responsibility of their titles of applied mathematicians.... They were owning their math identity." The developing STEM identities that Mr. K was speaking to were constantly and continuously under construction.

According to Mr. K, this approach worked in part because students responded to the appellation, applied STEM practitioner. For him, this was evidence of a positive shift in students' STEM identities:

> Yes, I feel like this approach worked. It wasn't perfect, but I do think we reached these young men. How do I know? These young men, who described feeling singled out and picked on far too often, really responded to and tried to own up to the responsibility of their titles of applied mathematicians in my class. They would even check me from time to time: If they felt that I was lecturing them, and just giving them facts, they'd stop me to inquire how this information was applicable to them. For me, this was evidence that they were owning their math identity. It was like there were saying, look, I'm a mathematician, too; you can't just tell me stuff without providing space for me to push back and question of this applies to my life and how I can apply it to my life. It was beautiful. Not only were they taking ownership of their education, they were taking a measure of ownership over math!

> It's when they began to see themselves as applied STEM practitioners that they started really engaging and, and consequently, really beginning to understand the material [as evidenced by 16 of 17 of the focal students improving from pre to post on the math assessment].

Mr. S spoke to a similar shift in his course. He noted that students, initially, felt as though the entirety of the help that they could provide was to devise ways for people in need of help to find people or organizations willing and able to help. However, over time, students began to see themselves as the help. For him, this shift in identity as a socially conscious, applied STEM practitioner was proof that this approach was working:

Yes, I agree that this approach is working. We're still working it out, of course, but our foundation is solid. I am convinced it's working because I'm seeing transformations, from the beginning of the year until now, in these young people. Initially, these students were reticent to or unwilling to, or perhaps, unable to empathize with oppressed people outside of their immediate locale. When we started talking about providing help to poor people negatively affected by the typhoon in the Philippines, students asked me why they should care about people thousands of miles away when their city had so many problems. Of course, this is a great question. My role was to help them see connections and how the very existence of oppression and inequity threatens people everywhere. Over time, these same students, because they were beginning to see themselves as young people capable of making positive societal changes, began to develop concern for the people they described as their brothers and sisters in the Philippines. At this point there was a shift: instead of a remove, wherein they tried to locate help for people, they began to see themselves as the help. They decided to begin developing an app that would lead people to drinkable water and shelter. They were becoming socially-conscious or their social consciousness was expanding and along with it their identification with STEM as a tool for social uplift. When they began to see themselves as capable of using STEM for important issues, they became more confident.

The individual assessments of these two MAN UP STEM instructors are bolstered by the evidence presented above: data bears out that there was, indeed, a positive shift in the first year MAN UP students' identification of STEM. The focal cohort began to see themselves not only as young men who could do well in STEM in the present as well as moving forward; they also began to see themselves as young men who could "do" or apply STEM to make the world a better place. And, according to their STEM instructors, these shifts were instrumental in the focal cohorts' increase in competency with respect to their STEM courses. To develop a deeper understanding of the shifts in identity that took place within the focal cohort during the academic year, under investigation, I use the data that percolated up from case studies of five representative members of the focal cohort.

We have lift-off: Shakers, makers, and takers

Based on responses on the pre-identification survey, three categories of participation rose to the fore. Returning to the three components under measurement in this study as delineated in the research question, these categories of participation are informed by the respective components under investigation in this study. More precisely, students that only begin to develop a STEM competency in the interest of securing financial stability to purchase the material accouterments that they desired yet did not demonstrate an increased identification with STEM—as young people who can both learn and do STEM—were categorized as takers.

I chose takers as the appellation for this group because their association with STEM was predicated on STEM as a commodity capable of being a possession and/or investment that would "pay off" in the form of individual financial success as demonstrated by their ability to purchase the clothes, shoes, and videogames that they longed for. That is, based on their responses, they wanted to take in all available STEM knowledge so that they could transform their knowledge into scholastic success that would pay future dividends insofar as college majors and ultimately high paying STEM jobs were concerned. And, while this positionality is totally understandable as these are predominately low-income students who have seen their parents struggle for even the most basic needs, unlike both the shakers and makers, the takers rationale for pursuit of monetary success was wholly individual unlike the makers, who wanted to excel in STEM in order to achieve monetary success to take care of their families, or, shakers, who wanted to excel in STEM in order to challenge inequity and social injustice, respectively. Takers simply wanted to buy clothes and video games for themselves.

The maker category is similar to the takers in that makers are also interested in learning STEM, or becoming more competent, so that they too can earn high salaries in their future careers. The major difference, however, is that makers see themselves as familial caretakers whereas takers seemed to be concerned only with fulfilling their own, immediate, material desires. The shakers, based on their responses to the pre-identification survey seemed to suggest that they were desirous to use STEM as a tool to benefit either their respective local communities and/or their macro-level identificatory groups, primarily, young and/or urban Black males.

This group, the "shakers," represented the ideal because their answers on the pre-survey suggested that they were interested in shaking up the current, inequitable status quo by using STEM as a tool for equity. Initially, only one student seemed to fit the shaker profile. (The students involved were unaware of these appellations.) In the following section, I discuss these categories of participation by using individual or pairs of students as representatives of the three above mentioned categories of participation.

Initially, the majority (10 members of the 17-student focal cohort) of the focal cohort fit most closely to the makers profile in that they expressed interest in STEM only as a vehicle that would ensure STEM jobs and commensurate salaries that would allow them to provide comfortably for themselves and their families. The next group, the takers, consisted of six students. These were students whose pre-identification survey responses suggested that they only saw STEM as a way to earn enough money in order to purchase the material accouterments that they desired. With these six students, there was no mention of familial considerations or responsibility.

The shaker: Michael, was one of the majority of MAN UP's students that qualified for Free or Reduced Lunch (FRL); however, unlike the majority of MAN UP's students who were also classified as FRL students (80 percent), Michael came from a two-parent home. (Neither of his parents earned a college degree.) Michael was quite different in appearance, too: he is bi-racial (European-American and Afro-Caribbean) and as a result his skin tone fit closely with purportedly normative Eurocentric physiognomy. Nevertheless, Michael self-identified as Black. According to his mother, Michael was not being challenged in school. More precisely, his mother described a toxic classroom situation that in her estimation was functioning to stultify Michael, which was why she felt that he was having trouble realizing his full academic potential. Michael's grade point average, 2.56, was well below the average of the focal class (2.99); yet, his standardized test scores placed him in the Advanced Category in both Math and English Language Arts (ELA).

Because Michael's answers on the pre-identification survey suggested that his association with learning STEM was more expansive than an individualistic desire to be positioned to earn a high salary, or even to address his own immediate familial needs, like the makers, Michael wanted to pursue STEM in order to benefit "people of color" in general. For example, Michael answered the following pre-survey question "Why do you want to join a STEM Focused Saturday Program?" thusly:

> For me it's kinda important that people of color, or Black people, get to see people that look like them doing STEM careers and going to college for STEM, because a lot of times we hear that we can't do it—and we start to believe the lies. Plus, we can use STEM to kinda level the playing field some. So, I guess, I want to do STEM for those reasons.

It is clear from Michael's answer to this question that his desire to excel in STEM was predicated on his desire to respond to and even begin chipping away at the societal promulgation, on the one hand, and the internalization negative stereotypes by people of color regarding people of colors' (a term that was synonymous with Black people, for Michael) purported collective inability to excel in STEM, on the other. Michael is the only student from the focal cohort whose answer accounted for people beyond just familial/kinship relationships, i.e., "people of color/Black people."

The makers: The second student profile that I identified as the "makers" seemed to reflect a collective interest in doing better in (i.e., taking all available knowledge) STEM so that they could work to ensure upward mobility, measured monetarily, in order improve the socioeconomic realities for themselves and their families. Like the shakers, the makers also viewed STEM as a tool of sorts, albeit with different, more individualized applications.

Jeff was low income and came from a single-parent home; however, unlike most MAN UP's students who hail from a single-parent home, Jeff's mother had a college education. Jeff felt as though he was doing well in school. He went to a parochial school on scholarship. His grade point average was higher than the average GPA for the focal class (3.35). His standardized test scores for both Mathematics and English Language Arts were categorized as Proficient. When asked why he felt it was important for him to learn STEM, Jeff answered thusly:

> I want to do well in school, specifically in math and science, so that I can get a good job when I get out of college. I heard something the other day that said that most of the new jobs by the time I get out of college will be in stem, so it makes sense for me to be prepared to do well in stem. Maybe, my dream is to be a professional basketball player, but I guess if I do realize my dream need to figure out how to keep my money. Anyway, the real reason I want to do well is so that I can get a good job and help out my mom and my sister. My mom works really hard to pay for my sister's college tuition, and if I don't get a scholarship she'll have to do the same for me when I get to college. So, I want to be able to pay her back. That's really important for me.

Jeff, was interested in doing well in STEM so that he could "go to a good college" and eventually earn a high salary to position himself to buy his mother her first home. He also wrote about wanting to position himself to afford a big screen television and a fast car, but he was resolute in first taking care of his mother. Jeff, like the other nine members of the focal cohort that fit this identity profile wanted to "do better" in math and science so that he could position himself to make money to provide for his family—more precisely, so he could repay his mother, monetarily, for the sacrifices she endured in raising him up until this point in his life. This was true of all of the students who fit within this profile. This was, by far, the largest group, which is not surprising in that most of these students came from single-parent, maternal households. The makers' responses to the pre-survey questioned that asked them why they wanted to join this STEM focused program included one or more of the following terms: job/money/earn money; mother/mom, grandmother, family; sacrifice/hard work/work less, repay, pay back; new car/new home. For this group, the concerns of their families, and especially their mothers were paramount and cited in over 90 percent of the focal cohorts' responses as the primary reason for their desired success in STEM.

The takers: The third identity profile that I identified as the "takers," were like the makers in that they, too, were desirous of taking in all available STEM knowledge. In their words, they wanted to "do better in school" so that they could secure "good jobs" in order to comfortably afford material items (e.g., Jordan sneakers, True Religion Jeans, etc.). However, unlike both the shakers and the makers, the takers responses to pre-survey questions did not seem to suggest that they envisioned themselves as young people capable of doing STEM. Instead, it was clear that for this group, learning STEM so that they could demonstrate their learning on standardized tests was a paramount concern. For the takers, it seemed that learning STEM material in MAN UP was quite simply a means to an individualistic monetary end, and at least early on, they had no stated desire to use STEM for familial or societal uplift.

Stevie was one of the few students in the program that was born outside of the United Sates (Africa). He was also from a single parent home and qualified for Free and Reduced Lunch. However, his (divorced) parents shared custody: Stevie lived with his mother during the week and with his father on weekends. Stevie's mother did not have a college degree; and, she spoke very little English. Stevie's father earned a degree in Africa, but according to Stevie his father's degree "didn't count" here in America. Stevie was a stellar student according to his teacher at his school (all MAN UP applicants were required to submit letters of recommendation from their math teacher). Stevie, according to the pre-survey felt that he was doing well in school, yet, he indicated that he did not feel that his voice counted at his school (he "Disagreed" with the following question: At my home school, it is clear that my teacher welcomes my input). Stevie's GPA (4.0) was well above the average GPA (2.99) for his MAN UP cohort; and, his Standardized test score in math was a perfect 600. He was the only student in his MAN UP cohort that earned a perfect score on the math section of the CST (more than once).

Stevie's answers on the pre-survey as an aggregate seemed to suggest that, for him, doing well in STEM was a way to extricate him from poverty. He did not want to live where he lived. And, he wanted to position himself to buy whatever his heart desired. At this stage in his life, his heart desired video games. At just over 10 years old, Stevie was the youngest student enrolled in MAN UP. (I never confirmed this, but it's likely that he may have skipped a grade or two.) Stevie's response to the following question is demonstrative of the overall tenor of his responses to the pre-survey: Is it important for you to learn STEM? Why or why not?

Stevie's response: Yes, it's important, because engineers and doctors and people in tech… those are the people who make the best money. I mean, they get paid the most. So, I want to work and get paid a lot. I want to get paid so that I can buy a new PS4 (Sony PlayStation 4 video game console). Plus, I never really get new clothes; I just get stuff from my brother or my older cousins. I just want to buy my own stuff.

This answer is indicative of the students who were categorized, initially, as takers: for them STEM learning was a means to a monetary end; however, unlike the makers, the takers only expressed interest in increasing their earning potential through STEM for individualized gain. The makers were concerned with taking in STEM as well; however, their impetus was to provide for their families in addition to themselves. Six students' pre-survey responses suggested that they fit firmly into this category. Their responses to the question that asked why they wanted to join MAN UP featured one or more of the following terms: money/ pay; job; shoes/Jordan's (shoes)/True Religion (jeans); myself/me; buy/purchase; and or Play Station 4/PS4/video games.

Based on this discursive analysis, while similar, the argument can be made that the makers—more than the takers—are beginning to see themselves as people who can learn and *do* STEM, albeit for micro-level, i.e., familial benefit.

Over the course of the MAN UP academic year, the focal cohort moved, fluidly, through these three student profiles. There was only one student whose post identification responses suggested that his own material needs took precedence over the perceived needs of his immediate family (makers) and or his larger local, national, or global community (shakers). (This student had more than 15 siblings.) On the pre-Identification Survey, nearly all of the focal cohort fit within either the taker or maker profile (10 takers and 6 makers, respectively). However, 16 of the 17 focal cohort members' responses on the post-identification survey included one or more of the following words: family/global family/neighborhood/community/planet/environment; brothers and sisters. A response provided, in response to the question: "Is it important for Black males have a STEM program?" by one member of the focal cohort best captures the sentiment of this group:

> It's important because, as Black males we face issues that a lot of people here in this country don't face. But, we're not the only people in the world that face negative stereotypes or discrimination or racism. So, we can understand what other people go through. And, it's important that we're in a STEM program, learning; so that they can see us and know that they can do whatever they set their mind to, too—and—and like us, they can also be applied STEM practitioners who use STEM to lift people up.

The above quote is representative of the general feeling of the focal cohort. They expressed, time and again, that they had begun envisioning themselves as applied STEM practitioners who: "can not only fix problems in our own communities, but can also be role models for other Black boys and other stereotyped people. They can know that they have the power to change things they think are unfair— just like we do!"

Cases studies: From a taker to shaker and from makers to shakers

Malachi, like most MAN UP students was considered first in family, low-income, and hailed from a single parent home. Malachi's initial answer to the question of what he hoped to be when he grew up also demonstrated a shift in the way he identified with STEM. Initially, Malachi wrote: "I want to be a professional basketball player, so that I can buy whatever I want." This answer situated Michael within the takers profile as his focus is, entirely, on individual wish fulfillment. However, his response on the post-manhood concept inventory demonstrated an expanded purview and, simultaneously, a critical understanding of STEM as a potential tool for a socially just (future) applications of STEM: "I want to be any job in the black community that encourages young black boys to get an education, really. But, specifically, I want to be a math teacher so that I can share the math that I know with kids like me—my community and others like it."

Malachi's latter response pointed to his desire to affect not only himself but also his local and perhaps global community as well. Over the course of the academic year all 17 students from the focal cohort spent varied amounts of time in each of the three categories of participation. The profiles were fluid. However, by the end of the MAN UP academic year, students from the focal cohort irrespective of where they started within this continuum began to fit most closely with the shakers profile. In fact, most students' (16 out of 17) responses to this particular question not only including STEM career aspirations, but also included mentions of their local, national, and global communities. More specifically, students made connections between their future STEM aspirations and the potential ameliorative power it holds. What is more, 16 of the 17 responses to this question featured one or more of the following words or phrases when students described why they wanted to take up STEM majors and, ultimately, STEM careers: help/aide/encourage/teach/model/make/smash. These words were used by students to describe what impelled them to pursue STEM; that is, they wanted to help/aide/teach the following people: marginalized/stereotyped/persecuted/racialized people. (The word "smash" seems somewhat out of place, but it was used in reference to "smashing" negative stereotyping.)

Further evidence of Malachi's identificatory shift can be gleaned from his responses to the pre and post manhood concept inventory. The question, Is race real?, initially stumped Malachi. He responded to this question by writing: "I don't really get this question. Of course race is real!" His response on the post manhood concept inventory is especially poignant and, simultaneously, indicative of the ethos that describes the shakers profile: "No! Race isn't real. It is a system that was created to keep people apart. It has real consequences, but really, the only thing that should matter is whether we help fill in the cracks we made in the world, not our 'race'. And, in MAN UP, we learned that we can fill these cracks using math and science and tech." So, then, Malachi's move from a self-interested taker to a young person who was interested in "filling the cracks he creates in the world" represented his move from a taker to a shaker. Malachi's answer on the post manhood concept inventory demonstrated care and concern for a cause larger than his own individual gain. This response suggests that Malachi recognized social inequity as "the cracks in the world", and that he recognized himself as someone capable of applying STEM to begin filling these fissures of social injustice.

Malachi's responses on the post-identification survey and RAM concept inventory indicated a shift in his critical understanding of who can be an applied STEM practitioner (ASP) and what an ASP can and should do. This critical perspective was also evident in his response to the question: Who defines Black manhood? Malachi's powerful response demonstrated an understanding of societal ills, and injustices, which begs address. He wrote, "Those who defines black manhood are those that do not know what African-American males are capable of and can do to better their lives." His connected response to the following question, What is Black manhood?, clearly demonstrated a clarity of thought regarding the positionality of African-American males in our society. He wrote, "Black manhood is the ability to know that you are better than those who hate your race, and that no matter what people say—we can change the world…we can be doctors, engineers, chemist, statisticians—whatever we want". His initial response to this question was telling in its simplicity: "black manhood is being a black man".

From makers to shakers: Maxwell and Jeff's, both low-income, first in family students who hailed from single parent homes, respective responses to the question (on the pre-survey) of what manhood is situated them squarely within the makers profile. Makers seemed to reflect a collective interest in doing better in (i.e., taking all available knowledge) STEM so that they could work to ensure upward mobility, measured monetarily, in order improve the socioeconomic realities for themselves and their families.

Maxwell's GPA was slightly above the focal cohort average (3.05); he was considered Proficient in both math and ELA as determined by his prior year STAR test scores. In response on the pre-identification survey regarding his future aspirations, initially wrote that he wanted to be either a basketball or football player when he grew up so that he could "repay my [his] mom for all of the sacrifices she'd made for him and his four siblings." And, while never losing sight of the importance of providing for his family, Maxwell's answer to this same question on the post-identification survey demonstrates a substantial shift in his subjective identification with STEM. To the question, What you want to be when you grow up?, to Maxwell responded thusly:

> I want to be a scientist, because that way I can show other African-American males that we can do this. It's important to me to be a role model if I can be. And, I can work on things that are problems for black people, like heart disease, and diabetes and stuff like that. And, not just us, but other marginalized people, too.

Jeff, who like Maxwell was low-income, first in family and hailed from a single parent home, responses also demonstrated growth: "When I grow up I still want to be a math teacher, but I think I also want to get a Ph.D., in math so I can be a math professor, too. That way I can teach teachers, like Mr. J and Mr. S, so that they won't continue to stereotype Black boys, especially in STEM." These two responses are indicative of what I have termed the critical contextualization of STEM: that is, when students began to recognize that they could be applied STEM practitioners capable of appropriating and using STEM for social justice, i.e., to positively affect their local, national and or global community.

Maxwell's response to question 1, What is manhood?, on the pre-manhood survey was: "Manhood is the maturity to get an education so that you can provide for your family." His response to the second question, "What do you want to be when you grow up, and why?" further illustrates his drive to be successful in STEM: "I just want to be successful and have kids look up to me and make a lot of money. My mom and dad and family have done a lot for me and I want to show them appreciation by doing well."

Jeff's response to this question was like Maxwell's: "Manhood is when you take care of your responsibilities like making sure that your kids have enough to eat and are taken care of and that they're happy." Like Maxwell, Jeff's response to the question regarding what it is that he wants to be when he grows up further illustrates his drive to be successful, monetarily: "Really, I just want to have a job where my mom doesn't have to work so much. I want her to be able to go on vacations like other people's mom's and have a new car and not always have to worry about bills. So, whatever job I can get maybe like an engineer, that's what I want to do." Of all the focal students, it was these two that, perhaps, demonstrated the greatest shift. In responding to the same questions on the post survey, there was the clear presence of a critical perspective—that is, a perspective that was far more expansive than what they demonstrated on the pre-survey.

In answering the question, five months later, What is manhood?, arguably, Maxwell's critical context had been expanded. Maxwell wrote: "Manhood it is understanding that you can take care of yourself and your family, and that you have a responsibility to your community as well." Jeff also demonstrated a shift in the locus of his concern, moving from individual and familial concern to a broader concern for mankind. Jeff wrote: "Manhood is understanding that you have a responsibility to your family and your planet; for example, like when we figured out was how to use STEM knowledge to help our brothers and sisters in the Philippines. That's manhood to me." This connects, conceptually, the work done in the RAM course with the work done in the CS course, and is indicative of these young men's shifts from makers to shakers.

For Jeff, it was clear that his socio-political understanding of the place of a man in society had shifted and become more expansive. His critical understanding of context, which was initially limited to only his immediate family, had grown to now encompass his global family as well. And, what is more, he included STEM as part and parcel of this newfound understanding. This is a prime example of the critical contextualization of STEM.

As evidenced by the focal cohort, shifts in profiles were largely predicated on varying levels of identification with STEM. The students who began to see themselves as young people capable of wielding their STEM knowledge to make the world a more socially just place, irrespective of where they began in this spectrum, eventually most closely aligned with the shakers profile. That said, a desire an ability to critically apply STEM for social justice was a concomitant virtue of all students that ended up in the shakers category. Nevertheless, this was true for all members of the focal cohort: once they began to believe that not only could they do well (or continue to do well) in STEM (as evidence by their increasing competence) but also that they could do STEM (in high school, college and as a career), or effectively apply STEM to equity issues that they felt were important, it became abundantly clear that they readily accepted the appellation of "applied STEM practitioners". Once they self-identified as applied STEM practitioners, they were, necessarily, shakers. This process from makers or takers to shakers is the instantiation of the critical contextualization of STEM.

Of course, while it was important to analyze whether this process took place, it is equally important to attempt to understand what precipitated or catalyzed these shifts in the first place. Focal students' own words on the program year-end program satisfaction survey (YPSS) and yearend individual and focus group interviews provide valuable insight into this question. These two metrics where designed to get at identity generally, by soliciting student responses that spoke to their STEM attitudes and aspirations and their self-efficacy vis-à-vis STEM. While the criterion for the categories of participation were somewhat rigid, as expected, there was movement between and across profiles for the students in the focal cohort as evidenced by the case studies provided above. In fact, all but one of the 17 focal students, by the end of the academic year, were shakers.

Context matters: Further connecting STEM identities in the courses

In all three MAN UP courses, emphasis was placed on positioning students as "applied STEM practitioners." This was seen, in part, in the work on final projects that the students completed for each class. For math class the focal students used linear equations to create a symbolic mathematical representation in the form of a crest or insignia to represent them as young scholars to the outside world. The symbol they created was a mallet breaking a large wall. At the year-end celebration, the class described the mathematical processes they mastered to create their insignia along with its symbolic implication. Speaking for the group, one student explained, "We created a mallet because in this program we are creating symbols using math…. If that doesn't smash stereotypes about us, I don't know what will…. We like the mallet because rubber is malleable…. We are, too!"

CS final project: In Computer Science, the focal cohort contributed to the creation of a mobile application to raise environmental awareness that was led by the 8th graders. The focal cohort also contributed to its creation. Though the focal class did not lead this project, their understanding of their identities as STEM producers rather than consumers was reinforced through it. In focus group interviews, for example, one focal student reported that he now "feels connected to the producer role" because in developing this app he was "doing the producing instead of just talking about it." Another focal student commented that this process had "convinced" him that can and he will be a video game engineer that "creates [produces] good video games with positive Black male role models, unlike GTA [Grand Theft Auto]."

RAM final project: Proposed project presentation: Similarly, the final project in the RAM class was to curate a production of diverse digital narratives modeled after the museum installation called "Question Bridge Black Males." This project reinforced STEM identities in the focal students in a variety of ways. A member of the MAN UP instructional team served as one of the advisors for the development of Question Bridge Black Males <http://questionbridge.com/>. This member introduced the rest of the MAN UP instructional team to this exhibit, and the program eventually took all the students on a field trip to see it at a local museum.

In RAM, the goal of addressing issues of identity was explicit, and the students brought what they were learning about rhetorical analysis to the "re-production" of a Question Bridge as a final class project. The focal students videotaped themselves and students in the other two classes addressing questions of Black male identity and life experiences as modeled in the museum exhibit. When asked why they chose this project, students talked about how they wanted to smash stereotypes around Black males in STEM and how they felt that using technology to counter stereotypes of Black males was analogous to "performing their argument."

Mr. K:	"Please provide the panel with the synopsis of the project that you're proposing."
Student 2:	We want to create a project that's like the question Bridge project. We want to ask the same questions that they presented on the website and some that we saw at the exhibit. We're going to answer the questions and we want the seventh and eighth graders to answer the questions, too.
Mr. K:	What do you hope to accomplish with this presentation?
Mr. J:	What's your thesis?
Student 1:	"Okay, we know that there are a lot of stereotypes, negative stereotypes connected to African-American male youth. People say that we're lazy, violent, do drugs, stuff like that or that we can't work together. So, the thesis is that we want to smash the stereotypes by showing people who see this video that we know how to use technology, and STEM, just as well as they do.
Student 2:	"That's right, and the rhetorical piece, or what Mr. J calls performing our argument, is that not only are we talking about how we could do all these different things with STEM, we're actually doing it by producing are all the [technology-based presentation] like Question Bridge and, by doing this, other kids like us—that are unfairly stereotyped can be encouraged."
Student 1:	"And, this is how we can uplift not just ourselves, but also our community, too."
Student 3:	"It's like stereotypes force us to consume negative stuff about ourselves. Now we can use this video project to produce positive images of Black males."
Mr. J:	WOW! That's powerful, bro!
Student 2:	Mr. J, are you crying?
Mr. J:	"Maybe…this is powerful stuff. I've never heard 6th graders talking like this."
Student 1:	"That's right, you have to remember that we're the experts now…."
Student 3:	"Yep, and we're going to use our expertness [expertise] to breakdown these wack stereotypes so that other young brothas [brothers] will know that they can do this, too."
Student 2:	"And their teachers will know, too."

The above conversation took place towards the end of March 2014, which was the midway point of the second semester. The ethos demonstrated in the way that the focal cohort presented their project plan was in stark contrast to their initial conception of manhood as evidenced by the Manhood pre-survey administered January 2014. The following quote, below, demonstrates this conceptual movement. Initially a first-year MAN UP student on the pre-survey defined manhood thusly:

> Manhood is the state of being a man rather than a child. Manhood in my opinion is taking care of your family, being responsible and being successful. Being a man takes a lot of responsibility, you have to take care of your wife and kids protect them and treat them with respect.

This quote captured the general feeling of the entire focal cohort as pertains to their definitions of manhood. In fact 16 of 17 focal students included the following words on their respective replies to this question: provide, protect/protection, family/kids, wife/women/lady. (The lone student who did not use one of these words simply stated that manhood is—"just being a man".) On the post-survey, however, while still deeply invested in the protection of their future families, the focal cohorts' conception of manhood had been broadened, 16 of 17 students, in addition to the abovementioned words also included the following words: community/communities, neighborhood, culture/society, environment, and planet. This shift in contextual understanding was eloquently captured by the following focal student's response on the post-manhood survey: "Manhood is understanding that you have a responsibility to your family and your community, and your planet." This particular conceptual shift in this student's understanding of manhood was indicative of the focal class by and large. Ultimately, I found that because MAN UP students were encouraged, empowered, and equipped to question seemingly axiomatic conceptions of manhood generally, and Black manhood specifically, this criticality bled over into their association with STEM learning as well.

Commensurate with MAN UP's pedagogical approach, the MAN UP instructional team was interested in devising ways to contribute to the development of MAN UP students' agentive voices, by function as active listeners, while contributing to increases in their STEM related identification, competency, and socially just application of science, technology, engineering, and/or math. Based on this project as well as the projects that were birthed in students' STEM classes, I found that this was indeed taking place, and, I found that students were intent on using their agentive voices, their STEM knowhow, and their power to change the world—for the better.

Practically, by creating a digital media project using the five-paragraph essay format and the rhetorical triangle, the focal cohorts' understanding of argumentation was strengthened (as demonstrated by their work on their RAM-specific final project). For example, the RAM Question Bridge Development Team, all members of the focal cohort, created a video project that interrogated the pernicious stereotypes that have been sutured to Black males in STEM and in other pertinent issues like familial and community relations. When presenting their work, this group of students identified and explained instances where their film demonstrated the themes covered in the RAM course:

Mr. K:	"So, why did your group settle on the three or four questions that your video brought to the fore (Why should Black Men learn STEM?; What is the role of the Black man in his community; and, Whose responsibility is it to raise Black children; and, lastly, As a Black man in America, are you truly free?)?"
Student 1:	"Well, we wanted to make sure that our argument was rhetorical[ly] balanced."
Student 2:	"Yeah, we didn't want our argument to be too pathetic—I mean too emotional, or offer just logical information [logos]."
Student 1:	"Right, we also want to make sure that it's clear that we know what we're talking about, so that our credibility—our ethos—is also covered."
Student 3:	"Exactly, the question about freedom is, like, our emotional question. We knew that the conversation would get heated when we asked groups to argue each side. [The RAM group asked students, irrespective of their personal beliefs, to argue or discuss each question.] We also knew that the question about raising our children would appeal to the audiences' emotions and kind of open them up so that we could share positive facts about the power of the Black family."
Student 4:	"That way, we could deconstruct the negative stereotypes that claim that there's something wrong with us and our families."
Mr. K:	"Okay, so, someone please sum up for me what it is that your project is hoping to achieve."
Student 1:	"I'll take this one [his group agrees with head nods]. We viewed this project as a message within a message, but I'll get back to that later. We constructed this like a five-paragraph essay. The problem that we're addressing was that people see the Black male experience as one thing and that that thing is negative, because it's based on stereotypes like we're not smart, or we're violent, or we're lazy and we don't love our kids and families. So, our thesis was [this]: if we can show the ways that young people—us—are thing about these things, thinking critically that is, then, and people will understand that those stereotypes are untrue. So, we picked questions that asked the same question differently. I mean, at the end of the day, we wanted to answer the question: does the Black man have a role in society, with a 'yes'."

Mr. J:	"Say more, please."
Student 1:	"Okay, it's like this…"
Student 2:	"I'll say more. All of the questions act as body paragraphs in the five-paragraph essay format. But like (Student 1) said, they all ask the same question so that they can help us demonstrate our argument: that the Black man has a huge role in family, community, STEM, and society. Because, when we all asked and you all debated these questions, it demonstrated how deeply we can think about these issues. It's not lost on us. That's how we concluded—by showing that we see the ways that we, a group of young Black men of the future, are paying attention to all of this and that we are smart enough and we care enough to plan to do something about it."
Student 3:	"Plus, like Mr. J always talked about with us: we preformed our argument by using tech to construct our argument."

Rhetorical argumentation for these students was no longer merely a rubric to follow; instead, this multimodal, digital project helped them arrive at a conceptual understanding of what it means to create and develop a cogent argument. In addition, by using the circle of critical praxis (Duncan-Andrade & Morrell, 2008) to develop this project, students were introduced to the engineering and design process. What is more, this technological project was catalyzed by students' desire to infuse constituents of rhetoric and composition in the creation of a STEM focused project that they designed to create more equitable, more socially just reality.

The Medium is the Message: As evidenced by the exchange above, these students went on to construct a narrative that featured a strong logical appeal, a strong emotive, or pathetic appeal, and that was predicated on an ethical appeal based on their expertise as middle school Black males in STEM. Throughout this project, it became clear that Mr. K's words were true: these students were taking ownership of their identities as applied STEM practitioners. They were desirous to demonstrate to their potential audience that they were a group of young men fully capable of applying STEM to a matter that was of utmost importance to them, individually, and to their community of other "negatively stereotyped people" more broadly. What is more, they had begun to connect their understanding of manhood to the pursuit of global equity, which is commensurate with the spirit of the program's name. Making this nuanced, yet important connection allowed these students to "perform their argument". By using technology, in this instance to deconstruct and later correct negative, stereotypical depictions of Black males, they instantiated their argument as well as the overall argument of MAN UP. They demonstrated our core belief that urban, predominately low-income Black middle school males are fully capable of learning and, subsequently, using STEM to address issues that are important to them and that inhere on social justice.

Chapter 4 review: Considerations and questions

Consideration:

In this chapter I discussed MAN UP students' shifts in their demonstrated under-standing of STEM (competency), the ways in which they see themselves as young men that can pursue STEM degrees and careers (STEM identity), and their will-ingness and ability to use STEM to make their neighborhoods and even the world a better place (socially just applications of STEM). In charting their movement in these three areas, I talked about three distinct, graduated student categories: *Shakers, Makers, and Takers.*

Questions for students:

1. Which one of the three student identities, shakers, makers, or takers, do you feel best describes you right now? Where do you hope to be by the end of this year?
2. Do you think that it is important for students to identify with one of the identity categories more than the other two, or, does it make sense that students go back and forth between these identities depending on their circumstances?
3. Much of the focus on STEM education is on students' individual success: do you think it is also important to focus on the ways that students can use their personal STEM success to improve their communities (why or why not)?
4. Which of the students mentioned in this chapter do you most closely identify with (please explain)?
5. Have you used STEM to address issues in your individual, family, and or community (please provide an example)?

Consideration:

In Chapter three, I presented an analysis of and findings from my data by analyzing the focal cohort's math pre-and post-test scores, their shifts in their Manhood Development Concept Inventory, shifts in their Rhetorical Analysis Concept Inventory, as well as shifts in their CS/Mobile Apps course: Technol-ogy for Social Justice Concept Inventory (CS), respectively. To assess the shifts in STEM competency, identification, and the student-derived development of socially just STEM applications, I was compelled to create two new terms. The first, socio-academic synergy is an educational atmosphere wherein students' real life considerations, affinities, and concerns are part and parcel of the educational atmosphere they are participating in. Socio-academic synergy—as evidenced by the data presented in this chapter—is a prerequisite to the critical contextualization of STEM, which is when students appropriate STEM by using their STEM knowledge and expertise to create STEM-based interventions of interruptions that benefit their local, national, and/or global communities.

Questions for educators:

1. Are there ways that you have or are currently working towards creating an atmosphere predicated on socio-academic synergy in your classroom, after/out of school program, course, or in the student services you provide (please provide an example)?
2. How can you or do you support both critical contextualization and the critical contextualization of STEM (where applicable) in your current pedagogical practices?
3. How do you or can you carve out spaces for students to use their expertise, whether it be academic, cultural, linguistic, etc., to contribute to the overall knowledge construction and meaning making that takes place in the educational space/s that you are responsible for?
4. How do you (or will you) create equitable educational opportunities for your traditionally marginalized students, including Black males, to develop both their academic and STEM identities (where applicable)?
5. How do you (or will you) create equitable educational opportunities for your traditionally marginalized students, including Black males, to use the knowledge and competencies they gain in your class to create innovative ways for them to address societal issues that they deem worthy of redress?

Keywords:

Socio-academic synergy, applied STEM practitioner; Shakers, Makers, Takers; STEM identity, STEM competency, socially just applications of STEM

References

Duncan-Andrade, J., & Morrell, E. (2008). *The art of critical pedagogy: Possibilities for moving from theory to practice in urban schools.* New York, NY: Peter Lang.

Mahiri, J., & Sims, J. J. (2016). Engineering equity: A critical pedagogical approach to language and curriculum change for African American males in STEM (55–70). Z. Babaci-Wilhite (ed.), In *Curriculum change in language and STEM subjects as a right in education.* Rotterdam: Sense Publishing.

5

Showing out

Developing competencies in STEM and beyond

The idea of showing up and showing out is of importance to traditionally marginalized students. This is a reconceptualization of a pejorative term. In my youth, whenever I was misbehaving my (Black) mother would warn me that I was "showing out", which meant that if I did not soon correct my behavior—there would be consequences. In both planned parent-teacher conferences as well as unplanned parent teacher "conferences", primarily in conversation with Black mothers and grandmothers, this term came up often. For many parents and guardians, the first thing they wanted to know about their son, nephew, or grandson was this: has he been showing out? Aware of this term, we, MAN UP instructional faculty and MAN UP students decided to appropriate and re-conceptualize this term. Instead of it signaling undesirable behavior, for us showing out meant: demonstrating an understanding of and identification with STEM and how it can be used to positively affect society. Implicit in this new definition was the notion that showing out was a direct challenge to negative stereotypes that hold that Black males cannot excel in STEM. In addition to developing the cohort's STEM identities, the MAN UP program also focused on developing specific STEM competencies required for college and careers. These two measures are not disparate. In fact, this programmatic structure of MAN UP argued that the development of a positive STEM identity was essential to the development of STEM competency. To assess shifts in math learning, a core "concept inventory" based on California State Standards and the Common Core State Standards was used. Different concept inventories were developed for CS and RAM that reflected specific content addressed in those classes. Like the pre and post surveys, the concept inventories (except for the RAM class) were administered at the beginning and end of the 2013–14 academic-year. In addition to the above-mentioned metrics, I discuss data collected from the YPSS to underscore the focal cohorts' shifts in confidence, which positively informed their demonstrated gains in competency as well as their positive shifts in self-efficacy. However, prior to analyzing the data provided by the YPSS, it makes sense to illuminate the gains that the focal cohort demonstrated based on their course-specific concept inventories.

Of course, data derived from standardized metrics only tell part of the story regarding the positive shifts demonstrated by MAN UP students. In addition to measurable growth in STEM competency, many of these young men also grew in confidence as well as civic engagement, empathy, and a critical understanding of the socio-political climate that they were enmeshed within.

"It was easier for me to learn here because I felt like what I said mattered"

The math course aimed to prepare students to continue to be successful in grade-level math and provide foundational skills and dispositions necessary to be successful as they advanced to higher levels of math. The math concept inventory captured the focal cohort's pre and post knowledge in three content areas: ratios and proportions, geometry, and statistics. All 17 students in the focal class completed the pre-MAN UP math assessment, which was administered September 2013. All 17 students in the focal class completed the post-MAN UP math assessment administered in June 2014. Pre- and post-MAN UP math assessment data were available for all 17 students in the focal cohort. The results of the pre-post math concept inventory were very encouraging: 94 percent (16/17) of the focal cohort demonstrated growth in mathematics performance from pre- to post-MAN UP. The focal class increased by an average of five items, or 14 percentage points (47 percent to 61 percent). Students eligible for Free/Reduced Price Lunch (FRPL) had the highest post-math scores, demonstrating growth of 8 percentage points compared to non-FRPL eligible students (2 percentage points), therefore bucking a seemingly ironclad trend. This is vitally important because low-income Black males are seemingly permanent fixtures on the bottom rung of the latter of educational achievement, due to myriad reasons that have little or nothing to do with their intrinsic ability.

What is more, the focal cohorts' responses in focus group interviews and on the YPSS indicated that they also saw increases in their confidence regarding math success, too. For example, all but one reported that they had learned a lot and that the program had improved their math skills. They spoke highly about ways that Mr. K's math course affected them. Many noted that they were ahead of the math they were learning in school because of participation in MAN UP. As one student said, "When I went to my math class, everyone was struggling except me because I had already learned it here." Another shared, "I always really liked math, but Mr. K helped me explore math and what it is and how to use it instead of just learning it." Students, when asked whether they felt that they could learn math more easily at MAN UP on the final focus group interview, pointed to MR. K's excellence as an educator as well as the overall atmosphere represented by MAN UP. For example, one student commented: "It was easier for me to learn here [MAN UP] because I felt like what I said mattered and I also felt like Mr. K was willing to help me, even if it took me a while to get the concepts." This sentiment was echoed by another student who stated: "Being here with other black males who are good in math and with male teachers who always push us to be our best. At my school, I'm the only Black male in my math class. And, my teacher is smart, but he does all the talking. We don't get to say much. It's different here [at MAN UP]."

Similar developments in STEM competencies were achieved in the Computer Science/Mobile Apps class. Mr. S taught students how to design and build Mobile Apps using App Inventor programming language. However, beyond learning to program, the course focused on big ideas of computing including abstraction, design, recursion, simulations, and the limits of computation. The Mobile Apps concept inventory consisted of 8 items asked students to evaluate their skill level and ability to complete skills tasks, based on a 3-point Likert scale ranging from "not at all true" to "very much true." The students showed significant gains in their knowledge and skills with increases on every item including understanding how to create a storyboard and implementation plans for apps, knowing what a mock-up is, understanding how to create a design rationale, and understanding how to use app programming software. These increases were best captured by the focal cohorts' invaluable contributions to the eighth-grade cohorts' conceptualization, development and actualization of an environmentally conscious, sustainability mobile application. The focal cohort helped storyboard and conceptualize the eighth-grade project, relying heavily on their newfound understanding of the design process (which was the focus for the 1st Year Cohort). The focal cohort's interview and YPSS survey responses confirmed that they felt they were developing important STEM competencies.

Achieving socio-academic synergy: Yearend Post-Satisfaction Survey (YPSS)

MAN UP was intended to be rigorous and a vehicle that resulted, ultimately, in measurable college-readiness for the students enrolled. There are several programs that do this type of work. The difference for this program, however, was a laser-focus and undying determination on creating an atmosphere that was built upon trusting, nutritive relationships within the MAN UP community. The strong feeling was that if middle school Black young men were in a STEM-focused educative program that celebrated who they are and developed a curricular foci and pedagogical approach that was based on their lived-experiences, concerns, interests, etc., they would not only improve in STEM scholastically, but that they would begin to do STEM. From a programmatic standpoint, this survey provided information for the MAN UP educational team to use for program improvement; for the sake of this study, this survey afforded a view into the ways in which the focal cohort recognized and identified with the atmosphere that MAN UP sought to engender and how it informed the development of a positive STEM identity for the focal cohort.

According to this survey, the focal class recognized that there was a difference in the way that MAN UP STEM instruction positioned them. For example, 15 out of 17 members of the focal cohort agreed that MAN UP challenged them to think about the way that they think in regard to their roles in society and how they can use STEM to be agents on positive social change. It is my belief that these shifts in STEM identity were precipitated on the critical-reality pedagogical approach that MAN UP instantiated. This approach to STEM education, intentionally centered the lived-experiences, culture, concerns, issues and ways of being that these young men instantiated. Data suggests that students recognized that this approach was different than what they were used to in their respective schools. For example, 76 percent of the focal (13/17) cohort felt that race and culture were connected to STEM course content within MAN UP. Conversely, only 23 percent (4/17) of the focal cohort felt as though their schools connected race and culture to STEM course content. Additionally, 88 percent of the focal class (15/17) felt that issues around equity and justice were connected to STEM course content within MAN UP. Conversely, only 23 percent (4/17) of the focal cohort felt as though their schools connected race and culture to STEM course content. Nasir's (2011) work demonstrates that there is reciprocal relationship between students' increases in (math) competency and increases in (math) confidence, and the obverse holds true as well. And, 94 percent of the focal class felt that MAN UP made them feel as though they could excel in STEM, versus only 23 percent feeling that their schools prompted this kind of confidence, respectively. The following data also speaks to the effect that that MAN UP pedagogical approach had on the focal cohort: 100 percent of the focal class reported that MAN UP improved their math skills; 88 percent of the focal class (15/17) reported that they learned "a lot" or "some" about mathematics in MAN UP; and, 88 percent of the focal cohort (15/17) reported that MAN UP increased their interest in Mobile Apps. In addition to these findings, the data also bears out that 76 percent of the focal cohort (13/17) reported that they learned how to create Mobile Apps in MAN UP; 76 percent of the focal class (13/17) learned "a lot" or "some" about Mobile Apps in MAN UP. And, 94 percent of the focal cohort agreed or strongly agreed that they felt that their confidence in their ability/ies to excel in STEM helped them do better in STEM.

These statistics provide valuable insight into what may have catalyzed the focal cohorts' shifts in STEM competency: as their confidence in not only learning but also doing STEM increased, they, in turn, began to see themselves as young people who could both learn and do STEM. This was the first step in the development of their STEM identities as applied STEM practitioners that do STEM well.

We can do math, too: Yearend focus group interviews

Returning to a discussion of STEM competency, data pulled from the yearend focus group interview bears out that students experienced increases in their attitudes and aspirations relating to mathematics, Computer Science, college and career in STEM fields, and their own study patterns. As Michael remarked, "I think about my future more" and Jeff shared, "It made me think about being a creator, not just a user." Students found themselves striving to succeed because of the program, describing how it "makes me want to do better on my math so I can stay here next year and keep my grades up." Because the program also stressed the importance of college and careers, according to the yearend focus group, the focal cohort reported that they felt more committed to their futures with students sharing statements such as, "I knew math was important from the beginning, but coming here as an African-American, I know it is more important to show them that we are smart and we can do math," which is commensurate with the work that students were undertaking to dispel negative stereotypes. Another student added: "MAN UP made me more interested in building things, like mechanical things or wooden things or technology."

This sentiment was consistent throughout the focal cohort. In fact, members of the focal cohort claimed that they were interested in wanting to "go to college earlier" and attend "a better college" than they had originally anticipated. Furthermore, students gained a new perspective on high school, sharing that the program "helped me because before when I thought about high school, I thought about work, work, and more work, but it [MAN UP] let me know that it isn't as hard I expected." Similarly, one young man stated that the program prepared him for high school, and more specifically "what expectations are there, and how I can be mature, and give it my all to make the most of it." All of this is the direct result of students beginning to self-identify as young people who can both learn and do STEM.

This is evidenced by the focal students repeatedly describing the extent to which the program helped them think about STEM careers, or "new career options I didn't know about." For instance, Jeff discussed how the program showed him "there are more tech jobs, and how tech can be useful, to help you and help the community. There are more jobs I didn't know about that I might want to do, like Google jobs and Mobile Apps and creating cars that drive themselves." Michael explained that "talking about high school and college, it made me think about what I am going to do in the future, and made me think more about options for what I wanted to do in my life, like science, math, and technology." Both Jeff and Michael's comments are indicative of the focal cohorts' positive shifts in their STEM-specific attitudes and aspirations. These positive shifts are concomitant with increased self-efficacy in STEM. All of this suggests that attitudes, aspirations and self-efficacy in STEM appear to be necessary steps in gaining competency in STEM (Mahiri & Sims, 2016).

Decoding success: Computer science course concept inventory

An example of connections between attitudes/aspirations and self-efficacy in STEM is in the fact that, 16 of the 17 students agreed that the program taught them a lot about Computer Science and that they now felt that Computer Science was interesting and fun. As one student noted, "I've never had a Computer

Science class before. This was all new to me. Mr. S was so patient, and he really knows his stuff. I'm beginning to think that I really can be a video game designer." And, related to the focal students' increases in CS competency, they felt that this course encouraged, empowered, and equipped them to devise and, later, develop technology that would benefit not only their own immediate communities, but also similar communities worldwide. During the yearend focus group interview one student commented that "Mr. S helped me think differently about the roles that I can play in society. Like, now I think about ways to fill in the cracks that make life harder for certain people." This student's statement is indicative of the overall feeling of the focal cohort: 16 of 17 members of the focal cohort agreed, on the YPSS, that the CS course helped them think of new ways to use STEM for positive social change. In addition to helping to foster a critical (theoretical) understanding of the ways in which STEM can be applied for social amelioration, the CS course also taught students how to develop their "hard" computing skills like storyboarding, developing mock ups, and employing the design process, for example. The focal cohort increased from pre to post on their CS concept inventories. In analyzing this data, increase from pre to post is defined as: movement from students self-selecting the "Very Much" option on the pre CS concept inventory versus the number of students from the focal cohort that selected "Very Much", for a given question, on the post CS concept inventory. The focal cohort experienced significant gains in their self-perceived familiarity and expertise with each of the questions represented on the two-part CS concept inventory. These gains are significant precisely because they demonstrated the focal cohorts' increasing confidence in doing CS (STEM), which is a both precursor for and indicative of the development of a positive STEM identity (Nasir, 2011).

Our voices matter: The rhetorical analysis of manhood

Language arts instruction, like STEM instruction (as with education writ large) is, intrinsically, an issue of social justice. Myriad issues are borne out of the quest to foment a more equitable, culturally relevant pedagogy that will eventually lead to a re-envisioned critical language arts paradigm. Language instantiates culture (Rickford, 1998) maybe not in its entirety, however, it is indispensable to both the communicability and continuance of culture. If this is in fact true, then, the linguistic repression/oppression that many marginalized ethnic minority students are subject to, needs redress. Linguistic oppression forces young people to check their culture at the door of their respective classrooms, so to speak. And, in so doing, it assures them, perhaps non-consciously, that the compulsory educational spaces that they inhabit are not reserved for them. This hierarchical differentiation then forcibly positions them as "others", who are deemed, simultaneously, non-standard and, therefore, inferior. This can be likened to linguistic oppression. The alienation that this exclusionary paradigm foments and ensures, while not the whole story, undoubtedly informs and exacerbates the seemingly intractably enduring achievement gap.

Linguistic oppression is enacted when deficient views of marginalized students' language, because it purportedly lacks the dominant languages legitimate features, results in psychological and material sanctions within an educational milieu. Contiguously, ideological linguistic oppression is being enacted whenever its use in, educational (traditional) setting, leads to further marginalization, forced remediation, and subordination (Freire & Macedo, 1987). For Freire and Macedo (1987) it is especially problematic because it disallows the realization of marginalized students' ontological vocation: to become critically conscious, reflexive, and transformational, i.e., to become more fully human. What is more, students' voices are their discursive means to make (and re-make) themselves heard in the world and to redefine themselves as authors of their own world; their agentive voices allow them to tell their story, in their words. However, this is not a luxury that linguistically oppressed students enjoy, for the most part, in our current educational milieu.

Therefore, the RAM class designed to offer a unique space for seeing how the first-year cohort was developing competencies in STEM as well as critical language skills. This course explored conceptions of manhood generally, and conceptions of Black manhood specifically in terms of definitions; individual, group, and societal perceptions; and the power relationships and media representations that influence these considerations. The students learned to use principles of rhetorical analysis to understand and critique the various considerations of manhood surrounding Black males and honed their presentation and technical skills through the Question Bridge like video project.

The initial concept inventory for RAM was administered at the beginning of the second semester as opposed to the start of the first semester for the other two classes, and the post concept inventory was administered at the end of the program. The 19 questions (See: Appendix B) on this inventory sought to ascertain students' conceptions of manhood. Data from these questions indicated that many students initially understood manhood as a static positionality that was predicated exclusively on the ability to provide both financial and physical security for women and children. This static conception of manhood shifted over the course of the second semester to a more malleable understanding of manhood as connected to being a caretaker, but also having responsibilities to improving the larger community. This shift was captured in an interview response of one of the 6th graders who noted, "Manhood is understanding that you have a responsibility to your family and your community, and your planet."

Across all three classes and across the various sources of data, there were clear indications that the MAN UP program had significant impacts on developing competencies as well as identities in connection with STEM subjects and careers. As one participant concluded in a focus group interview, "It's a great way to spend my Saturdays and stay off the streets because I bettered myself and my STEM skills."

Chapter 5 review: Considerations and questions

Consideration:

This chapter chronicles the focal cohorts' shifts in STEM competency in order to highlight the ways in which their increases in STEM identity contributed to academic success in their MAN UP STEM courses. In this context, increases in STEM identity meant that students were beginning to see themselves as young people that could not only excel in STEM at their current grade level, but also potential STEM majors and potential and potential STEM professionals. However, unlike most STEM interventions, this kind of progress was not the main goal. Instead, I wanted to measure whether MAN UP students were beginning to identify as applied STEM practitioners, or shakers. Soon it became apparent that they were, in fact, progressing towards becoming shakers. And, what is more, the data revealed that these students were also experience increasing levels of academic success in their two STEM classes. This chapter worked to illuminate a link between these two seemingly connected phenomena.

Questions for students:

1. Are you provided with opportunities to "show out", i.e., opportunities to demonstrate your understanding of and identification with STEM, at your school (please provide an example/s)?
2. Do you think that an increase in STEM identity is necessary to do better in STEM classes?
3. Have you ever been in a class where your teacher provided opportunities for you to develop your academic and/or STEM identity? (how did she or he do it; and, how did it make you feel?

4. Which of the students mentioned in this chapter do you most closely identify with (please explain)?
5. Have you used STEM to address issues in your individual, family, and or community (please provide an example)?

Consideration:

In this chapter I chronicled the focal cohorts' shifts in STEM competency as well as their shifts in competency in their non-STEM, RAM course to speak to the ways in which their increases in STEM identity contributed to their demonstrated increases in competency vis-à-vis the courses offered at MAN UP. I worked to illuminate the potentially powerful connection between the intentional development of a positive STEM identity—as an applied STEM practitioner—to their confidence and demonstrated ability to excel in the STEM course content covered in MAN UP.

Questions for educators:

1. Are there ways that you have or are currently working towards creating an atmosphere predicated on socio-academic synergy in your classroom, after/out of school program, course, or in the student services you provide (please provide an example)?
2. How can you or do you support both critical contextualization and the critical contextualization of STEM (where applicable) in your current pedagogical practices?
3. How do you or can you carve out spaces for students to use their expertise, whether it be academic, cultural, linguistic, etc., to contribute to the overall knowledge construction and meaning making that takes place in the educational space/s that you are responsible for?
4. How do you (or will you) create equitable educational opportunities for your traditionally marginalized students, including Black males, to develop both their academic and STEM identities (where applicable)?
5. How do you (or will you) create equitable educational opportunities for your traditionally marginalized students, including Black males, to use the knowledge and competencies they gain in your class to create innovative ways for them to address societal issues that they deem worthy of redress?

Keywords:

Socio-academic synergy, competency, linguistic oppression, identity, rhetorical analysis, computer science, math

References

Freire, P., & Macedo, D. (1987). *Literacy: Reading the word & the world.* New York, NY: Continuum Publishing.

Mahiri, J., & Sims, J. J. (2016). Engineering equity: A critical pedagogical approach to language and curriculum change for African American males in STEM (55–70). Z. Babaci-Wilhite (ed.), In *Curriculum change in language and STEM subjects as a right in education.* Rotterdam: Sense Publishing.

Nasir, N. S. (2011). *Racialized identities: Race and achievement among Black youth.* Stanford, CA: Stanford University Press.

Rickford, J. R. (1998). The creole origins of African-American vernacular English: Evidence from copula absence. In S. S. Mufwene, J. R. Rickford, G. Bailey, & J. Baugh (Eds.), *African-American English: Structure, history, and use* (pp. 154–200). London: Routledge.

6

STEM for good

*Creating socio-academic synergy for
the development of socially just
applications of STEM*

For whatever reason, the lunch room at MAN UP seemed heavy. Granted, it was what was at that time a rare rainy day in the East Bay Area (because we had been mired in a year's long drought). But, the lunch room was dark. It felt humid and morose. This was aberrational, because whenever the MAN UP scholars entered this room—and every other room—they did so with a mix of boisterous and cacophonous aplomb. This day was different. Mr. K, Mr. S and I recognized the seeming melancholy right away. We had already spent between six months to two years with these dynamic young men; we could tell individually and collectively that something was in the air. So, we decided to forgo lesson plans and just talk. One young man, Malcolm, volunteered that he was struggling because his father, seemingly out of nowhere, decided to challenge his mother for custody. Malcolm told us that while he and his father were on good terms, he did not want to leave his mom. He also told us that he told the judge hearing his case that he did not want to miss MAN UP. (The issue at hand was bi-monthly weekend visitation.) We had incredible input from committed, caring MAN UP fathers; however, these men were the exception—not the rule. We decided to refocus. Instead of discussing STEM in any detail, we opted to have a discussion on fatherhood. MAN UP students, one-by-one, talked about what they think fatherhood should entail. We then asked them to "speak" to their fathers. Here is a poignant exchange that is indicative of the conversation that this impromptu activity encouraged:

Mr. J:	If you could talk to your father right now, what would you say?
	(Several students raise their hands.)
Mike:	I guess, I would say…um, thanks, dad, for always being there for me. That's what I would say. My dad is my best friend.
Talik:	(tears streaming down his face): Dad, where are you? We need you? My mom needs help. Daddy, I need you!
Anthony:	Why did you leave?
Darius:	Dad, where are you?
Sammy:	Dad, why did you leave us? What did I do?
Alex:	Who's going to teach me how to be a man—my mom?

Many of the questions were chocked full of emotion. Most of the responses spoke of absence and or loss. We know that there are systemic, systematic mechanism that have delimited and delegitimized the Black father from slavery until this very day. I am not including this section to further penalize, castigate, or pathologize Black fathers. Rather, I am using this example to illuminate the necessity of an educational space that is acutely attuned to the needs, concerns, dreams, issues, etc., of Black boys. Seemingly, towards the end of this conversation there was not a dry eye left. We, the MAN UP instructional team, cried; our students cried. Then, we formed a hug line. We gave hugs. We dapped. We acknowledged our students while simultaneously allowing them the space to acknowledge our loss and our pain. This moment, which lasted more than two hours, solidified the atmosphere at MAN UP. We were a brotherhood not simply because many of us had suffered loss, but because we confronted the loss by working together to address the individual and collective loss of our respective communities. We invited our students real-lives into our curriculum long before this event. However, this event was concrete evidence that our students felt appreciated, safe, and valued in our communal space. We were not merely interested in being our scholars' friends, though this was important to us. Rather, our goal was to create an educative atmosphere wherein our scholars, our traditionally marginalized, educationally maligned, low-income Black boys could feel loved, safe, and sufficiently challenged. We curated this educational atmosphere by endeavoring to strike a kind of socio-academic synergy.

Socio-academic synergy is a process in which students' real-life issues, concerns, joys, and respective socio-cultural and socio-historical ways of being are intentionally integrated into the curricular material of a given educative milieu such that their identities are part and parcel of the meaning making processes taking place in spaces of educative knowledge construction. The expressed goal of working towards an educational atmosphere predicated on socio-academic synergy is arriving at a synchronicity between students' real-lives, outside and inside of educational spaces, and the material covered in a given educational milieu. Socio-academic synergy paves the way for and invites students to increase in competency in canonical knowledge by working through issues that are important to them. When students are encouraged, empowered, and equipped to be their authentic selves—especially traditionally marginalized students—while wrestling with canonical knowledge apprehension and construction via a pedagogical lens that centers their lived experiences, the stage is set for them to begin critically contextualizing the disciplinary material covered in a given class.

Equity by design

The MAN UP instructional team worked collaboratively to design the courses and activities such that the students would not only be learning STEM, but also doing and applying STEM to equity and social justice issues that the cohort identified as important. To position students to do this kind of STEM-mediated social justice work, by applying STEM to societal inequity, the MAN UP instructional team knew that we needed to focus not just on curriculum or pedagogy, but also on the atmosphere that our curricular and pedagogical approaches would be housed within. We knew that we had to develop an authentic socio-educational atmosphere in concert with our critical-reality based pedagogical approach if we wanted to carve out a space for all MAN UP students to feel valued, appreciated, and loved. We soon found out that this kind of community building could not be limited, exclusively, to classroom interactions. One early example set the stage for the realization of socio-academic synergy at MAN UP.

The MAN UP instructional team along with four parent chaperones took 39 MAN UP scholars to a popular, interactive science academy in San Francisco. This science academy featured a multitude of interactional science exhibits. Seemingly, most everything at this science academy was manipulatable. As we arrived it became abundantly clear that all eyes were on us. Our group made up nearly the entire population of people of color at the academy on this day. No long after our arrival, I was met by a clearly agitated middle-aged White man. He walked toward me and angrily asked, in front of a dozen of more MAN UP scholars: "are you the leader of this group?" I acknowledged that I was. Before I could finish my sentence, he cut me off saying: "well, these boys (pointing to the increasing large group of MAN UP scholars forming behind me) are playing with this water fountain!" My response was short. I said, "Okay, and?" Now, this man was nearly irate.

Looking towards the MAN UP scholars present, he yelled: "the water fountain says do not play with it!" Seeking to ascertain the source of his angst, I then asked him if he worked for the science academy. He did not. He then asked me, confrontationally, what I was going to do about my students perceived misbehavior. I looked at my guys; they looked nervous. So, I took a step towards this man, further distancing him from the scholars and I told him that I planned to do nothing at all. I said: "everything in this place invites students to manipulate it—so why would the water fountain be any different? I'm fine with them playing with the water fountain. What I'm not fine with is you having any kind of conversation with my guys. If you have something to say—say it to me, and me only." I looked him in eyes to make sure that he fully understood me. At this point, he promptly turned and stormed off in a huff.

When I turned again to check on the scholars, I was greeted with several smiles and nods. Then, in unison, I was saluted with a chorus of: "Thanks, Mr. J!" I told them that while they were in my presence, they never had to wonder whether I would have their backs. I told them that while I expect a certain level of decorum, in moments like this I will always advocate for them and physically protect them, if necessary. We may have to have follow-up conversations about their behavior, but those discussions will only take place in our loving, nutritive environment—never in front an angry accuser. Many students identified this as a seminal moment in developing a feeling of belongingness within the MAN UP community. This incident was seminal for me, too, because it made me realize that true advocacy cannot not be limited to the classroom or the confines of our program.

Socio-academic synergy: Cultivating and curating an educationally nutritive atmosphere

The MAN UP critical-reality pedagogical approach was predicated on a phenomenon I termed socio-academic synergy: Socio-academic synergy is a synergistic relationship between students' lives outside of educational settings and the curricular goals, course content offered at MAN UP, and the pedagogical approach employed by MAN UP instructors. The goal was to curate a positive, educationally-nutritive, and empowering atmosphere, which the YPSS data suggests represents a very different educational atmosphere than the atmospheres represented by the schools that many the focal students attend. This approach is derived from and commensurate with culturally relevant pedagogy (CRP); however, there is a clear aim to not only make students comfortable in an accepted educational space, but also to encourage, empower, and equip them to use their agentive voices for positive societal change. CRP is an incredibly powerful educational paradigm, and I believe that it was further strengthened by working to shift MAN UP students' concerns beyond their own subjective levels of comfortability by positioning them as change agents able to extend their critical contextual understanding of their socio-political environment to issues that plague other hyper-marginalized people, too. So, this approach as an extension of CRP is not something implemented top down, from teachers to students'; instead it was co-constructed based on students lived experiences in and outside of the classroom. My presupposition was that for students to begin behaving as applied STEM practitioners, they had to be afforded a space where this identity was readily available and even encouraged. By most of these students' (and their families') admission, they schools that they were enrolled in did not feature this kind of nutritive atmosphere—at least not for them.

Several questions on the YPSS were geared to unearth students' experiences with this approach in differentiation from what they experienced at their respective schools. More specifically, students were asked to rate their experience with the purposefully cultivated MAN UP atmosphere vis-à-vis the atmospheres they encountered at their schools. The data collected was illuminating and provides valuable insight as to explanations regarding the focal cohorts' increases in STEM identity, STEM competency, and in their self-directed creation of socially just applications of STEM. To be clear, the goal if this survey was to devise new ways to improve MAN UP by working to address student-perceived holes in the educational atmosphere and concomitant experiences at their regular schools. My intention was not to sour them in any way to their home schools, which is why the YPSS was administered at the end of MAN UP, which was also the end of the focal cohorts' school year.

As evidenced by the YPSS, 16 out of the 17 focal students agreed that they were treated fairly by their MAN UP instructors versus only 6 of 17 of the focal cohort with regards to the instructors at their respective schools. This is particularly illuminating because it directly informs the next statistic: 16 of 17 members of the focal group agreed that the felt a sense of belonging at MAN UP as opposed to only 4 of the 17 members of the focal cohort agreeing that they felt a sense of belonging at their schools. Contiguously, 16 of 17 students agreed that they enjoyed attending MAN UP versus only 6 of 17 agreeing that they enjoyed attending their home schools. This is important because MAN UP meets on Saturdays, a time where these students could be involved in other (non-academic) activities; and, what is more 15 of the 17 members of the focal cohort agreed that MAN UP's curricular content was more challenging than what they were receiving in their schools. So, as evidenced by the data presented above, when taken together, what became clear is that these vibrant, busy young men would rather spend six hours, two Saturdays per month (for a total of 12 hours per month) in a program that, for most them, featured academic work that was more challenging that the work that they encountered at their schools. And, while this is cause for celebration for the MAN UP instructional team, this is also, simultaneously, an indictment of the experiences that they, urban Black males, are forced to encounter traversing the contested terrain built atop a white supremacist agenda—that many of their schools represented. Despite this oppressive reality, these students still thrived at MAN UP; in fact, 100 percent of the focal cohort agreed that MAN UP helped them develop confidence in learning and excelling in STEM as well as applying STEM to issues that are important to them. This newfound confidence helped the focal cohort become more self-efficacious and begin to see themselves as the powerful change agents, or in MAN UP vernacular, as the applied STEM practitioners that they truly are.

Doing for self: Positive shifts in self-efficacy

The focal cohort continually remarked that they felt the program had an impact on how they think of themselves. They described having "more confidence" and that the program helped them to "feel smarter, like I could do it." Malcolm stated that the program transformed how he sees his math abilities, saying, "I never thought I was good at math, but I think I did well here.... When I first came here, I kind of didn't know anything, and as the teachers worked with me, I found out that I was smarter than I actually thought I was." The entire focal cohort agreed that they felt that they found their voice because of participating in the program. For example, one student shared, "I learned not to be shy here, because it was an inclusive environment. The instructors encouraged inclusiveness, and people that don't normally participate at school participated here." As a result, 16 of 17 students' self-efficacy was positively impacted, with one student explaining, "This program made me feel, instead of just having ideas about things and not building them, like I can actually build them and get the right materials instead of just thinking it. Like one time I had an idea of building a robotic arm and now I feel like I could build it." Similarly, Jeff shared, "It [MAN UP] made me feel that high school and college will be easier since I know what to expect and what to do."

Furthermore, students repeatedly mentioned the development of increased pride. Malachi, a member of the focal cohort, commented that "We are raising expectations…since there aren't a lot of African-American males in STEM, and opportunities can open up because of what we are doing here" and Jeff remarked that the program helped him to "have pride in young African-American men and seeing what we can do." Lastly, as cogently explained by Thomas, "I have never been in an environment that is even close to MAN UP, where we learn to help ourselves and our community by using STEM as tools."

The MAN UP atmosphere was built around and predicated on the lived-experiences of urban, predominately low-income, middle school Black males. Data from the YPSS suggests that students recognized this approach and that this intentional focus resonated with them. For example: 15/17 of the focal class and agreed that MAN UP challenged them to think about the way that they think about their roles in society; 16/17 of the focal class and agreed that the can use their STEM knowledge to make their neighborhoods better; and, 15/17 of the focal class and agreed that the can use their STEM knowledge to make the world a better place. Additionally, 16/17 of the focal class and agreed that the instructors at MAN UP helped them see a connection between STEM and Social Justice; 16/17 of the focal class and agreed that the instructors at MAN UP helped them see a connection between STEM and Race; and, 15/17 of the focal class agreed that MAN UP helped them think about STEM differently. Perhaps the most telling statistic was this: all but one (16/17) of the focal cohort agreed that MAN UP instructors connected STEM to their (the students) lives; conversely, none of the members of the focal cohort felt that instructors at their schools connected STEM to their (the students') real life concerns.

Overall, the focal cohort reported high levels of satisfaction with the MAN UP program on the YPSS. Actually, of all three cohorts, the first-year MAN UP students reported being most satisfied with MAN UP: they repeatedly shared various experiences relating to what they enjoyed about the program. In addition to academic knowledge gained, they repeatedly described extensive satisfaction and growth because of being around same-race, same-gender peers and role models. Furthermore, students remarked that they felt they "benefited mentally seeing role models of my color skin" and that MAN UP is "a good thing for African-American boys." One student said he feels "less shy" because of the program, because he has "never been in an environment like this." Another young man stated, "It is a great way to spend my Saturdays and stay off the streets, because I bettered myself and my STEM skills." This was attributed to "getting together with kids my age and race to do work" and "getting help from teachers who inspired me and were my role models."

According to the YPSS students within the focal class looked up to the MAN UP instructors as mentors, with one young man stating, "I really didn't have a role model and now I have three [the MAN UP Instructional Team]." Another explained, "I never thought of African-American scientists and they [instructors] introduced me to some and I saw what we could do and it changed my perspective on my role models." This growth occurred throughout the school year, as described by, Maxwell another member of the focal cohort:

> Before I came here, I never thought of a Black male as a role model, because I am not super into sports so I wouldn't say Kobe Bryant or anything, but now it opened my eyes to all the good and important things Black males have done and it made me think about who my role models are.

What is more, MAN UP students even found themselves developing into role models for their peers; as one young man stated, "my friend now thinks of me as an inspiration" (Stevie, 1st year MAN UP student). This data suggests that students recognized that there was something different about the curricular foci and pedagogical approach, both of which congealed to form an atmosphere that hinged on socio-academic synergy. And, more importantly, students realized that they had the latitude, and were even encouraged to be successful in STEM without being forced to change who they were. This sentiment was best captured by a student's responses to the final focus group interview question: Do you think MAN UP was successful? Why or why not?: "I know MAN UP was a success. A lot of us felt like we were okay or even good in math. But, I don't think many of us thought we could *do* math until we joined this program." Another student followed: "I always felt respected here, I mean, I feel like my voice mattered. So, I think that that gave me a lot of confidence that I could really be an applied STEM practitioner. I mean that I *am* and applied STEM practitioner". Contiguously, another student remarked, "This was so different from school: 40 plus Black males doing math together. No one was telling us to sit down and be quiet, or just listen. We got to teach, too. I know this helped me become someone who can *do* STEM, not just learn it."

All this suggests that socio-academic synergy (SAS) is integral to student success. SAS is predicated on multi-cultural education. It is inclusive; and, it is also prescriptive. Again, the goal of MAN UP was to create a safe space where urban, African-American males were not required to check their culture at the door to be considered successful students. It was clear, for example, by his own and his as well as his father's admission that a student like Chisulo felt welcomed, protected, and loved in this space. As his earlier story demonstrated, this was not the case at the school that he spent the majority of his waking hours within. The MAN UP instructional team cultivated our educational space/s by focusing on three overarching components of the program: relationships, relevance, and rigor. In leading the charge for the design of this program, I was determined to create a program that was predicated on healthy, empowering, and educational relationships between the young men served and the MAN UP instructional team. Therefore, as I mentioned previously we were intentional about our curricular foci in that everything that we did needed to be in some way connected to the students' real life experiences. For example, when time for the assessments arose, we made sure that students knew doing well in these assessments was part of their civic duty. We made sure that they were aware that the work that they did on these assessments were directly affecting their neighborhoods in a positive way, because if we could make the argument that this program helps them improve scholastically, then, not only with this program persists, but the eventuality of other programs being created to serve more students like them becomes a strong reality as well. So, again, even in taking the assessments that the parent organization required as an auspice of the program's funder, the students were positioned as change agents with the potential to use STEM to better their local national and global communities. In this way, these assessments along with the MAN UP curriculum were made relevant while maintaining rigor. And, it was because of the relationships established with these young men that we could have a frank conversation regarding their role in contributing to the educational achievement of young men that will, potentially, follow in their footsteps. This conversation started on the first day of the program.

MAN UP was a rites of passage program in many respects; however, being fully aware of the (sometimes misinformed) critiques of many rites of passage programs that exist for African-American males, we were guided by the desire to provide the students with not only a relational and relevant experience, but also a rigorous academic experience as well. As stated in the previous section, 94 percent of the focal cohort agreed or strongly agreed that the work that they do in the MAN UP program is more difficult than the work that they receive at their home schools. But, unlike the home schools that many of the students attend, we did not simply give them curricular material in a way that is consistent with the banking model of education. Instead we asked them to take the curricular material from the RAM course, and their math course, and their CS course, and not only learn it but also to apply it to situations that they felt were important—situations that were relevant to them based on their lived experiences. We wanted to model critically contextualized curricular and pedagogical practices so that they would begin to critically contextualize their STEM learning, in return. What this looked like, practically, was groups of students working collaboratively in Socratic seminars, questioning, reckoning, reasoning and, ultimately proto-typing and designing solutions to the problems that they felt were most pressing. And for each session there were always student presentations in each group. Even the opening warm-up activity, which was always a complex math problem, was done collaboratively by the students; then, each group of students was afforded the opportunity to present along with their group on why it is they felt that they had arrived at the correct answer.

And, while there was an explicit emphasis on rigor, MAN UP, did not over-determine the importance of academic success. It was simply part and parcel of the holistic approach that MAN UP represented. Not only did we challenge the young men to "work together and work smart" using STEM for societal uplift, we also ate with these young men. We also brought our families to meet their families during MAN UP get-togethers. We built community with the young men served at MAN UP. This was the setting. In the three years that I guided the MAN UP program, even though we know the saddening statistics regarding Black male suspensions and expulsions from school and how these disciplinary actions correlate with fighting in particular (Freeman, 2013), I was never forced to remove a student for behavioral issues. What is more, there was never any-thing close to an altercation at MAN UP. MAN UP was a brotherhood; more than anything this word, brotherhood, accurately described the MAN UP atmo-sphere. Even though this program was predicated on complex theoretical terms like critical pedagogy and reality pedagogy and featured rigorous course material, these aspects congealed into a socio-academic synergy because the brotherhood community of MAN UP was nurtured, cared for, insisted upon and as a result it was strong. This was a brotherhood where the concerns, the joys, the successes, the challenges, the lived experiences of urban, African-American middle school males were what animated and impelled this program. All of this resulted in the fact that these young men were beginning to see themselves as applied STEM practitioners, ready, willing, and able to use their STEM knowledge to better their local, national, and global communities. This meant that their culture was no longer deficient—at least not in this space. Instead, their culture, their lives, their ways of being were re-positioned as valued assets. They began to realize that no one could speak to their unique perspectives like they could. This is captured by Jeff's pellucid response to the (YPSS) question: Why is it important for you to do STEM?:

It's important because I have a unique perspective as a 6th grade Black male. I'm tired of always having other people speak for me, for us. We need to tell our own story. And, we can't expect someone who is totally different—who has a different life to understand us and fix our problems. We can do it ourselves. We just have to work together and support each other and not tear each other down.

In math, this was realized through Mr. K connecting learning to larger societal inequities on one hand while centering it in the lived experiences of the students on the other. A key aspect of his pedagogical approach was to engage the students in critical dialogues about how math is crucial to engagements in personal and cultural group contexts beyond classwork in schools. Starting with simple examples like how frequent attempts have been made by unscrupulous merchants to short-change some Blacks based on assumptions that they might not be able to accurately count their change to the roles of math calculations for understanding the complexities of wealth accumulation as it is affected by things like credit scores, credit card debt, differential interest rates, taxes, stocks and bonds, and other kinds of math driven investment instruments.

Putting the tools to work: Examples of socially just applications of STEM

One of the many examples of Mr. K's focus on socially just applications of math was his unit on the role of fast food in health disparities suffered by Blacks. The guiding question for the unit was, "Is there a connection between poor health and poverty"? Students could choose any topic for which they felt they could use math to facilitate understanding and positive change. They decided to use statistical analysis to arrive at a list of healthy food alternatives for low-income people. They researched the number of calories, fats, saturated fats, proteins, sugar, and sodium in the foods that they normally ate because according to one student "we all eat, pretty much, the same junk." These projects culminated in PowerPoint presentations to the class, but they also hoped to share their findings at their respective schools as well as at community events so that they could in the words of one focal student, "educate their brothers and sisters how important diet is." Ultimately, the focal students saw their experiences learning math in the MAN UP program as "better and more challenging" because it was "math in real-life situations" that was "more hands on and more interaction than regular class and more active." Because this work resonated with them, they were engaged and committed. Their engagement, then, lent itself to positive shifts in their math competency—in this example—because they were doing work that was critically contextualized in that it was predicated on issues that were important to them as Black peoples.

Math final projects: During student work on their final projects, which was audio-video recorded or recorded, data on students' understanding of how to use STEM to address issues of social justice arose. I used field notes to collect data in the rare occurrences where A/V equipment was unavailable.

The final project in the math class required the focal class to create a crest or insignia using linear equations. This symbolic mathematical representation was intended to be emblematic of how the students saw themselves and how the wanted to present themselves to the outside world. During the presentation at the year-end event, the audience was wowed by students' ability to explain the process they undertook in creating the sophisticated insignias. Each grade-specific cohort completed a math specific final project. The focal class created a symbol of a large hammer or more accurately, a mallet destroying a large wall. When students asked why they created this symbol, Michael spoke for the group:

> We created a mallet because in this program we are creating symbols using math, I mean, if that doesn't smash stereotypes about us, I don't know what will. And, we like the mallet because rubber is malleable, it's flexible, not a steel hammer. That's important because we are flexible. There's not just one way to be an African-American male, to be Black. Sure, we can try to do sports or music or whatever. We can do anything we set our minds to. And, we can also do STEM. I think it's important that we know that all of us know that. That's why we choose this symbol to represent us.

Though, perhaps, unaware of the proper nomenclature, this student is speaking to the ways in which the focal class sees themselves not only destroying stereotypes, but also smashing the essentializing narratives that these insidious stereotypes are predicated and reliant on. And, the impetus of this group's project, consistent with McLuhan, Fiore, and Agel's (1967) argument that the medium is the message, created their presentation based on a very astute observation. In this case the medium, the use of linear equations to create a symbolic representation of these predominately low-income, urban, middle school Black males' strength, resiliency, and power—as the student above noted—was truly the message. This group understood the performative aspect of their work as evidenced by the first line of the above quote. So, then, the argument can be made that these students were alloying conceptual aspects of the RAM course, which dove deep into ideas of Black male representation, with both math and technology. Evidence of this kind of conceptual transference also came to the fore in the focal cohorts' conceptualization of the final project for their CS course.

In the Computer Science class, a critical pedagogy approach to engaging the cohort in mobile app development was taken throughout the school year. CS integrated technology and computer programming with political and societal issues to expand students' thinking on how technology can be leveraged to address the big problems of our day, and how contributions to community justice can be made through the design and creation of technology. Over the course of the school year, Mr. S noted that he saw a definite shift in students' perspectives about the roles and values of technology in contributing to social justice. Initially, his students felt that the extent of help they could provide to their communities was to devise ways for people to find resources or organizations that were able to help people in need. Over time, however, the focal students began to see themselves as the help. For Mr. S, this shift in the students—that is their becoming socially conscious, applied STEM practitioners—was one clear way that the critical-reality pedagogy approach was working.

One of several examples of this was in the focal class' extensive participation in the 8th grade class' design and construction of a mobile app to raise environmental awareness for middle and high school students. The app was designed and played as a football game wherein the running back gained yardage with each right answer selected regarding sustainability, global warming, and environmental awareness. When asked, in the yearend focus group interview, what he enjoyed about working through this project, Jeff shared: "I liked working on video game production, because I play video games, a lot. But, this time I'm not just consuming—I'm producing, or helping to produce a game that helps our environment." The RAM course discussed the dueling roles of consumer versus producers in detail. This is the same conceptual transference that became evident in the focal cohort's work on the math final project.

As noted earlier, my implementation of critical-reality pedagogy in the RAM class was key to how the students were facilitated to cognitively wrestle with the applications and ethics of STEM knowledge and skills in conjunction with their emerging STEM identities. By continuously tackling different notions of manhood that are deeply entrenched in our national ethos, the students were positioned to also critically question other axiomatic conceptions. They did this by working through the rhetorical triangle to identify logical, emotional, and ethical arguments that were being put forth. My undergraduate degree is in Rhetoric and I attempted to put it to good use by equipping MAN UP students with the rhetorical/analytical tools necessary so that they were empowered to consider and assess the myriad arguments they encounter on a day to day basis.

This approach began with the very first assignment in the RAM course in which the students searched Google Images for the word manhood and Black manhood. They, then, were told to select one of the first 15 images that popped up, with the lone proviso being these images could not have words. For each search result students were asked to deconstruct the implicit argument underlying their selected images using the rhetorical triangle as an analytical tool. Additionally, they were asked to lend a perspicacious eye to the notions of European maleness vis-à-vis Black maleness that were being promulgated. Eventually, they began applying this critical framing to their STEM courses. So, where STEM had initially been neutral and axiomatic, the students began to ask more critical questions by applying the tools of rhetorical analysis to their STEM learning. They wanted to know: STEM for what, and, STEM for whom?

The impact of his approach on student learning is partially captured in the final class project to create a Question Bridge like video documentary (noted earlier in this chapter) that would reveal the diverse views on young Black men on the positive possibilities and intricate dimensions of manhood. Guided the focal cohort on storyboarding the project by using design principles learned in the Mobile Applications course. Before filming their classmates, the students developed a critical focus for the project utilizing elements of the rhetorical triangle and the circle of critical praxis that were central to the RAM curriculum. Once they concretized the arguments that would undergird the documentary, they then developed questions to ask the students who would be featured the video.

This project exemplified several core components of the MAN UP program simultaneously. It reflected the utilization of digital technology in the production of video documentary in conjunction with developing the students' understanding of how to use STEM to achieve social justice goals. Importantly, there was substantial cross-fertilization of development of the focal students across all three courses such that they were reinforced through work in Math, CS, and their RAM course to increasingly see themselves as capable producers of positive social change. Essentially, they learned to see themselves as young men that could use STEM to make the world a better place. Or in MAN UP vernacular, they became applied STEM practitioners (i.e., shakers).

The final projects that provided the best vantage point to determine whether individual members of the focal cohort had made their way into the shakers profile. Shakers were shakers because not only did they understand that STEM was a tool for social justice—they also devised ways to use STEM for social justice. MAN UP's critical-reality pedagogical approach, which challenged students to not only think outside of the proverbial box but also to consider the box itself and how its existence and positioning either negatively affected or privileged certain groups, was instrumental to catalyzing these shifts. Over the course of this academic year, I found that students in the focal cohorts increased ability to apply STEM for social justice was proof that students had successfully critically contextualized STEM, because the critical contextualization of STEM is manifested when students who have appropriated STEM begin to use it for societal uplift, or, social justice. More precisely, students' ability to demonstrate socially just applications of STEM was predicated on their critical contextualization of STEM; and, what I found to be the case was this: the presence or absence of this ability was the best indicator as to where the focal students ended up on the takers, makers, and shakers continuum.

Based on this criterion, when alloyed with the data that highlighted shifts in student identification and determined by both group and individualized work on course work and final projects as well as individual and groups interviews and surveys, at the end of the academic year all but one student from the focal cohort fit within the shaker profile. This student was unwavering in his belief that STEM was his way out of poverty, and at no point in the semester, on any of the measures above, did he move past an individualized relationship to and with STEM. For example, on the post identification survey, in differentiation from all his cohort mates, when answering the question why is learning STEM is important, he did not use words like: community/family/culture/brothers/sisters/world/neighborhood, which are collective terms and were used by the focal cohort to describe their goals in applying STEM for social justice. This student, however, only used individualized terms like: I/my/myself/mine, in speaking to the importance of his learning STEM. His answer was as follows: "STEM is important because I can use it to get a good education and a good job so that I can buy whatever I want for myself and won't have to depend on anyone else. I'll be able to buy my own stuff, that'll be mine." And, while my survey data did not reflect a discernable shift towards a more equitable, socially just STEM orientation, this young man did show identifiable shifts in both his confidence and competence in the STEM material covered in MAN UP, which is a its core the pragmatic goal of this program.

Chapter 6 review: Considerations and questions

Consideration:

In this chapter discussed the ways in which the intentional atmosphere developed and curated at MAN UP facilitated and/or contributed to the focal cohorts' desire, willingness, and ability to apply their increased STEM knowledge for social justice as well as their self-directed applications of STEM for social justice. When

MAN UP students began using their STEM knowledge to make their neighbor-hoods, communities, and eve the world better it was clear that the critical contex-tualization of STEM was taking place. Our goal was never to merely teach MAN UP about STEM and critical thinking (metacognition); rather, our goal was to help them think about the ways that they think about STEM and their place in the world as fledgling STEM experts. We wanted to do this because the goal of MAN UP's curricular approach was to position students to think about the ways that they could apply their knowledge to real life issues that were important to them. We did not want them to simply "bank" information until it was time to make a cognitive withdrawal on some standardized test.

Questions for students:

1. This chapter is arguing for an educational atmosphere that invited the language, culture, concerns, pains, joys—the real lives—of Black males into the classroom: In what ways does this kind of atmosphere seem important to you?

2. In this section, I recounted a story where I defended a MAN UP scholars in front of someone who was, aggressively, accusing them of misbehav-ing. Has anyone advocated and or defended you from accusations from a teacher or administrator or even one of your peers? How did that make you feel?

3. Related to question number 1, have you ever been in a classroom setting where you felt like you were being valued for who you are and that you did not have to change anything to be viewed as a capable, intelligent student? Which of the students mentioned in this chapter do you most closely identify with (please explain)?

4. If you answered, yes, to question number 2: how did this make you feel? What was your reaction?

5. And, if you answered, yes, to question number 2, did this happen in a STEM specific class (if so, please provide an example)?

6. This chapter includes conversations form MAN UP students—which student quote resonates most with you?

Consideration:

In this chapter, I chronicled the steps that contributed to the atmosphere, predi-cated on socio-academic synergy, that MAN UP developed and curated and the effects that it had on the focal cohort based on their own accounts of its efficacy as well as what they demonstrated in their course specific yearend final projects. Additionally, this chapter also looked at the effects of synergizing atmosphere that worked diligently to include students' voices and their lived-realities into the curriculum as well as the overall ethos of this program. This chapter also speaks to the importance of centering critical-reality pedagogy in STEM and understanding the power of student agency via application, and why it is that a critical-reality based STEM pedagogical approach is a matter of social justice. I concluded this chapter by making the argument that the critical contextualization of STEM was in fact taking place and was evidenced by the focal cohorts' positive shifts in STEM identity, competency and in their socially just applications of STEM.

Questions for educators:

1. How do you or will you begin to enact critical-realty pedagogy in your teaching and instruction; what does this look like for you?
2. How do or will you create spaces for students to cultivate and hone their agentive voices?
3. How do or will you connect your course content to social justice?
4. How do or will you work towards creating opportunities for all of your students to critically contextualize STEM such that they are encouraged, empowered, and equipped to apply their STEM knowledge for social justice?
5. In what ways are you catalyzing a nutritive educational atmosphere that works to ensure socio-academic synergy between students' real lives and the course content (please provide an example/s).
6. In this section, I recounted a story where I defended a group of MAN UP scholars in front of someone who was, aggressively, accusing them of misbehaving. Have you ever been in a position to advocate for and or defend a student from accusations from a fellow teacher or administrator? How did you respond? In retrospect, is there anything that you would have done differently?

Keywords:

Equity, self-efficacy, socio-academic synergy, critical contextualization, socially just applications of STEM

References

Freeman, A. (2013). *8 Disturbing truths about suspensions in America*. Retrieved from http://www.takepart.com/photos/8-disturbing-truths-school-suspensions-america/school-suspension-rate-dilemma.

McLuhan, M., Fiore, Q., & Agel, J. (1967). *The medium is the massage*. New York, NY: Bantam Books.

Love conquers fear

The efficacy of critical-reality pedagogy at MAN UP

To discuss and further amplify these findings, this chapter will assess the pedagogical atmosphere that characterized this program and how it created a nutritive educational space that afforded the focal participants the opportunity to become applied STEM practitioners by critically contextualizing STEM. In researching programs that were STEM focused that also served middle school Black males, the first noteworthy finding was that in area that MAN UP was housed, which has one of the highest absolute numbers of Black males on the West Coast in the feeder school district, there were no other programs exclusively for this group that were in anyway STEM based even though the hub for technological advancement, Silicon Valley, is not all that far away. There were, however, several programs for Black males that work to connect them to their history through the arts. So, from the onset this program was different. What made it even more innovative and, perhaps, even more rigorous was its focus on issues that inhere around social justice. There were programs in the general vicinity of MAN UP that focused on social or restorative justice; however, not one of these programs sought to develop an intersection between STEM and social justice. Another aspect of MAN UP that made it innovative was the pedagogical approach, which centered critical-reality pedagogy. This approach was necessary to facilitate the focal cohort's (demonstrated) growth in their social political understanding of their lived contexts. We were convinced that they could, eventually, extend their understanding of social justice and equity such that they began to envisage ways to use their STEM knowledge to address and redress issues that affected them as well as other marginalized groups—which is demonstrative of the critical contextualization of STEM. Critical contextualization of STEM is not just attitudinal or aspirational, however: it should result in measurable shifts in STEM competency as well. And in this study, the data suggests that it did.

Paradigm shifting approach to STEM education

To be clear, deciding to take a critical-reality pedagogical approach to learning, identity, and skill development of Black middle school students was viewed as somewhat radical by the host organization of the MAN UP project. However, the MAN UP instructional team was convinced that connecting STEM learning to social justice would be crucial to the effectiveness and success of the program, and I believe this is reflected in the findings reported. I, along with the MAN UP instructional team, was also clear on the possibilities of our approach to STEM learning from the work of scholars like Moses and Cobb (2001) with the Algebra Project, Gutstein's (2005) work on mathematical literacy as a critical literacy for increasing equity in society, and Blikstein's (2008) work on the use of science and digital technology as necessary tools for fulfilling Freire's vision of humanization and societal transformation. This work argues, and I think the MAN UP program demonstrates, that mere access to STEM subjects and careers is not enough. Instead, critiques of the roles of STEM in the processes of oppression must accompany considerations of the potential for STEM to be used to mitigate oppression as part of the process for opening wider access to STEM as a civil and human right.

Throughout this program, the MAN UP instructional team was careful not to push students into thinking that they needed to be future STEM professionals to be successful. Instead, students were encouraged to ask critical questions as to why STEM education is important in the first place and what is it about STEM education that has prompted all of the attention about racial and demographic differences in outcomes? Rather than encouraging them to simply identify with STEM majors and careers, students were invited to ask critical, epistemological questions about the roles of STEM in larger societal processes and problems. Instead of passively receiving or absorbing STEM knowledge, they were empowered, encouraged, and equipped to relate whatever knowledge they received to their daily lives and the lives of other marginalized people. In so doing, our hope was that they would be able to flip the script and co-construct along with their instructors new possibilities for STEM and for themselves.

Data from the preceding two chapters, when taken together, seem to point to a synergistic relationship between the atmosphere and pedagogical approach featured at MAN UP and the real-life concerns of the young men in this program. As I mentioned earlier on: this is not happenstance. The impetus of this program was to create a STEM enrichment program that was, simultaneously, a safe space for urban, Black males to not only maintain their identities as such, but also to further develop their identities as applied STEM practitioners—fully capable of learning and doing STEM for their individual benefit as well as the overall benefit of their local, national and global community. However, this philosophical positioning was not enough for the funders. And, quite frankly, this goal was not enough for the MAN UP educational team either. Urban Black males, even at the middle school level, face deeply entrenched, structural bulwarks of white supremacy that delimit their access to the type of quality education that leads to material upward mobility. However, often this reality is obfuscated with rhetoric that is based on deficit model thinking, and/or oppositional culture (Fordham & Ogbu, 1986), whereupon these young men, these children are, essentially, blamed for increasing the achievement gap—even to their own educational detriment. Or their parents, who have had to endure the same inequity are made to be completely culpable for raising their children within a so-called culture of poverty. Thus, we were committed to creating a program that at least in some small measure began to chip away at this inequity. This, of course was a tall task. However, I am encouraged by the focal cohorts' near unanimous positive shifts in STEM identity, which led to their personal and collective instantiations as applied STEM practitioners as evidenced by 16 of 17 students fitting within the shaker criterion by the end of the academic year.

These young men have the potential to not only do well scholastically, they also have the potential to advocate for themselves and other hyper-marginalized students like them because their critical consciousness around STEM was raised as evidence by their emerging critical contextualization of STEM. So, then, not only did 16 of 17 members of the focal cohort experience gains in STEM competency, they also grew in their demonstrated ability to apply their STEM knowledge in the amelioration of social inequity and injustice; or, more specifically—to envision themselves as and behave as applied STEM practitioners (or shakers in MAN UP parlance).

Why the critical contextualization of STEM mattered

At the end of the academic year, as evidenced by the data collected and analyzed throughout this study, 16 of the 17 members of the focal cohort aligned most closely to the shakers student profile (which is analogous to the role of an applied STEM practitioner), precisely because they demonstrated not only the ability but also the willingness to use STEM for societal uplift in the interest of social justice. These 16 students' ability and willingness to use STEM for social justice was contingent upon both an increase in their STEM identities, as applied STEM practitioners and in their ability to devise socially just applications of STEM, which spoke to their increases in STEM competency, respectively. And, what is more, all 16 of the students who ended the year as shakers also improved in that math-specific and CS concept inventories, respectively, which further strengthens the proposed corollary between the critical contextualization of STEM and increases in STEM competency. This is important because it suggests that there is a positive relationship between these students' feelings of belongingness, in that, in contradistinction to ubiquitous, negative stereotypes of Black male failure in school and in STEM specifically, they succeeded in STEM when working with a group of peers who were also excelling in STEM and who were deeply invested in devising ways to critically apply STEM for social justice. According to the YPSS, 16 out of 17 members of the focal cohort agreed or strongly agreed that they felt more comfortable at MAN UP than they did at their schools. And, the same number of students agreed or strongly agreed that they felt "smarter" after their first year attending MAN UP, versus only 3 of the 17 agreeing that they felt "smarter" because of their previous year spent in their regular schools.

To be clear, it was never my goal to sour MAN UP students to their regular schools; instead, my goal in designing questions that juxtaposed MAN UP with students' regular schools was so that I could design future iterations of MAN UP so that they would continue to fill in some of the atmospheric gaps that students experienced at their schools. Thus, it was important to know whether students felt empowered, equipped, and encouraged at MAN UP vis-à-vis their regular schools.

Time to switch it up: Focus on relationship building

The MAN UP instructional team was intentional in our goal to create and curate a positive academically rich atmosphere for MAN UP students, because as a team, we were convinced that relationships were king, so to speak. We adhered to the old educational adage: "kids don't care about what you know until they know that you care." More precisely: we did not want the Black males that we served to feel as though they had to check their identities as urban, Black males at the proverbial door of the classroom. We needed them to know that they could be exactly who they were and still be successful academically without sacrificing their ways of being or language or cultural affinities by donning a "white mask" (Fanon, 1968). Thus, we encouraged students to think about what it meant to be applied STEM practitioners, because inherent in this term was the thought that applied STEM practitioners are, in fact, change agents. We referred to them as applied STEM practitioners because this recursive linguistic shift over more common terms like student/s, for example or even simply STEM practitioners, fully captured the essence of the work they were being asked to do. These young men were being asked to learn STEM, but not learn STEM in the way that there were most accustomed—via the banking or absorption model. Rather we were asking these young men to learn STEM while doing STEM, that is, while wielding STEM as a tool for social justice. There is a direct analog between the appellations applied STEM practitioner and shaker; however, the focal cohort was never made aware of this terminology (i.e., shaker, maker, taker)—they were, nevertheless, routinely referred to as applied mathematicians and/or applied STEM practitioners.

Real talk: Focusing on students' real lives in and out of school

Also, this pedagogical approach, unabashedly, sought to situate STEM learning vis-à-vis the subjective experiences, concerns, affinities, interest, etc., of urban, middle school African-American males. This is what Emdin (2010) referred as cosmopolitanism (Hull, 2003), that is, the purposeful integration of students' environments into a given educational space. This philosophical and spatial (re) positioning is derived from multicultural educational approaches. The MAN UP pedagogical approach built on this framework. However, instead of simply integrating the students' lives into educational spaces while still covering decontextualized course content, we made every effort to use student experiences as the starting point for the curricular material; and, we invited students to do the same. For example, the first question we posed to MAN UP students was why a program like this needed to exist; and in doing so, we invited students to begin making connections between race and STEM opportunity, access, and achievement. The year-end MAN UP survey asked students to juxtapose the atmosphere at MAN UP with the atmosphere at their respective schools. This was an attempt to determine whether the atmosphere at MAN UP, which encouraged students to maintain their identities, even though their identities are considered non-normative or even worse, are systemically pathologized, was markedly different from what they experienced at their respective schools. The importance of this atmosphere is best captured by an emotive conversation I had with Michael, a first year, sixth grade MAN UP student.

Mr. J:	Michael, you are a little loud, bro—take it down a few notches, please.
Michael:	Okay, Mr. J. My bad.
	(Moments later I noticed Michael yelling in excitement.)
Mr. J:	Michael, come here [Michael walks to Mr. J]. Did you notice what happened with that group when you walked over here?
Michael:	No.
Mr. J:	You notice they're much quieter now, right?
Michael:	Yes, Mr. J. Sorry.
	(Michael beginning to walk away, but now he looks dejected. So, I call him back.)
Mr. J:	Mike, are you okay? You look down. (Michael is looking down, at the floor.) Bro, I'm not trying to single you out to make you feel bad. I know that lunchtime is your time to catch up with your friends. I'm just asking that you do it a little quieter.
Michael:	I get it, Mr. J. It's just that everywhere I am, especially at school, people are always telling me to sit down and be quiet. I never felt that here; here I feel like I can be me. I mean, I feel like my voice counts.
Mr. J:	You're right, Mike. I apologize for not really hearing you. So, what should we do now? Your voice counts. How can we move forward? Because outside of this space, like at school for example, raising your voice that much will probably get you in trouble, right?
Mike:	Yeah. That's why I'm quiet at school. I guess I can be quieter here, too, if it makes you feel better.
Mr. J:	You're fine, bro. Just enjoy your lunch.
Mike:	Thanks, Mr. J; I'm glad that we can talk about stuff like this. At school, I just get detention, or, they'll say they're going to call my mom—which is way worse than detention!

This conversation was quite revealing, and I must admit quite convicting. Here I, along with the MAN UP instructional team, had worked to curate an atmosphere where students felt as though their voices counted, and as perspicaciously noted by Michael, I was trying to regulate his personhood by diminishing his voice. Of course, classroom decorum is important, but this conversation happened at lunchtime, where all cohorts along with the instructional staff eat together. We often held lunchtime whole group conversations, but this was not such an occasion (lunches were always provided by MAN UP). This conversation spoke to the importance of MAN UP as a safe space for the students served. At MAN UP, Michael felt welcomed, respected and appreciated—he felt as though his true voice was being heard, perhaps for the first time in an educational setting.

In fact, these four words: respected, appreciated, welcomed, and heard, occurred most frequently when students described their impression of MAN UP during the yearend focus group interview. This pedagogical approach was innovative and it was vitally important because it led to the realization of socio-academic synergy, which was manifested in an educational atmosphere that valued these students for who they were. We were also challenging them to excel academically in STEM so that they could benefit, individually, while making the world more socially just (i.e., becoming a shaker), which, again, is the goal and realization of the critical contextualization of STEM. This was possible because as evidenced from the exchange above I, just like my fellow MAN UP instructors, Mr. S and Mr. K, was willing to listen and even humble ourselves in order to really hear our students.

Chapter 7 review: Considerations and questions

Consideration:

In this chapter, I discussed the ways in which the intentional atmosphere developed and curated at MAN UP facilitated and/or contributed to the focal cohorts' desire, willingness, and ability to apply their increased STEM knowledge for social justice as well as their self-directed applications of STEM for social justice. When MAN UP students began using their STEM knowledge to make their neighborhoods, communities, and even the world better, it was clear that the critical contextualization of STEM was taking place. Our goal was never to merely teach MAN UP about STEM and critical thinking (metacognition); rather, our goal was to help them think about the ways that they think about STEM and their place in the world as fledgling STEM experts. We wanted to do this because the goal of MAN UP's curricular approach was to position students to think about the ways that they could apply their knowledge to real life issues that were important to them. We did not want them to simply "bank" information until it was time to make a cognitive withdrawal on some standardized test.

Questions for students:

1. This chapter is arguing for an educational atmosphere that invites the language, culture, concerns, pains, joys—the real lives—of Black males into the classroom: Does this kind of atmosphere seem important to you?
2. Related to question number 1, have you ever been in a classroom setting where you felt like you were being valued for who you are and that you did not have to change anything to be viewed as a capable, intelligent

student? Which of the students mentioned in this chapter do you most closely identify with (please explain)?

3. If you answered, yes, to question number 2: how did this make you feel? What was your reaction?

4. And, if you answered, yes, to question number 2, did this happen in a STEM specific class (if so, please provide an example)?

5. This chapter includes conversations form MAN UP students—which student quote resonates most with you?

Consideration:

In this chapter, I chronicled the steps that contributed to the atmosphere, predicated on socio-academic synergy, that MAN UP developed and curated and the effects that it had on the focal cohort based on their own accounts of its efficacy as well as what they demonstrated in their course specific yearend final projects. Additionally, this chapter also looked at the effects of synergizing atmosphere that worked diligently to include students' voices and their lived-realities into the curriculum as well as the overall ethos of this program. This chapter also speaks to the importance of centering critical-reality pedagogy in STEM and understanding the power of student agency via application, and why it is that a critical-reality based STEM pedagogical approach is a matter of social justice. I concluded this chapter by making the argument that the critical contextualization of STEM was in fact taking place and was evidenced by the focal cohorts' positive shifts in STEM identity, competency and in their socially just applications of STEM.

Questions for educators:

1. In what ways are you catalyzing a nutritive educational atmosphere that works to ensure socio-academic synergy between students' real lives and the course content (please provide an example/s).

2. How do you or will you begin to enact critical-realty pedagogy in your teaching and instruction; what does this look like for you?

3. How do or will you create spaces for students to cultivate and hone their agentive voices?

4. How do or will you connect your course content to social justice?

5. How do or will you works towards creating opportunities for all of your students to critically contextualize STEM such that they are encouraged, empowered, and equipped to apply their STEM knowledge for social justice?

Keywords:

Critical contextualization of STEM, efficacy, relationships, relevance, rigor; paradigm shift

References

Blikstein, P. (2008). Travels in Troy with Freire: Technology as an agent of emancipation. In P. Noguera & C. A. Torres (Eds.), *Social justice education for teachers: Paulo Freire and the possible dream* (pp. 205–244). Rotterdam, The Netherlands: Sense.

Emdin, C. (2010). *Urban science education for the hip-hop generation: Essential tools for the urban science educator and researcher.* Ithaca, NY: Columbia University Press.

Fanon, F. (1968). *Black skin, white masks.* New York, NY: Grove Press.

Fordham, S., & Ogbu, J. U. (1986). Black students' school success: Coping with the "burden of 'acting white'." *The Urban Review, 18*(3), 176–206. doi:10.1007/BF01112192

Gutstein, E. (2005). *Reading and writing the world with mathematics: Toward a pedagogy for social justice (Critical social thought).* New York, NY: Routledge.

Hull, G. (2003). Youth culture and digital media: New literacies for new times. *Research in the Teaching of English, 38*(2), 229–233.

Moses, R. P., & Cobb, C. E. (2001). *Radical equations: Civil rights from Mississippi to the algebra project.* Boston, MA: Beacon Press.

It takes a village

Highlighting the indispensability and strength of the three-fold cord

Our goal at the MAN UP program was to create a reciprocal caring community by constructing a three-fold cord consisting of the students, their parents/guardians, and us, the MAN UP instructional staff. Parental involvement is important for all students; and, this is especially true for hyper-marginalized Black boys that are often tasked with navigating educational spaces that think less of their ability, aptitude, and perceived intelligence (Mahiri & Sims, 2016; Vakil, 2014). What is more, a disproportionate number of Black children live in households that are both low-income and single-parent. These households also feature caretakers with lower than average levels of educational attainment who are disproportionately unemployed as a result. These realities delimit Black parents' ability to advocate for their students. Not because they are incapable of doing so, but, because often the schools that their children attend are not as attentive to their needs and in some cases the schools are resistant to and hostile towards the advocacy of Black parents—especially poor, "uneducated" Black parents (Noguera, 2008). According to Johnson (2010), many Black parents have been made to feel as though they are not equipped to effectively advocate for their students because of the condescending treatment they receive from school officials. And, for single parents there is a confluence of limitations for effective advocacy: they may feel dismissed and because they are the sole breadwinners in their families, often, they simply do not have the time to tackle the intentionally obtuse bureaucracy of their child's school and or school district. According to Dauber and Epstein (1993), because of this constellation of unfortunate circumstances, Black parental involvement, traditionally, does not rely on direct school contact.

This is important because accord to Jeynes (2010) and others, parental involvement is perhaps the most powerful predictor of a child's academic success. Obviously, advocacy is not limited to direct school contact. Advocacy can and should be a demonstrated belief, manifested as high expectations, in a child's ability to excel academically. According to Jeynes, this is especially important for Black children because Black children, starting early on in their educational journeys, are bombarded by racist, discriminatory stereotypes—passed off as axioms—about their perceived, innate academic ability. Jeynes argues that high expectations from parents can disrupt, for children, the internalization of negative academic stereotypes (2010).

What's love got to do with it: Two contrasting tales of parental advocacy Justin and Judah

I witnessed this "dance" play out for many of the parents of our MAN UP scholars. One situation in particular really struck me because the resolution this situation was drastically different than the resolution of a situation that we faced with our firstborn son, Judah. Justin is an incredibly bright, boisterous young man. He is a natural leader, whether he ever wanted to be one. He has a magnetic personality because of his wit, and he was armed with a 50,000 watt smile to boot. According to his mom, Carroll, Justin was struggling in school. Carroll was a hardworking single mother. She had what she described as a decent job, but had mentioned to me that she was thinking about going to school to earn a (college) degree. Justin's father had been in and out of jail for much of Justin's life. Justin was Carroll's only child. His math teacher called to warn her that if Justin did not quickly right the ship, he was doomed to fail. This was news to us at MAN UP because Justin, while sometimes rambunctious, seemed genuinely engaged and even excelled in math. I confirmed my suspicions with Mr. K, the MAN UP math instructor. Mr. K agreed. The following week we met with Carroll.

Mr. K: Justin sometimes takes a little while to settle down, just like many of our guys. But, he's one of the stronger students. Actually, he functions as a kind of TA [teacher's assistant] when others need help. He gets the material, and, this material is a year ahead. We met with Carroll and told her about Justin's performance at MAN UP.

Carroll:	See, I'm surprised: his teacher made it seem like he was struggling because the material was over his head, like he couldn't get it. (Carroll hands Mr. K one of Justin's recently graded exams.)
Mr. K:	We've already covered this stuff. Last semester. Judging by this, if anything, Justin is probably bored out of his mind in this class.
Mr. J:	We're happy to reach out to his math teacher if you think it'll help. We can try to tailor Justin's work to address the needs his teacher feels he has while also helping the teacher get a better understanding of Justin's ability.
Carroll:	Thank you for offering that. I told Justin that you two would be willing to do something like that, but he said that he didn't want that because it might make it worse for him in class.
Mr. K:	Like Jeremiah said, if we can help in anyway let us know. I can tell you that he gets the concepts. I hate to say it, but it may be his teacher.
Carroll:	I have a meeting with the Assistant Principal (AP) next week. I'll let you know how it goes.

Following her meeting with the Justin's AP, Carroll told us that she was told that nothing could be done. She said that the meeting was only 15 minutes long. She said, "I never really got to say all the positive stuff you guys told me; it seemed like he wasn't interested in what I had to say." Clearly, Carroll, like many low-income, non-college educated Black parents before her felt as though her voice was neither welcomed nor valued at her son's school. She ended this interview by saying, with an unmissable resignation in her voice:

It's always like this; I guess they just don't have time to meet with all of the parents that have issues—you know? I tried to meet with the principal. They always make me meet with the AP. He told me that he has the full support of the principal—so, there's really nothing else I can do if the principal already, like, gave power to the AP permission. I mean, if the principal is on board, what am I supposed to do? It's his school.

This outcome is very different than a situation that I felt compelled to address with my own son, Judah. Judah, like Justin, is extremely bright. Judah was speaking in full, coherent sentences by eight months old; he began reading at 15 months old. Judah, who is in the first grade, is an 11th grade level reader and he is already working through pre-algebraic math material. We were in position to send him to a private school for kindergarten. This private school was unable to meet his needs, even though he was one of only eight students in his class. And, while we received tuition assistance, this school was still quite expensive and far from where we reside. So, we decided to send him to or local elementary school instead because that way we could work closely with his school. Judah has a very different reality than in many ways. Like Justin, Judah has a Black father; however, unlike

Justin, Judah has two parents with advanced degrees in Education. Initially, we were hands off because we wanted Judah to acclimatize to his new environment absent our direct influence. It quickly became apparent that the work that Judah was required to do was too easy for him. He could complete four to five worksheets in under five minutes. There were many nights where he cried because he felt that the work he was being asked to do was so boring. Fearful that this stultifying work could dull Judah's love of learning, I decided to reach out to both his teacher and the school's principal. I was told that the rigor of his work would soon increase. And, to his school's credit, the rigor did increase albeit incrementally. It was still not enough, however.

Not long after my initial meeting with Judah's teacher and principal, I politely informed both Judah's teacher and principal that he would no longer do the work assigned by the school, but instead, I would create cognitively appropriate work for him (and any other student that would benefit from more rigorous work). Just like that, this situation was resolved. The difference in these two situations are glaring. Because of my training, I knew how to "play the game" in the interest of advocating for my son

I provide these two disparate accounts of parental advocacy to illuminate the dichotomous responses to Carroll and my own respective attempts to advocate, face-to-face, for our sons. I love my sons dearly—with everything that I am, in fact; and, I am convinced that the same is true for Carroll—she loves Justin with every fiber of her being. So, the question was never whether she had her son's best interests at heart. Rather, the question was and is whether the institution of K12 schooling, microcosmically represented by Justin's school, valued her input regarding the educational journey of her son. Clearly it did not. What is more, they may not have valued my voice all that much either, but I was intimately aware of how the school power structure works. For example, I know that the principal does not have final say; and, unlike Carroll, I knew whom to reach out to if the principal is unwilling to lend me a sympathetic ear. Carroll's struggle is true for most parents of color whose children attend under-resourced schools in low income communities (Noguera, 2008).

Therefore, the MAN UP program was designed to bring parental involvement to the forefront. We did not expect parents to simply and unproblematically support the work that we were attempting to do with their sons, grandsons, and nephews, which in my experience in K12 education is the underlying request when teachers lament the lack of parental support their students receive. This line of thinking is often offered as an explanation of the continued struggles of students of color. I have been brought into school spaces as a professional development consultant numerous times. There is an easily identifiable refrain when I ask teachers why some students struggle more than others in their classes that goes something like this: It is difficult for me to truly engage these students, whether it be Black boys or Black girls or Latinx students, because education is not valued at home. All the progress I achieve is undone by their parent's disdain for school. Nevertheless, at MAN UP, we decided to actively challenge what we felt to be an erroneous narrative regarding the level of parental commitment for parents of Black boys.

Setting the stage: Every year, after the selection of a subsequent cohort, we convened the parents/guardians of all three cohort, sans their MAN UP scholars. We spent three hours together to build community prior to our first session. During this time, I asked parents the following questions:

1. What do you bring to the MAN UP community that will be a resource for our scholars as well as the entire community?
2. What do you need us to do so that we can best work together in the interest of your scholar?
3. How would you plan to support all our scholars on a session by session basis?
4. Are there any activities that you would like to lead during the academic year?

These questions were discussed among the parents/guardians, then, they captured their thoughts on large PostIt papers, which were hung specifically for this meeting. The goal of this exercise was to invite parents to help us develop an environment that was supportive of their students and supportive of them, too. Many parents, in response to the first question, offered intangible yet altogether indispensable assets to the MAN UP community like love, patience, and a warm smile; other parents offered material wares like food, cookies, and hot chocolate. Still others offered professional connections. All of the parents present throughout the three years that I was at the helm of this program offered their real authentic selves to not only this discussion, but also this program writ large. Their input, knowledge, love, and patience were invaluable.

Returning to Johnson's (2010) work, which found that many Black parents felt as though they were ill-equipped to effectively advocate for their students because of the condescending treatment they receive from school officials, we know that this condescension while painful does not stop Black parents from advocating for their students altogether. It does, however, contribute to an unwillingness for some Black parents to seek out opportunities to interface with school officials in face-to-face situations. Just think back to Carroll's story above. Her story, while egregious, was indicative of her relationship with Justin's school as evidenced by what she said: "it's always like this; I guess they just don't have time to meet with all of the parents that have issues—you know…there's really nothing else I can do." Her unmistakable resignation is the direct result of the way that Justin's school interacts or does not interact with her. That Carroll felt summarily dismissed is a material manifestation of deficit model thinking on the part of Justin's school. This is precisely why it is of the utmost importance to involve and integrate parents into any program designed to reach Black boys (Jeynes, 2010). Black boys are under constant threat of stereotype threat (Steele, 2010) as well as corporeal threats of incarceration, which is akin to a psycho-social death, and/or actual, physical death (Alexander, 2010; Sharpe, 2016).

A commitment to becoming a more critical, emancipatory, social justice centered educator is wholly necessary, but, a psychological commitment is not enough: There must be action. To begin to address the myriad considerations necessary to provide safe spaces that also challenge, supportively, Black boys, we must enlist, accept, and welcome the input of the people that care for them most. Therefore, we worked diligently to form a tight, three-fold cord or braid between MAN UP Scholars, their parents, and the MAN UP instructional team afforded us an opportunity to realize socio-academic synergy. As evidenced by the data below, MAN UP parents were on board, and their input was integral to our overall success.

We elicited parental feedback on the overall efficacy of the program. Between 90 and 100 percent of all MAN UP parents (not just the focal cohort) agreed or strongly agreed with the following statements:

- The MAN UP Instructional team made me feel that my input was welcomed (100 percent).
- The MAN UP Instructional team made me feel like I was part of the team (100 percent).
- MAN UP staff did their best to accommodate my scholars' schedule (100 percent).
- MAN UP staff responded to my questions and/or concerns in a timely manner (92 percent).
- MAN UP offers activities that my child finds enriching and enjoyable (98 percent).
- My child has gained new skills and/or knowledge during the after-school program (94 percent).
- Staff treat us equally and respectfully (100 percent).
- I would recommend the MAN UP program to my friends and family (100 percent).

As evidenced by the data presented above, parents functioned as a part of the MAN UP Instructional Team and as a result their perceptions, supported by data on increased competency provide in the previous chapter, were that their scholars were engaged and learning. In addition to this, parents shared their thoughts on specific aspects of MAN UP as well as the overall efficacy of this program. The parental comments discussed below are important because they provide insight into what parents believe the needs of their students are. This context is important because sometimes, as educators, we think we know what students need because our graduate level course work has told us as much. The quote below suggests that both students and parents recognized that this was an inclusive atmosphere:

> My son and I like that he can be around other boys who have the same interest and positive role models such as the teachers. We both love the atmosphere at MAN UP; it was so supportive. We parents felt like we were wanted. Additionally, the program gives him a chance to be with exceptional role models and with a large group of intelligent young men of color. The opportunity to get together with positive African-American male role models—peers and instructors (Mother of 6th grade MAN UP Student).

U-N-I-T-Y: Working against racial isolation for our scholars

The above quote points to a recognition MAN UP's quest to arrive at socio-academic synergy. However, at the same time it speaks to issues that many of our MAN UP scholars had to face—racial isolation in their STEM courses. This quote speaks to the isolation that high-achieving Black boys sometimes experience. We had a wide range of achievement at MAN UP. Within that range we had scholars that routinely scored in the 99th percentile on standardized tests in math. Michael was one of these young men. He often lamented the fact that in all his classes he was the only Black male. Michael saw this as a problem. Not just because all his friends were "white and Asian", but because he felt that, perhaps, something else was going on:

> I know some of my Black friends that are just as good as me in math, but they're not in my class—I guess because they kind of get in trouble a lot for stuff that other people don't get in trouble for. It's kinda messed up. It's like the teachers just don't want them in the class, even though I think they can do the work.

Many of the parents' comments in the end-of-semester survey, yearend program satisfaction survey, in the yearend focus group, and in regular conversation highlighted just how important it was for parents and for their scholars for their sons, grandsons, and nephews to be amongst other young men of color, especially while working through STEM material. Because we worked with students and parents, we were able to begin developing and strengthening an atmosphere of collegiality and brotherhood. Both characteristics are indispensable in the pursuit of socio-academic synergy. And while we thought that we, the MAN UP instructional team, was providing ample opportunities for our scholar to build bonds of brotherhood, it turns out that the scholars wanted more opportunities to work together not simply in their own cohorts but also across cohorts. And, clearly, their parents wanted more opportunities for these kinds of interactions as well. However, this information did not come our way from students. Instead, we, based on parental feedback, determined that while the students largely enjoyed the curricula, they wanted more opportunities to simply be amongst their peers because for many of them, doing STEM alongside other Black boys was a rarity. The following quote provided on the End-of-The 1st Semester Parent Survey, is indicative of much of the feedback we received from parents regarding their scholars' desire to work in collaboration with other Black boys:

> My child and I equally enjoy the enrichment opportunity that this program has to offer. My son finds it highly enjoyable to work with so many young men who are equally interested in the same subjects in school. He attends this program, knowing that each session will afford him the chance to learn something new, in a way that he may have never thought of before. We are contentiously grateful for this opportunity. (Mother of 6th grade MAN UP Scholar)

Unlike the quote above from a first year MAN UP parent, the following quote is from a parent whose son had already been in MAN UP for two years, which means that the "novelty" of an educative atmosphere filled with Black males doing STEM had not simply worn off for her or for her son. Rather, that she still mentions the importance of both student and adult role models speaks to the unwavering necessity of these two programmatic characteristics:

> I believe my son loves just being around more young men his age. I love the fact that he is surrounded by young educated men of color and is being encouraged to travel the same path. He is in need of these role models. We like the program because it has positive male role models, teaches him about math and he has made new friend. (Mother of 8th grade MAN UP Scholar)

Because we asked for and received parental feedback, we were able to build in more opportunities for scholars to work together within and across cohorts. Parents/guardians also highlighted the importance of role models and how important role models were to the overall MAN UP atmosphere:

I love MAN UP because I appreciate the effort that is being given towards our male children of color in light of the obstacles they will face throughout their lives. I love that MAN UP is providing insight into the STEM career fields and constantly teaching them how to think and analyze situations. I love the positive environment, information and uplifting that is provided. My son loves it for the information he is receiving as well as looking up to and admiring his teachers as role models. (Mother of 7th grade MAN UP Scholar)

Another parent support this thought as well: "I love everything about the program. My son is in a single parent household and I am honored to have such excellent male role models for him. Best program ever (Mother of 6th grade MAN UP Scholar)!" Yet another parent highlighted what he identified as the familial atmosphere that MAN UP featured: "I love the family like support system that is provided to my son as well as opportunity to receive academic support and enrichment (Father of 8th Grade MAN UP Scholar)."

These quotes speak to the importance of working with the whole community in the interest of serving Black boys in STEM and in life. The parental feedback, as evidenced by the above-mentioned data, is, in my opinion, the direct result of the ways in which we invited, welcomed, and insisted on input from the parent community on the shape and form of the MAN UP program. Because we have been cemented as the antithesis for whiteness in this country, Black men and boys face obstacles that other groups do not. This is a sad, undeniable reality. To adequately address both the scholastic and human needs of the Black boys we serve, we must enlist the help of the community. There are two purportedly African proverbs that best encapsulate this tripartite approach to student success: "If you want to go fast, go alone; but if you want to go far, go together." And, perhaps the most famous of all, one that we recited on several occasions: "It takes a village to raise a child." At MAN UP, we enlisted our scholars' parents because we were convinced that the cooperation, wisdom, and experience of our entire MAN Up village was necessary to create an atmosphere predicated on socio-academic synergy that began to prepare our scholars for the road ahead.

Chapter 8 review: Considerations and questions

Consideration:

In this chapter, I discussed the necessity and benefit of integrating parents/guardians into both the construction and maintenance of the intentional atmosphere developed and curated at MAN UP. Again, a commitment to becoming a more critical, emancipatory, social justice centered educator is wholly necessary in this work. It is also wholly necessary to work alongside and in solidarity with students and parents. We cannot continue the trend of presupposing that we know exactly what our students need to feel safe and encouraged to being realizing their fullest possible potential. Instead, we have to create opportunities for students and parents/guardians, respectively, to help shape the educational atmosphere by listening to and addressing the issues, concerns, and needs of both the students and their primary advocates.

Questions for students:

1. Feeling confident in your ability to speak up and advocate for yourself as well as others should be part of every class you take in your educational journey. This is called "agency". However, often this is not the case for us. Please provide an example of a time in class where you exercised your agentive voice (i.e., your agency) to advocate for yourself or for one of your classmates? What caused you to speak up?

2. Related to question number 1, can you tell about a time when you were in a classroom setting where you felt like you were being valued for who you are and that you did not have to change anything to be viewed as a capable, intelligent student?

3. In what ways do you feel that your school values your input?

4. Give an example demonstrating how you feel that your school values your parent/guardians' input?

5. Taking your education seriously by exercising your agentive voice to insist on equitable educational opportunities and by doing everything in your power (e.g., committing to studying, speaking to teachers about grading criterion, etc.) is integral to academic success. This is what is referred to as self-efficacy. Knowing that advocating for yourself is important, how will you begin demonstrating self-efficacy?

Consideration:

Black boys (and men) have been positioned as the antithesis for whiteness in this country; and, as a result, for much of our history Black men and boys have been forced to overcome obstacles that other groups do not. This is a sad, undeniable reality. If this book is any indication, we must be willing to enlist the help of the community, not in a way that pathologizing to further marginalizes community member. But, in a way that works in solidarity in the interest of all the students we serve. More specifically, to adequately address both the scholastic and human needs of the Black boys we serve, we must eschew deficit model thinking regarding both our students and their families.

Questions for educators:

1. How do you (or will you) actively work against perceptions of Black deficiency in both students and families in your class and in your school site?
2. How do you create opportunities for both students and parents to contribute to the overall educational atmosphere featured in your class?
3. How can will you position parents as resources in a way that is neither perfunctory nor dismissive? That is, how will you provide opportunities for parents to provide input on the teaching and learning that is characteristic of your class?

Keywords:

Threefold cord, parental involvement, parental advocacy, Black parents, schools as a fortress, village, community

References

Alexander, M. (2010). *The new Jim Crow: Mass incarceration in the age of colorblindness.* New York, NY: The New Press.

Dauber, S. L., & Epstein, J. L. (1993). Parents' attitudes and practices of involvement in inner city elementary and middle schools. In N. F. Chavkin (Ed.), *Families and schools in a pluralistic society* (pp. 53–71). Albany, NY: SUNY Press.

Jeynes, W. (Ed.). (2010). *Family factors and the academic success of children.* New York, NY: Taylor & Francis/Routledge.

Johnson, L. (2010). Rethinking parental involvement: A critical review of literature. *Urban Education Research and Policy,* Annuals (3), 77–90.

Mahiri, J., & Sims, J. J. (2016). Engineering equity: A critical pedagogical approach to language and curriculum change for African American males in STEM (55–70). Z. Babaci-Wilhite (ed.), In Curriculum change in language and STEM subjects as a right in education. Rotterdam: Sense Publishing. Noguera, P. (2008). *The trouble with Black boys: And other reflections on race, equity, and the future of public education.* San Francisco, CA: Jossey-Bass.

Sharpe, C. (2016). *In the wake: On Blackness and being* (Kindle Edition). Durham, NC: Duke University Press.

Steele, C. (2010). *Whistling Vivaldi: And other clues to how stereotypes affect us.* New York, NY: W. W. Norton.

Vakil, S. (2014). A critical pedagogy approach of engaging urban youth in mobile app development in an after-school program. *Equity & Excellence in Education, 47*(1), 31–45.

The revolution will be digitized

In the third stanza of the 1970 poem, by Gil Scott Heron, *The Revolution will not be Televised,* Heron seems to be challenging the potential and even imminent co-optation of the civil-rights centered, cultural revolution that was taking place at the time of his writing. Clearly, Heron is also urging potential revolutionaries to resist becoming deluded by the endless inculcation that a televisual medium allows for. In simpler terms, the work of catalyzing a revolution in human rights, social justice, and equity necessitates on the ground work, in real life. The revolution will not come to fruition if the workers allow themselves to be seduced and inundated by the hegemonic imagery that mass media promulgates. Contrastively, Branch (1988) argues the obverse of Heron's point. Branch contends that the televisual medium was instrumental in helping Reverend, Dr. Martin Luther King, Jr., work towards the realization of his American dream: social justice and equality for all. Brach argues that television provided opportunities for people all around the world to see with their own eyes the atrocities that Black people in America were being terrorized by. Branch (1988) argues that Television created a viewpoint wherein the eyes of the world were forced to bear witness to police dogs savagely attacking Black children. These images led to worldwide outrage. This outrage helped to catalyze the civil rights revolution. In this book, I am calling for a paradigm-shifting revolution in the ways in which STEM pedagogy is conceptualized and, subsequently, delivered to hyper-marginalized students. STEM education must be connected to the real-life experiences, concerns, and joys of Black males (and other traditionally marginalized students). And, because of our fast-moving, technological economy coupled with an overdetermined National focus on scientific and technological innovation, STEM education must be central to this curricular and pedagogical revolution (McLaren, 2015).

The revolution will be digitized, riffs on Heron's famous poem, above. The definition of digitized is: to convert (pictures or sound) into a digital form that can be processed by a computer. While this book speaks, briefly, to some considerations around computer science education, CS is not the focus of this book. Rather, the concept of digitization is used a metonymically to represent STEM. The argument of this book is this: a revolution in STEM education, specifically STEM pedagogy, will create opportunities for Black boys, specifically, and other hyper-marginalized students generally, to use their knowledge—in this case their STEM knowledge—to reimagine their local, national, and global communities in ways that address their specific needs, issues, and concerns. This book is an attempt to provide both evidence of and precedence for a dramatic shift in STEM pedagogy, especially for Black males. This dramatic, paradigm-shift in STEM education, if it is to benefit Black boys, must invite the language, culture, and general ways of being into the learning spaces that they occupy throughout this country. MAN UP endeavored to create learning spaces that worked to benefit Black boys. And, as evidenced by the data covered in this book, we found some success. The focal cohorts' competency in the STEM subjects covered in MAN UP grew both individually and collectively as evinced by their improvement on the course concept inventories conjoined with the focal cohorts' feedback on the YPSS and the yearend final focus group. In fact, all but one student improved from pre to post on his math assessment and Computer Science assessment. Along with their growth in competency it was also evident from their own personal accounts that their confidence grew in not only learning STEM but also doing (or applying) STEM for social justice.

That said, MAN UP represented in many ways an ideal atmosphere for these young men to thrive. The MAN UP instructional team was, firstly, composed exclusively of men of color (two of which were low-income, urban Black males like the majority of the MAN UP students). And, the MAN UP instructional team because of the university connection of two of the instructors received (free) professional development and advising from Professor Jabari Mahiri, whose research focuses on urban education, on pedagogy as well as the overall structure of the program. And, what is more, the entire instructional team understood critical race theory, critical-reality pedagogy, and were attuned to and vitally interested in the plight of

Black males. This educative situation is rare in K-12 education because, 80 percent of teachers in the United States are European American (65 percent of teachers in the US are European American women). So, the question becomes: how can these experiences translate into academic success in STEM for urban, Black males who are for whatever reason unable to attend programs like MAN UP—where they meet, exclusively, with other Black male peers who share their excitement regarding STEM, and/or their commitment to using STEM to first improve their own communities before working to improve the entire world?

All power to the people: Cultivating student voice through critical-reality pedagogy

In our work at MAN UP, the pedagogical work was sutured to and even the byproduct of the socio-academic synergy that we worked diligently to ensure. By creating an atmosphere, predicated on socio-academic synergy, where hyper-marginalized Black males did not have to check their variegated cultures at the door of the classroom, we were able to build relationships that gave us insight into their interests, concerns, and aspirations so that we could co-develop rigorous STEM course material with them and for them. This is a crucial point and may be the most pivotal part of the success that this program enjoyed: we co-constructed not only meaning within the courses offered to MAN UP students—we also co-constructed our curricular scope and considerations based on the interest of the students being served. I cannot stress this enough: because of our "frontend" work to cultivate an educative atmosphere that invited students to co-develop both the curricular considerations and course material, student buy-in was not hard to obtain, which meant that engagement was high and behavioral issues were almost non-existent. This socio-academic synergy worked because we saw the work of connecting what we termed the Three R's: relationships, relevance, and rigor as indispensable to these students' scholastic success and to the strengthening of their agentive voices.

However, often times educators are lead to believe that they are some type of messianic figure whose commission is to rescue hyper-marginalized students from their immediate environments, which are admittedly, far too often, sites that are potentially deleterious. However, we must bear in mind that for these students, there is also beauty—even if our eyes are not attuned to see the radiance that they see. Emdin (2016) talked about giving youth cameras in the projects in New York: his expectation was that they would come back with pictures and video of old, dilapidated buildings and weathered, oxidized windows. This would have suited his needs nicely, as he hoped to talk to them about weather processes and pollution and the like. Instead, Emdin (2016) noted that these students came back with pictures of rainbows in the projects that they lived in and pictures of familial tenderness, e.g., big brothers walking their younger sisters to school. My point is this: we educators cannot unproblematically foist our sensibilities and/or our worldviews on the students we serve. We need to make our sensibilities jive with theirs' if we truly hope to reach them; this positionality will allow us to hear our students' voices. It is important to note that that these students do not need us to help them find their voices, which is a romanticized narrative that pervades rhetoric around teaching and learning in urban communities: they have incredibly powerful, transformative voices. They merely need someone who is willing to listen to and value what it is that they say. This study suggests that focusing on cultivating an educational atmosphere predicated on socio-academic synergy is integral to providing a space for hyper-marginalized students to not only increase their competence in STEM, but also to both recognize and apply the power that they have to use STEM for the amelioration of inequitable societal realities (i.e., for social justice). At the same time, we have to maintain high expectations for Black boys both academically, in general, and in SYEM, specifically.

Expect the unexpected: The importance of high standards for Black boys

According to Encyclopedia of Educational Research 1992, "Teachers who produce the greatest learning gains, accept responsibility for teaching their students. They believe that students are capable of learning and that they (the teachers) can teach them" (1992, p. 45). This is vitally important. Educators must expect that all of their students can succeed. A major factor contributing to low self-image of many Black youth is the institutional racism found in schools and society. Institutionalized racism is systemic and systematic and thus can be subtle yet pervasive. Furthermore, according to Darling-Hammond (2010), institutional racism creates situations in which Black students are enrolled in less challenging educational programs. Moreover, lowered educational expectations create psychosocially unsafe environments where Black boys receive the message that they cannot succeed. I would argue that few educators are intentionally sending Black students a "message that they cannot succeed"; however, I do believe that many educators, perhaps unwittingly, often send black students the "message" that they are not *expected* to succeed. This is institutionalized racism. This racism promotes a low self-image in marginalized youth, which then creates a psyche where high expectations are unrealistic. According to Knowles and Prewitt (1969), "The possible consequences of low self-image…can be a fear of failure and rejection of success" (p. 43). They go on to say, "…when these kinds of practices are embedded in school systems, schools can act to perpetuate the class differences and racial discrimination that are prevalent in society at large" (p. 43). Institutionalized racism in schools is sometimes hard to identify because it informs the normalized practices or culture of a given school. It does not only inform students' behavior in the face of it; it also contorts and perverts teacher behavior as well as other organizational norms so that they are commensurate with white supremacy, which serves only to lower Black students' individual and collective self-image.

These behaviors and norms are made manifest in curricula construction and pedagogical approaches that are incongruous with a Black student's cultural preferences. These norms also normalize the salience of White culture with simultaneously denigrating Black culture. This perverse negation of Black culture takes many forms; often it is reflected by absence of materials which include Black content and role models and stereotyping and the resulting low or negative teacher expectations (http://www.maec.org/achieve/2.html). At MAN UP, alongside our students, we openly challenged the negation of Blackness in STEM by encouraging, empowering, and equipping our scholars to question, deconstruct, and reimagine who can create and what should count as normative knowledge. Therefore, if we truly want to make a difference in the lives of Black boys, we must be the ones that expect greatness from them precisely because we plan to support them in their pursuit of their ontological vocation (Freire, 1997): the realization of their full humanity made manifest by their realization of their full human potential. If this is our goal, of we want to keep it 100, so to speak, we have to fight in solidarity with our students against the many instantiations of educational inequity that they are confronted by and with.

So, the goal must be to create educational spaces for hyper-marginalized students to be who they are—to not have to check their culture at the doors of their classrooms—and still be treated as students full of promise and potential, not students who need remediation simply because they come from a purported culture of poverty. An educational approach that uses Black male students' as well as other hyper-marginalized students' lived experiences as the starting point of instruction is not only important, it is exigent.

Finally, in returning to this specific study, the findings from this study provided evidence that there was indeed a shift in identity taking place for the focal cohort. This is important because we know from the work of Nasir (2011) and others that there is a positive correlation between the development of an academic identity and increased levels of math competency, for example. The findings illustrate connections between socio-academic synergy and positive STEM identity development and increased competency in math and Computer Science and the creation of Mobile Apps, also. Additionally, the findings suggest that our critical-reality based pedagogical approach was important in helping the students critically contextualize STEM, i.e., to devise ways apply STEM for social justice purposes. This frame, complete with a purposeful emphasis on conjoining relationships, relevance, and rigor, was central in helping students feel empowered, encouraged, and equipped to develop their positive STEM identities while gaining competency and using their knowledge to improve their local, national and global communities. The three R's when instituted critically, equitably, intentionally, and in-line with students' lived-experiences have the potential to produce an educational atmosphere where socio-academic synergy can hone their agentive voices.

Nevertheless, it is no secret that Black males are grossly underrepresented in STEM. This inequity is neither happenstance, nor the result of any intrinsic cognitive deficiency endemic to Black males as Herrnstein and Murray (1996) erroneously argued. The truth is much more pernicious: Black males have been systemically excluded from realizing their full potential in STEM due to a lack of opportunity to do so. This opportunity gap has precluded far too many Black males from developing a positive STEM identity. Therefore, the shifts in identification with STEM, discussed in this study, are incredibly important if there is ever to be a measurable shift in STEM access, opportunity, and success for Black males throughout K–12, college, and in their future careers. Moreover, while I am heartened by what the data suggests my goal in developing this program was not merely to aid in the growth of Black male technocrats. Rather, the shared goal of the MAN UP instructional team was to contribute to the growth of Black males who are equipped to succeed academically in STEM while, simultaneously, developing a critical, social consciousness so that they use their STEM knowledge to better their local, national and global communities. The data suggest that we were able to achieve this goal in 16 of 17 of the focal students.

In conclusion: Please, allow me to keep it 100 with you

For Black males, in this country, the threat of violence is ever present—so much so that it is part and parcel of our lived-experience. I know this to be true, first-hand. When I was young, I saw so much growing up in the East Bay Area. There was lots of beauty here, too; we were only a 15 minute BART ride away from one of the most beautiful cities in the world, San Francisco. But, there was also so much despair and death. For those of us that grew up in Richmond, California, we had to be hypervigilant to avoid getting "caught slippin'" (i.e., so oblivious to our surroundings to become vulnerable). Education is the primary way for Black males to escape the perilous environs that they are forced to navigate. Of course, my goal is not for them to leave and never turn back. The goal of the MAN UP program was always to position them to better their communities from within and without. This is my personal goal as well.

Like many of the young men that I have been blessed to work with over the years, violence was never far away from me because I grew up like them: in a single parent home in the inner city, poor and Black. Like them, I have always been negotiating the death of my Blackness in some form (Sharpe, 2016). Like them, my stepfather was an abusive alcoholic. I saw him treat my mom as though she was his sparring partner, repeatedly. He was a heavily-muscled former Marine; my mom was not. Because of him, we were homeless. Because my mom finally mustered the strength to leave him, we had to leave our support system. We ended up living in a Battered Women's shelter.

At this shelter, the kids were continually warned to never eat candy before going to sleep. I figured that it had something to do with cavities. It did not: More than 30 years removed from this incident, I still recall it vividly. I remember waking up to a bloodcurdling scream. I ran along with my mom to see what was going on because the staff at this shelter had to guard against abusers entering the premises and further harming the women and children protected within the gray-ish, peeling walls of this safe space. This time, however, the issue was a different kind of giant rat (rats are big in San Francisco) that had chewed the sugar residue off a little girl's lip, biting through her lip in the process. I remember the women there. Several of them had their mouths wired shut because their jaws, previously broken by men they once trusted, needed healing—just like their souls. Some of the young men I was blessed to serve had experienced homelessness, too. This was their reality. They were working to be phenomenal students for themselves, for their families, and for their communities. Some of them were doing this while unsure of their family situation, their living situation and/or whether they had access to three square meals.

I am older now, married with four beautiful boys of my own. I no longer live in Richmond, California, though I am not that far away—at least geograph-ically. My family lives in a safe city. But I still worry about the violence, the ever-looming specter of symbolic, psycho-emotional, and physical death that seems to doggedly pursue young men of color. I am probably overprotective as a result; I hope that one day my sons understand. I guess I escaped Richmond in some ways—though the memories still haunt me from time to time. Just two weeks ago, I was informed that a young man that I worked with in a different STEM program took his own life. Mike was 19. I do not know what led this beautiful, young Black man to take his life. But, I do know that the specter of death is part and parcel of the lived experiences of poor, urban Black males here in the "Land of Opportunity" (Sharpe, 2016).

In this book, I am calling for a paradigm-shifting revolution in the ways in which STEM pedagogy is conceptualized and, subsequently, delivered to hyper-marginalized students including and, perhaps, especially for educationally-maligned poor, urban Black boys. STEM education must be connected to the real-life experiences, concerns, and joys of Black males (and other traditionally marginalized students) precisely because STEM education has been exclusionary throughout our National history. STEM is presented as the exclusive domain of Eurocentric males (Kuhn, 1970). If the findings presented in this book are pre-dictive it holds that a revolution in STEM education that encourages students to critically contextualize their STEM pedagogy will lead to a revolution to tra-ditionally marginalized students' both their commitment and aptitude in using their STEM knowledge for social justice. This book is an attempt to provide both evidence of and precedence for a dramatic shift in STEM pedagogy, especially (though not exclusively) for Black boys.

This revolutionary, paradigm-shift in STEM education, if it is to benefit Black boys, must invite the language, culture, and general ways of being into the learning spaces that they occupy throughout this country. So, though I am not yet sure if the revolution will be televised, I am sure that the revolution will be digi-tized. And, if the study highlighted in this book is any indication, the atmosphere developed at MAN UP, when coupled with a critical-reality based pedagogical approach has the potential to empower, equip, and encourage students—perhaps especially hyper-marginalized students—to become world shakers by critically contextualizing STEM. After all, creating positive, nurturing educational spaces for urban, Black male students to succeed in STEM is not just the order of the day: it is a matter of social justice.

Keywords:

Revolution, paradigm shift, cultivating. Atmosphere, student voice, agency, rigor, high expectations

References

Alkin, M. C., and American Educational Research Association. Encyclopedia of Educational Research. 6th ed. New York; New York: Macmillan; Toronto; Maxwell Macmillan Canada; Maxwell Macmillan International, 1992. (Ref LB 15 E48 1992, p. 45)

Branch, T. (1988). *Parting the waters: America in the King years, 1954–63*. New York, NY: Simon and Schuster.

Darling-Hammond, L. (2010). *The flat world and education: How America's commitment to equity will determine our future*. New York, NY: Teachers College Press.

Emdin, C. (2016). *For white folks who teach in the hood…and the rest of y'all too: Reality pedagogy and urban education*. Boston, MA: Beacon Press.

Freire, P. (1997). *Pedagogy of the oppressed* (20th century anniversary ed.) (Myra. Bergman Ramos, Trans.). New York, NY: Continuum Publishing.

Herrnstein, R. J., & Murray, C. A. (1996). The bell curve: Intelligence and class structure in American life. New York: Simon & Schuster.

hooks, b. (1992). *Black looks: Race and representation*. New York, NY: Oxford University Press.

Knowles, L. L., & Prewitt, K. (1969). *Institutional racism in America*. Englewood Cliffs, NJ: Prentice-Hall.

Kuhn, T. (1970). *The structure of scientific revolutions* (2nd ed.). Chicago, IL: University of Chicago Press.

McLaren, P. (2015). *Pedagogy of insurrection: From resurrection to revolution*. New York, NY: Peter Lang Publishers.

Nasir, N. S. (2011). *Racialized identities: Race and achievement among Black youth*. Stanford, CA: Stanford University Press.

The New London Group. (1996). A pedagogy of multiliteracies: Designing social futures. *Harvard Educational Review, 66*(1), 1–31.

Sartre, J.-P. (1964). *Colonialism and neocolonialism*. New York, NY: Gallimard.

Sartre, J.-P. (1984). *Being and nothingness*. New York, NY: Gallimard.

Sharpe, C. (2016). *In the wake: On Blackness and being* (Kindle ed.). Durham, NC: Duke University Press.

Final consideration (Epilogue)

Finally, it seems that the "struggle" always ends at equality, and never harmonious distinction. Seemingly, only uniformity can usher in harmony. This is the implicit argument for standardization. And, in this case the standard is a Europocentric, patriarchal, heteronormative aesthetic that values ways of being, thinking, and acting that are commensurate with, derived from, and supportive of whiteness. For proponents of this view, only standardization can bridge the "unbridgeable" gap that exists between African Americans and Whites. Consequently, equality becomes a kind of indeterminate purgatory, an "unrealizable" nowhere (Sartre, 1964). This is precisely because equality in this context is the working out of the Melting Pot ideal. We have to realize that Blacks will no more be equal to Whites than Whites to Blacks, not culturally at least. This is not a negative, because if we were all to be made "equal" then all cultural differences and distinctions must be abrogated. There would be no room for multiculturalism, for multi-voicedness; on the contrary, we would all be amalgamated into one amorphous people, with the dominant culture free to determine what is and what is not normative. Uniformity is not a synonym for equity, peace, or social justice. We must remember this: we don't have to all speak the same, standard, distinctly Eurocentric language to be "equals"; instead, we must work for an equality that does not devalue cultural difference in favor of the dominant class (Freire, 1997).

Rather, educators must work towards a more dialogic, multi-vocal, culturally sensitive pedagogy (Freire, 1997; hooks, 1992). A pedagogy that does not alienate and devalue, but rather one that celebrates and investigates the panoply of cultures that the United States is home to. We need a pedagogy that allows for multiliteracies, a pedagogy that "develops an epistemology of pluralism that provides access without people having to erase or leave behind different subjectivities" (The New London Group, 1996). Critical-reality pedagogy is an attempt to make this kind of educational equity realizable. More specifically, critical-reality pedagogy is a pedagogical approach that seeks to encourage, empower, and equip all students, but especially hyper-marginalized students to "benefit from learning in ways that allow them to participate fully in public, community, and economic life (NLG, 1996)." This type of pedagogy will lead to a departure from the ideology that cultures and languages other than those of the mainstream represent a deficit (NLG, 1996), and will help to address real deficits, such as a lack of access to social power, wealth, and symbols of recognition and equitable educational opportunities.

Running the race: A level playing field is not enough

Equitable education is not about leveling the proverbial playing field. Or, more specifically, I should say it's not only about leveling the playing field. Let's take for example a hypothetical relay race, where the prize is an affirming, nutritive, quality education that ensures viable avenues for upward mobility. Team one has been allowed to prepare and many of this teams' members have received specialized training to be fully prepared to win this race. In addition to specialized training, this team has been told since birth that they will succeed because this race was created for them to succeed; the track was built by their forefathers to accentuate their natural gifts and to mitigate, ignore, or elide any individual or collective shortcomings they may have. Furthering their unmerited advantage, this race will take place in the backyard of the captain of Team 1. Then, there is Team 2. Each member of Team 2 has had their feet and ankles bound from birth, so that the muscles necessary to run are atrophied; and, they have been told all along that their inability to run has nothing to do with having their feet bound from birth, but is instead due to their innate inability to run. Not only that, they are constantly bombarded via mass media and told that they are incapable of running because they are less qualified, less intelligent, and altogether innately inferior. These messages are buoyed by actual policy that requires them two run while bound. In this example, what difference does a level playing field really make?

This is the case with Black boys in this country. Sticking with the relay race metaphor, not only have they been physically handicapped, which is akin to being routinely sick and malnourished due to inequitable access to healthy food and health care, they have also been told that no matter what they do or how hard they train they won't succeed at the same level of the people that they're competing with based on intrinsic, innate deficiencies. In this instance, in the instance of poor Black boys, leveling the playing field is not enough. We have to work to understand, address, and ultimately remove the specter of failure, criminalization, and even death that haunts young Black boys. Just working towards equal educational opportunities is not enough. We must work towards educational equity, because educational equity requires us to not only remove the shackles from the feet of the ready runners it also requires us to pursue, alongside the runners, an environment where they can heal and become healthy enough to run to their fullest potential. Moving away from the race metaphor to talk about race, insofar as ethnic and cultural differences are concerned, Black males, scholastically, have been told that they cannot succeed because they are just not as smart as their Asian-American and European American counterparts. In addition to this, for much of our history here in the United States, Black people were disallowed to read, a crime punishable by death, and therefore disallowed to aspire towards any level of real academic success. So, again, giving everyone the same opportunity is not sufficient. Rather, to provide equitable educational opportunities, we have to account for and seek to redress the pernicious environments and circumstances that many Black boys, by focusing on creating socio-academic synergy in our classrooms.

Clearly, there needs to be more work done to understand how to develop urban Black males as well as other hyper-marginalized students' positive academic identities so that they begin to see themselves as young people fully capable of excelling in STEM, and using their STEM knowledge to improve their communities as well as similar communities throughout the world in the interest of shrinking both the achievement and opportunity gaps. I do not have a definitive, sweeping solution for this conundrum. Traditional approaches to STEM education, which are plenteous in low-income, urban school systems throughout this country, have systemically delimited Black males as well as other low-income underrepresented minorities from receiving critical and empowering STEM education that encourages, empowers, and equips them to develop not only their STEM competence but also their (requisite) STEM identities. In MAN UP, we worked diligently to create opportunities for socio-academic synergy: we concentrated on involving MAN UP students in planning what it is that they would be doing in their courses as well as on the final projects that emanated from each course. We also endeavored to move students away from simply creating a catalogue of inert facts by empowering, equipping, and encouraging them to apply their newfound STEM knowledge in the amelioration of issues that were germane to their lived-experiences. Eventually, they began to devise ways to ameliorate social injustice that was outside of their immediate context. That is, they began to shift their critical contextualization understanding of socio-economic, socio-political, racial, educational, cultural, and environmental differences, which then afforded them space to begin applying their STEM knowledge as a tool for social justice (which is the actualization of the critical contextualization of STEM).

This process revealed two important, even indispensable educational implications: firstly, that a critical-reality based pedagogical approach was instrumental in contributing to students' increases in competency, identity development, and demonstrated ability to apply STEM for social justice. And, secondly, in much the same way that even the most state of the art powerboat is powerless and incapable of realizing its potential outside a body of water, a critical-reality based pedagogical approach must be placed within an educational atmosphere working to develop socio-academic synergy for its potential transformational power to be realized. To alloy MAN UP's critical-reality based pedagogical approach to STEM education with an educational atmosphere predicated on socio-academic synergy, we focused on building relationships that were nutritive and supportive while involving students in the meaning making and curricular processes so that course material was relevant to them. And, we made sure to push them, while providing all necessary support, to critically contextualize STEM in a thoughtful and rigorous way. This is key. It is also key to realize that for Black boys' education can be a matter of life and death.

This is not just meaningful work, it's life and death

Earlier today (Dated 5/26/17), my closest friend—a man I consider to be a brother, the best man at my wedding, lost his second brother to gun violence. I am 40 years old, in good health. I do not smoke or drink and I am a vegan; yet, I think about my mortality more than I would readily admit. I started a family, purchased a home, solidified my career after earning advanced degrees from the Nation's preeminent public University, and, I am writing this book; yet, I still get text like this: "Bro, please PRAY for us! T got killed last night." T was claimed by fratricidal violence. Purposefully engendered and systemically/systematically promulgated by white supremacy, hopelessness (the nihilistic threat mentioned earlier on) leads to an abject lack of access to viable employment, healthcare, healthy food, educationally enriching activities, quality education, and/or access to levers for upward mobility. This hopelessness manifests itself through violence. This is not an excuse, but it is truth (Alexander, 2010). We do not have the luxury of patience. We have to go all in, right now. Love should impel us, not just love for our students, but also love for justice, equity, and fairness. Because the circumstances for many inner city, low income Black males is dire—in fact, it is life and death.

So, I pray. I pray for T, who I knew well. T sat in my house, ate my food, played with my children. He was only two years removed from high school; but now his corporeal body is no more. I pray for Mike's family. I pray for my brother's family. I pray for my nephews. I pray for my sons. I pray for all of the young people that I have been blessed to encounter on my own journey. And, I work. I work to create equitable educational opportunities for the marginalized of the marginalized. If we are caring, committed educators—we cannot do this work when it's convenient or when we are comfortable. This work is life and death. It is that serious. We cannot afford to fail simply because we are unaware of the stakes. This is life and death for Black males. The stakes could not be higher. Nevertheless, I am not discouraged. I am sad, but not dissuaded. I am mourning, but I am not defeated. For me, this is the work that I have been called to do. These verses have always encouraged me:

[55] "O death, where is your victory? O death, where is your sting?"
[56] The sting of death is sin, and the power of sin is the law. [57] But thanks be to God, who gives us the victory through our Lord Jesus Christ.
[58] Therefore, my beloved brothers, be steadfast, immovable, always abounding in the work of the Lord, *knowing that in the Lord your labor is not in vain.*
1 Corinthians 15:55–58 (https://www.biblegateway.com/passage/?search=1+Corinthians+15%3A55-58&version=ESV)

Irrespective of the panoply of religious belief systems that guide people's lives, please pay attention to the words of the verses above. If you are an educator committed to improving the life possibilities for Black males, by working alongside them to eradicate the sting of psychological, emotional, symbolic, intellectual, and actual death in the afterlife of slavery (Sharpe, 2016), just know that no matter what the circumstances are, your labor is not in vain. Therefore, our expectations must remain as high as ever for Black boys in STEM. The concepts offered in this book, critical-reality pedagogy, socio-academic synergy, and the critical contextualization of STEM represent new ways to conceptualize work with Black boys in STEM. My sincere hope is that adding these terms to the important discourse on STEM pedagogy for Black boys will afford educators an additional way to interface with Black boys and work alongside them so that they are positioned to realize their fullest academic and human potential. This book was a labor of love. Thank you for taking the time to read it. For me these new terms are necessary and exciting. However, the real joy I derived from this book was functioning as a conduit to relay the struggles and successes of the brilliant young men that I was blessed to work with and to tell my story along the way. And, in so doing, I endeavored to honor the stories of all of the young men I have been blessed to serve by keeping it 100 with you all, the readers. Please remember that the young men both named and unnamed in this book are the real stories; and, their stories are just getting started!

Keywords:

Revolution, paradigm shift, cultivating. Atmosphere, student voice, agency, rigor, high expectations

References

Alexander, M. (2010). The new Jim Crow: Mass incarceration in the age of colorblindness. New York, NY: The New Press.

Freire, P. (1997). *Pedagogy of the oppressed* (20th century anniversary ed.). (Myra. Bergman Ramos, Trans.). New York, NY: Continuum Publishing.

hooks, b. (1992). *Black looks: Race and representation*. New York, NY: Oxford University Press.

The New London Group. (1996). *A pedagogy of multiliteracies: Designing social futures. Harvard Educational Review, 66*(1), 1–31.

Sartre, J.-P. (1964). *Colonialism and neocolonialism*. New York, NY: Gallimard.

Sharpe, C. (2016). *In the wake: On Blackness and being* (Kindle ed.). Durham, NC: Duke University Press.

Appendix A

Pre/post identification survey

- Please draw an engineer, present your drawing.
- Please draw a scientist, present your drawing.
- Is it important for you to learn STEM? Why?
- Does a STEM program just for Black males need to exist? Why?
- What do you want to be when you grow up? Why?
- What is social justice?
- How do you know if something is unjust?
- Why are there so few Black males in STEM professions?
- Is there a connection between STEM opportunities and race?
- Can you see yourself being a scientist, engineer, technologist or mathematician?
- Can YOU use STEM to improve your community? How?
- Whose job is it to improve your neighborhood?
- Is there a connection between STEM and social justice?
- Why did you sign up for this program?
- What do you hope to gain from this program?
- What do you think will be the biggest difference from now to the end of the academic year?
- Who can do STEM?
- Why is STEM for Black males important?

Appendix B

Manhood survey and rhetorical analysis concept inventory

- Please answer the following questions to the best of your ability: please make your thoughts/argument clear. Please provide a thorough/complete answer. Thanks.
- What is manhood?
- How do you define manhood?
- What is Black manhood?
- What makes a man a man? Please explain.
- Who defines Black manhood?
- How do you define race?
- How do you define racism?
- Is race real?
- Please explain your answer.
- What is a stereotype?
- What is stereotype threat?
- Is there a connection between race and STEM achievement? Please explain.
- Does race factor into STEM achievement and/or STEM excellence? Please explain.
- Is there a connection between race and STEM opportunity? Explain.
- Do certain races get more exposure to STEM based on their race?

- Is there such thing as acting white? Explain. If so, provide examples.
- What does acting Black mean? Please provide examples.
- Why do you think that there are so few AfAm males in STEM majors and in STEM careers?
- Does doing well in school mean that you are acting white? Please explain.

What do you want to be when you grow up? Why?

Rhetorical Analysis

What is the rhetorical triangle, define each part.

What is a syllogism?

What is an enthymeme?

What is a thesis statement?

What are the parts of the five-paragraph essay?

What is evidence?

Define critical thinking?

What does cogent mean?

Appendix C

MAN UP yearend program satisfaction survey (YPSS)

This survey is to get a gauge of what we are doing right and which areas need improvement for MAN UP (MAN UP)

Key:

1 = Strongly Disagree

2 = Disagree

3 = Neutral

4 = Agree

5 = Strongly Agree

STEM = Science, Technology, Engineering and Math

* Required

Top of Form

I have a good relationship with my STEM teachers at school.

	1	2	3	4	5	
Strongly Disagree						Strongly agree

At my school my teachers talk openly about race.

	1	2	3	4	5	
Strongly Disagree						Strongly agree

I feel comfortable at my school.

	1	2	3	4	5	
Strongly Disagree						Strongly agree

I feel like my "race" and culture are talked about and connected to course content in most of my classes at my school

	1	2	3	4	5	
Strongly Disagree   Strongly agree

The work I do at my school is exciting.

| | 1 | 2 | 3 | 4 | 5 | |
Strongly Disagree   Strongly agree

The work I do at my school is challenging.

| | 1 | 2 | 3 | 4 | 5 | |
Strongly Disagree   Strongly agree

At my school, most of my teachers are "good" teachers

| | 1 | 2 | 3 | 4 | 5 | |
Strongly Disagree   Strongly agree

Learning STEM is important.

| | 1 | 2 | 3 | 4 | 5 | |
Strongly Disagree   Strongly agree

I can see myself pursuing a STEM career

| | 1 | 2 | 3 | 4 | 5 | |
Strongly Disagree   Strongly agree

I feel comfortable at MAN UP (MAN UP).

| | 1 | 2 | 3 | 4 | 5 | |
Strongly Disagree   Strongly agree

At MAN UP, most of the instructors are "good" at bringing out my best.

| | 1 | 2 | 3 | 4 | 5 | |
Strongly Disagree   Strongly agree

MAN UP Instructors help me see myself as someone who does STEM, not just someone who learns STEM.

| | 1 | 2 | 3 | 4 | 5 | |
Strongly Disagree   Strongly agree

MAN UP instructors are patient.

| | 1 | 2 | 3 | 4 | 5 | |
Strongly Disagree   Strongly agree

My STEM teachers help me individually when I request help.

| | 1 | 2 | 3 | 4 | 5 | |
Strongly Disagree   Strongly agree

MAN UP is helping me improve my grades.

| | 1 | 2 | 3 | 4 | 5 | |
Strongly Disagree   Strongly agree

Racism is partially responsible for the lack of AfAm/Latino males in STEM.

        1   2   3   4   5

Strongly Disagree   Strongly agree

Laziness contributes to the lack of underrepresented minorities in STEM.

        1   2   3   4   5

Strongly Disagree   Strongly agree

Environment contributes to the lack of minorities in STEM.

        1   2   3   4   5

Strongly Disagree   Strongly agree

It is important for more underrepresented minorities and women to pursue STEM majors and STEM careers.

        1   2   3   4   5

Strongly Disagree   Strongly agree

At my home school, my individual voice is recognized and encouraged.

        1   2   3   4   5

Strongly Disagree   Strongly agree

At MAN UP, my individual voice is recognized and encouraged. That is to say, you know that you count as an individual.

        1   2   3   4   5

Strongly Disagree   Strongly agree

My school challenges me to think about the way that I think.

        1   2   3   4   5

Strongly Disagree   Strongly agree

I usually learn new things at my home school.

        1   2   3   4   5

Strongly Disagree   Strongly agree

I usually learn new things at MAN UP.

        1   2   3   4   5

Strongly Disagree   Strongly agree

STEM can be used as a tool to help people better their lives.

        1   2   3   4   5

Strongly Disagree   Strongly agree

I will be able to use STEM to help people live better lives.

        1   2   3   4   5

Strongly Disagree   Strongly agree

Appendix D

Teacher interview questions

- What does student empowerment look like?
- Did you design your course to facilitate the development of student agency? How so?
- Is agency important?
- Is it important to attempt to make STEM curriculum critical? Please Explain?
- What would you say to someone who claims that talking about inequity, racism, ageism, and or sexism creates victims?
- What did you do, regularly, to make sure that this wasn't the case?
- Do you think that your curriculum in concert with your pedagogical approach achieved the goals that you were after, personally, and that the program claims to be after, generally? Please explain.
- Do you think that the MAN UP educational approach is working? How do you know?
- Please provide a story where your ideological predispositions were challenged directly or indirectly from one or more students. How did this change your views? Or, if it did not change your views, why not?

- Please provide a narrative around one or more students experiencing an "aha" moment when either learning new material, or connecting material to existing issues of problems.
- Please provide a narrative of a time where one or more students connected their struggles or the struggles of middle school Black males to the struggles of someone or a group that is different from their own.
- Provide an example of one or more students using STEM to address a local, national, or global issue.

Appendix E

Yearend focus group and individual interview prompts

Please use this scale to respond to the following survey prompts:
| 1 | 2 | 3 | 4 | 5 |
Strongly Disagree   Strongly agree

- At MAN UP I feel like my voice mattered.
- At my school I feel like my voice matters.
- At my school we discuss social justice matters.
- At MAN UP we discussed social justice matters.
- MAN UP made me feel like I can succeed in STEM.
- My school made me feel like I can succeed in STEM.
- MAN UP made me feel like I was a successful STEM student.
- My School made me feel like I was a successful STEM student.
- MAN UP made me feel like I can be a role model.
- My school made me feel like I can be a role model.
- MAN UP talked about what it means to be a change agent.
- My school talked about what it means to be a change agent.
- MAN UP made me feel like I can be an applied STEM practitioner that can positively affect my community.

- My School made me feel like I can be an applied STEM practitioner that can positively affect my community.
- MAN UP challenged them to think about the way that they think about their roles in society.
- My school challenged them to think about the way that they think about their roles in society.
- MAN UP helped me believe that I can use my STEM knowledge and skills to make their neighborhoods better.
- My school helped me believe that I can use my STEM knowledge and skills to make their neighborhoods better.
- MAN UP helped me believe that I can use my STEM knowledge and skills to make the world a better place.
- My school helped me believe that I can use my STEM knowledge and skills to make the world a better place.
- My teacher/s at my school helped me see a connection between STEM and Social Justice.
- My teacher/s at my school helped me see a connection between STEM and Social Justice.
- My teacher/s at my school helped me see a connection between STEM and Race.
- The instructors at MAN UP helped me see a connection between STEM and Social Justice.
- The instructors at MAN UP helped me see a connection between STEM and Race.
- I felt more comfortable at MAN UP than I did at my school.
- I felt "smarter" after attending MAN UP.
- I felt "smarter" after attending my school.
- My ability to identify with STEM subjects and careers was highly impacted by having instructors who were themselves role models of STEM practitioners.
- Race and culture were connected to STEM course content at MAN UP.
- Race and culture were connected to STEM course content at my school.
- Issues around equity and justice were connected to STEM course content at MAN UP.
- Issues around equity and justice were connected to STEM course content at my school.
- MAN UP made confident that I can excel in STEM.
- My school made confident that I can excel in STEM.

- MAN UP improved my math skills.
- My school improved my math skills.
- I learned a lot about mathematics in MAN UP.
- I learned a lot about mathematics at my school.
- MAN UP increased my interest in Mobile Apps.
- My school increased my interest in Mobile Apps.
- I learned how to create Mobile Apps in MAN UP.
- I learned how to create Mobile Apps at my school.
- I learned "a lot" or "some" about Mobile Apps in MAN UP.
- I learned "a lot" or "some" about Mobile Apps at my school.
- I learned how to improve my community using STEM at MAN UP.
- I learned how to improve my community using STEM at my school.
- I was encouraged to think about my role in society at my school.
- I was encouraged to think about my role in society at MAN UP.

Index

A

"Absorption" model, 78
Academic achievement of Blacks, 10–13, 45.
    See also STEM education
    Black English and, 73–75
    consequence of low expectations and, 82
    discouraging academic environments and,
        53
    educational opportunities and, 20–21,
        56–57
    level playing field as not enough for
        equitable, 186–188
    opportunity gap and, 59–60
    real dialogue about, 56–57, 180–182
    (re)conceptualizing rigor in, 82–86
    in STEM fields, 52–53
    teacher expectations and, 75, 80–81
Adultification of Black males, 43–45
Advocacy, parental, 164–169
Agency, Black, 34–35
Alexander, M., 35

Althusser, L., 21, 59
American Chattel Slavery, 3, 17, 29
Aronson, J., 61–62

B

Banking model of education, 58, 63–64
Barton, A. C., 70, 72
Being-for-others, 24
Being in-itself-and-for-itself, 24
Beloved, 39, 40–41
Black agency, 34–35
Black communities
    fratricidal violence in, 42–43
    as ghettoes, 35–36
    "otherness" of, 33–35
    threats to, 30–31, 188–190
Black death, 2–4
Black English, 73–75
Blackface Minstrelsy, 19, 23, 30, 36, 37–39
Black literature, 39–42

Black males
  adultification of, 43–45
  consequence of low expectations for, 82
  conspicuous absence in STEM spaces of,
    52–53
  criminalization of, 53–55
  cultivating student voice of, 177–178
  demystifying stereotype threat and, 60–62
  educational opportunities for, 20–21
  educational outcomes for, 10–13
  importance of high expectations for, 178–180
  incarceration of, 18, 45
  insisting on high expectations for, 80–81
  internalization on imminent Black death,
    2–4
  level playing field as not enough for
    equitable education of, 186–188
  living conditions in the inner city, 1–2, 10–11
  parental advocacy for, 164–169
  (re)conceptualizing rigor and, 82–86
  STEM education and, 4–6
  stereotypes of, 18, 28–30, 60–62
  transmogrification of, 28–30
  working against racial isolation for, 169–171
Blackness
  as antithesis, 17, 18
  demystifying stereotype threat and, 60–62
  repudiation of, 35
  whiteness construction vis-à-vis Blackness, 23
Black on Black violence, 32, 42–43
Blikstein, P., 78–79, 154
Branch, T., 175
Brown, Michael, 29, 44
Brown V. The Board of Education, 63
Butler, J., 7–8

C

Capital culture, 21–23
Carson, Ben, 52
Carver, George Washington, 52
Civil-rights centered cultural revolution,
    175–176

Classification of "others," 19–20
Clinton, Bill, 30
Cobb, C. E., 63, 79, 154
Common Core State Standards, 124
Computer science course concept inventory,
    128–129
Cooper, M., 18
Criminalization of Black males, 53–55
Critical contextualization
  constitutive phases of, 99–100
  defined, 99
  emerging, 101
  evidence of emergent STEM, 101–102
  socio-academic synergy and, 100
  of STEM, importance of, 156
Critical-reality pedagogy, 8–10, 63–66, 186
  cultivating student voice through,
    177–178
  data analysis procedures for, 86
  in STEM education, 67–69, 154–155
Cultivating and curating an educationally
    nutritive atmosphere, 138–140
Cultural-linguistic identities and STEM
    competencies, 75–78
Culturally relevant pedagogy (CRP), 138–140
Cultural misidentification, 24–26
Cultural sustaining pedagogy (CSP), 66

D

Darling-Hammond, L., 178
Dauber, S. L., 164
Deficit-model thinking, 45
Delpit, L., 77
Denbo, S., 75, 76
Denzin, N. K., 86
De Tocqueville, A., 34
Digitization, 175–176
DiIulio, J., 18
Discouraging academic environments, 53
Domination and hegemony, 33–34
Double-consciousness, 25
Duncan-Andrade, J., 9, 45, 59

E

Education. *See* Academic achievement of Blacks; STEM education
Emancipatory education, 64, 71
Emdin, C., 9, 59, 68, 157, 177–178
Encyclopedia of Educational Research, 178
English Second Language (ESL) classrooms, 73
Epstein, J. L., 164
Equity, 185–186
   by design, 137–138
   excellence and, 65
   level playing field as not enough for, 186–188
Ernest, J., 23, 38
Exclusionary nature of traditional STEM education, 58–59
Eylon, B. S., 58, 64, 78

F

Fanon, F., 20, 24–25, 31, 32, 38–40, 68–69
Fatherhood, 135–136
Foucault, M., 19–20
Fox News, 43
Fratricidal violence in the Black community, 42–43
Freire, P., 8, 68, 154
   as anti-colonial thinker, 42
   on the banking model of education, 58, 63–64
   on discouraging academic environment, 53
   on love, 85–86
   on social justice, 78–79
Freud, S., 35

G

Gangs, 2
Ghettoes, 35–36
Giroux, H., 9, 78

Gramsci, A., 20, 59–60
Greene, D., 73–74
Gutstein, Eric, 59, 64, 69–73, 79, 154

H

Hale-Benson, J., 76
Halpin, D., 81
Harrington, M., 31, 35–36
Hate crimes, 19
Heron, Gil Scott, 175, 176
Herrnstein, R. J., 56, 180
Hyper-marginalized students, 10–11, 20, 64, 77, 79, 187

I

Identity development, 65
Ideological inculcation, 24–26
Ideological State Apparatuses (ISAs), 21, 27
Incarceration rates of Black people, 18, 45
Intercultural Development Research Association (IDRA), 62
Internalization on imminent Black death, 2–4

J

Jeynes, W., 164
Jim Crow laws, 17, 28, 30
Johnson, L., 163, 167

K

Kant, Immanuel, 31–32
"Keeping it one-hundred (percent)", 56, 180–182
King, Martin Luther, Jr., 66, 175
KKK, 17
Knowles, L. L., 179

L

Law enforcement, 29–30, 44, 54–55
Lee, C. D., 77
Leonardo, Z., 59
Level Playing Field Institute, 5
Lincoln, Y. S., 86
Linn, M. C., 58, 64, 78
Literature, Black, 39–42
Lynch, Marshawn, 10
Lynching, 17

M

Mahiri, Jabari, 176
Manhood, notions of, 7, 113–114, 117. *See also* Rhetorical Analysis of manhood (RAM)
   fatherhood and, 135–136
Manhood survey and rhetorical analysis concept inventory, 193–194
MAN UP (Male Aptitudes Nurtured for Unlimited Potential) program, 4
   case studies, 111–115
   centering the lived-experiences of students served, 12–13
   computer science course concept inventory, 128–129
   core classes in math, Computer Science and Mobile Apps, 6, 87–88
   critical contextualization in (*See* Critical contextualization)
   cultivating and curating an educationally nutritive atmosphere, 138–140
   culturally sustaining pedagogy and, 66
   curricular focus and pedagogical approach of, 98–99
   data analysis procedures, 86–88
   data collection, 89
   developing identification with STEM, 103–105
   equity and excellence in, 65

equity by design and, 137–138
fatherhood and, 135–136
focusing on students' real lives in and out of school, 157–159
focus on relationship building, 156–157
further connecting STEM identities in the courses, 115–119
high expectations for students, 179
identification and socially just applications of STEM, 90
identity development in, 65
instructional team, 176–177
manhood survey and rhetorical analysis concept inventory, 193–194
objectives of, 51, 60, 123–124
operationalizing critical-reality pedagogy, 8–10
"otherness" and, 33
parental advocacy and, 164–169
positive shifts in self-efficacy and, 140–145
pre/post identification survey, 105–110, 191
RAM (*See* Rhetorical Analysis of manhood (RAM))
(re)conceptualizing rigor, 82–86
and reimagining what it means to MAN UP, 7–8
shakers, makers, and takers, 89
shifts in students' STEM identities and, 102
social justice and, 69–73, 145–149
STEM competencies developed in, 124–126
STEM identification surveys, 25–26
student teacher relationships, 65
teacher interview questions, 104–105, 199–200
teaching the whole child, 65
working against racial isolation for our scholars, 169–171
Yearend Focus Group & Individual Interview Prompts, 103, 126–127, 201–203
yearend focus group interviews, 127–128

Yearend Program Satisfaction Survey (YPSS), 195–197

Martin, Trayvon, 17, 44
Marxist economic model, 74
Marxist universal consciousness, 27
McLaren, P., 78
Media, 18, 43
Military Industrial Complex, 72
Morrell, E., 9, 45, 59
Morrison, Toni, 39, 40
Moses, R. P., 63, 79, 154
Murnane, R. J., 76
Murray, C. A., 56, 180

N

Nasir, N. S., 59, 77, 127, 179–180
Nast, H. J., 34–35
National Center for Education Statistics, 52
National Council of Teaching Mathematics, 70
Native Son, 30
Nietzsche, F. W., 32
Nihilism, 31–33
  threat of, illustrated in Black literature, 39–42
Noguera, P., 5, 32

O

Obama, Barack, 19
Operationalizing critical-reality pedagogy, 8–10
Opportunity gap, 59–60
"Other America," 31, 35–36
Othering, psychological consequences of, 24–26
"Otherness" and the other, 33–35
  Blackface Minstrelsy and, 37–39
  in Black literature, 39–42

P

Paradigm shifting approach to STEM education, 154–155
Parental involvement, 163–164
  advocacy and, 164–169
  working against racial isolation for our scholars, 169–171
Paris, Django, 66
Persistent Traumatic Stress, 1
Philip, T. M., 60–61
Phobogenic neurosis, 24
Pre/post identification survey, 191
Prewitt, K., 179

R

Racism, 17–18, 23
  achievement gap and, 45
  of Blackface Minstrelsy, 19, 23, 30, 36, 37–39
  depictions of African Americans and, 19
  domination and hegemony in, 33–34
  portrayed in Black literature, 39–42
  repudiation of Blackness and, 34–35
  and working against racial isolation for our scholars, 169–171
Rationalism, 31–32
Reagan, Ronald, 36
(re)conceptualizing rigor, 82–86
Relationship building, focus on, 156–157
Repressive State Apparatuses (RSAs), 21
Revolution will not be Televised, The, 175
Rhetorical Analysis of manhood (RAM), 6, 10, 87–88, 103, 124
  language arts instruction and, 129–131
  STEM identities and, 115–119
Rice, Tamir, 29, 44
Rigor, (re)conceptualizing, 82–86
Roediger, D., 22, 27–28

S

Sabol, W. J., 18

Sartre, J.-P., 24, 33, 34, 38–39

Saxton, A. P., 38

Schilling, K. L., 75, 82

Schilling, K. M., 75, 82

Segregation, 17, 28

Self-devaluation, 20

Self-efficacy, 140–145

Separate but Equal Laws, 17

Shakers, makers, and takers in STEM
    education, 105–110
    case studies, 111–115

Shakur, Tupac Amaru, 1, 10

Sharpe, C., 3, 4, 29, 38

"Showing out," 123

Skinner, R., 5

Slavery, 3, 17, 23, 28, 29, 36
    Black literature and, 41–42

Snitman, A., 60, 72

Social justice, 10–11, 185
    identification and socially just applications
        of STEM, 90
    STEM education and, 69–73, 78–80,
        145–149, 153–154

Socio-academic synergy, 100, 126–127,
        136–137, 177
    cultivating and curating an educationally
        nutritive atmosphere, 138–140

Spradley, J. P., 86

"Stacking," 2

Standard English, 73

Steele, C., 58, 60–61, 75, 76, 85

STEM education. *See also* Academic
    achievement of Blacks
    Black males and, 4–6, 12–13, 20, 51–52
    case studies, 111–115
    competencies developed in MAN UP,
        124–126
    computer science course concept inventory,
        128–129

connecting cultural-linguistic identities
    and, 75–78

conspicuous absence of Black males in,
    52–53

critical-reality pedagogy in, 8–10, 63–69

cultivating and curating an educationally
    nutritive atmosphere for, 138–140

data analysis procedures for, 86–88

developing identification with, 103–105

educational gap in, 57–58

equity by design in, 137–138

evidence of emergent critical
    contextualization of, 101–102

exclusionary nature of traditional, 58–59

failures and efforts to correct, 97

focusing on students' real lives in and out
    of school, 157–159

focus on relationship building in,
    156–157

further connecting STEM identities in the
    courses in, 115–119

identification and socially just applications
    of, 90

importance of critical contextualization of,
    156

level playing field as not enough for
    equitable, 186–188

opportunity gap and, 59–60

paradigm shifting approach to, 154–155

parental advocacy in, 164–169

positive shifts in self-efficacy and,
    140–145

real dialogues about, 56–57, 180–182

(re)conceptualizing rigor in, 82–86

shakers, makers, and takers in, 105–110

shifts in students' STEM identities and,
    102

social justice and, 69–73, 78–80, 145–149,
    153–154

yearend focus group interviews,
    127–128

STEM identification surveys, 25–26

Stereotype threat, 60–62

Student teacher relationships, 65
Student voice, 177–178
"Superpredator" theory, 18

T

Tate, W. F., 77, 80
Teacher expectations, 75, 80–81
   importance of high, 178–180
Teacher interview questions, 104–105,
    199–200
Teaching the whole child, 65
Three-fifths compromise, 17
Three-fold cord, 163–164, 168
"Thugs," 28–30
Toldson, I. A., 60, 72
Transmogrification of Black males, 28–30

U

"Universal equivalent," 18–19, 21
Urban-colonies, 30–31

V

Voice, student, 177–178

W

Wacquant, L., 11
Walker, F., 73–74
Wells, Ida B., 30
West, C., 30, 32
West, H. C., 18
Westernized White reality, 21
"White masks," 24
Whiteness, 185
   abolition of, 26–28
   commoditized, 21–23
   construction vis-à-vis Blackness, 23
   as thesis, 17
   uncovering, 18–21
White privilege, 26–28
White supremacy, 17–18, 34–35
Williams, Daniel Hale, 52
Wofford, J., 74
Womanhood, 7
"Wretched of the Earth, The," 31
Wright, R., 30, 39–40

Y

Yearend focus group interviews, 127–128
Yearend Program Satisfaction Survey (YPSS),
    103, 126–127, 195–197

Critical Pedagogical Perspectives

M. Cathrene Connery and

Greg S. Goodman, *General Editors*

Educational Psychology: Critical Pedagogical Perspectives is a series of relevant and dynamic works by scholars and practitioners of critical pedagogy, critical constructivism, and educational psychology. Reflecting a multitude of social, political, and intellectual developments prompted by the mentor Paulo Freire, books in the series enliven the educator's process with theory and practice that promote personal agency, social justice, and academic achievement. Often countering the dominant discourse with provocative and yet practical alternatives, Educational Psychology speaks to educators on the forefront of social change and those who champion social justice.

For further information about the series and submitting manuscripts, please contact:

M. Cathrene Connery | Greg S. Goodman
cconnery@salisbury.edu | gsgoodman17@gmail.com

To order other books in this series, please contact our Customer Service Department at:

(800) 770-LANG (within the U.S.)
(212) 647-7706 (outside the U.S.)
(212) 647-7707 FAX

Or browse online by series at:

www.peterlang.com

CPSIA information can be obtained
at www.ICGtesting.com
Printed in the USA
BVHW091459040522
636085BV00025B/382